Claire Cross is currently Senior Lecturer in History at the University of York, where she has taught since 1965. A Cambridge graduate, she was County Archivist of Cambridgeshire from 1958 to 1961, and Research Fellow at Reading University between 1962 and 1965. Her previous books are *The Puritan Earl: Life of Third Earl of Huntingdon* (1967), *Royal Supremacy in the Elizabethan Church* (1969), and an edition of *The Letters of Sir Francis Hastings* (1969).

FONTANA LIBRARY OF ENGLISH HISTORY

Edited by G. R. Elton

The aim of the series is to reinterpret familiar and
unfamiliar aspects of English history. There will be a pair
of volumes on each chronological period which will throw
new light on the age in question by discussing it in
relation to contrasting themes.

ALREADY PUBLISHED
D. M. Loades, *Politics and the Nation, 1450-1660*

FORTHCOMING TITLES
Asa Briggs, *The Growth of Leisure 1815-1970*
H. E. Hallam, *Rural England 1066-1272*
Peter Heath, *England and the English Church 1272-1460*
J. R. Jones, *Britain and the World 1649-1815*
Malcolm Todd, *Roman Britain*
Anthony Tuck, *The Crown and the Nobility 1272-1461*

CHURCH AND PEOPLE
1450-1660

The Triumph of the Laity
in the English Church

CLAIRE CROSS

THE HARVESTER PRESS

By agreement with Fontana

THE HARVESTER PRESS LIMITED
Publisher : John Spiers
2 Stanford Terrace,
Hassocks, Sussex.

Church and People 1450—1660
This edition first published in 1976 by
The Harvester Press Limited
by agreement with Fontana Books
Fontana Library of English History, Volume 2

ISBN 0 85527 129 9

Printed in Great Britain by
Redwood Burn Limited,
Trowbridge, Wiltshire

CONTENTS

ACKNOWLEDGEMENTS

My indebtedness to the many historians who have written on the English Church in the fourteenth, fifteenth, sixteenth and seventeenth centuries is very great, and I regret that I can only acknowledge it, most inadequately, in the bibliographies at the end of this volume. I must, however, make special mention of the work of Professor A. G. Dickens who has done so much in recent years to emphasize the importance of the laity in the history of the Church at the time of the Reformation: had he continued his *English Reformation* into the seventeenth century this account would have been unnecessary. I would also like to thank the General Editor of this series for all his help and understanding.

The spelling and punctuation of quotations has been modernized throughout.

Vanbrugh College, University of York
Whit Sunday 1975   *Claire Cross*

CHAPTER I

PROLOGUE: LAY QUESTIONING
OF THE MEDIEVAL CHURCH

'We pray God of his endless goodness reform our Church, all out of joint, to the perfecting of the first beginning.' So in 1395 a group of Lollards ended their list of contemporary abuses in the English Church. Earlier in their manifesto they had declared that the 'holy Church of England' had been 'blind and leprous many years by maintenance of proud prelacy, borne up with flattering of private religion' and had submitted Twelve Conclusions concerning the present state of the Church. Their grievances fell into four distinct categories. They objected to certain theological developments in the medieval Church and what they considered to be erroneous practices; they deplored the way in which the ministry, intended by Christ to serve his people, had been distorted into an overbearing priesthood; they denounced the misuse of the endowments of the Church, and they called for a return to primitive simplicity and morality. None of these charges was new, and most had at different times been brought by the clergy themselves with equal vehemence. But the fact that some apparently humble laymen could ask the Lords and Commons in Parliament to lead the way to reformation heralds a significant change in religious practice in England. The laity in general, not merely the King and his ministers, or even the Crown together with the nobility and gentry, was beginning to demand a far more active role in the life of the Church.

The dissemination of Lollardy in the reign of Richard II, the first large-scale outbreak of heresy in England, marks an important stage in the emergence of an articulate laity. All kinds of men, not only in London but in widely-separated regions of the country, seized the opportunity to voice criticisms both constructive and destructive of the present state of the Church. Only a little more than a generation after the Twelve Conclusions had been posted up in English on the doors of St Paul's Cathedral and Westminster Abbey, a miller of Flixton in Norfolk, one John Skilly, confessed to holding beliefs which would have totally undermined the established hierarchy of the medieval Church. He admitted to episcopal investigators that he had once believed 'that confession should be made unto no priest, but only to God, for no priest has power to absolve a man from sin'. He then, under direction, went on to abjure such inflammatory statements as 'no priest has power to make Christ's body in the form of bread in the sacrament of the altar'; 'every true man and woman living in charity is a priest'; 'the pope of Rome is antichrist, and . . . has no power to bind or loose'; 'it is lawful for priests to take wives, and nuns to take husbands'; 'no pilgrimage ought to be done nor any manner of worship ought to be done to any images of the crucifix, of Our Lady, or of any other saints'. Lollards as outspoken as Skilly probably represented only a tiny proportion of the laity but their opinions, in a less radical form, gained a fairly wide acceptance at all levels of society, and the bishops, despite their efforts, never subsequently entirely succeeded in eradicating them. Laymen had begun a conscious quest for reformation.[1]

Ignoring the long hallowed theory of the two kingdoms under which the Pope and his bishops governed the Church while the Monarch and his lords ruled the secular state, the authors of the Twelve Conclusions assumed without argument that Richard II and his Parliament had the power and authority to reform the Church. The theme of this account is the long struggle of the laity, between 1450 and 1660, to gain supremacy in the English Church. In the course of the contest successive governments allied themselves with the upper clergy to repel dangerous popular demands, though at the Reformation Henry VIII exploited these pressures to secure the break with Rome. Once a national Church had been established, conservative monarchs like Elizabeth and her early Stuart successors tried to reassert their former right to rule the national Church through their bishops, only to discover that the laity would not willingly abrogate the rights they had briefly enjoyed in the Parliaments of Henry VIII and Edward VI. The laity's eagerness to determine the exact form of religion practised in England played a considerable part in the clashes between the Crown and the governing classes from the accession of Elizabeth to the beginning of the Civil War, and were perhaps at their most bitter when Charles I gave his support to the Arminian party among the clergy. Yet the rivalry between laity and clergy was never a simple one. It might seem in the 1630s that the laity stood united against the aspirations of the Laudian clergy, but fundamental divisions soon appeared among them once Laud and his supporters had lost power. Members of the Long Parliament wanted a uniform, national, Protestant Church under their control; the populace at large strove for the right of individual freedom of choice which, under Cromwell's protection, they gained to a very large degree for a decade. By the mid-seventeenth century the laity had won their ascendancy over the clergy but the final victory proved to belong to the parliamentary classes. In 1662 the Cavalier Parliament prevented Charles II from implementing his promises of toleration largely it seems because influential laymen had come to believe that political stability in England depended on the enforcement of religious uniformity. With the fifteenth-century bishops they failed to extirpate dissent, but not for many years did they acknowledge their failure. Universal religious toleration in England, the logical consequence of the laity's triumph, remained several generations away.

Jealousy of the privileged position of the clergy may well have been endemic among the laity from the time that Constantine recognized Christianity as the religion of the Roman Empire. Confrontations between the rulers of Church and State had taken place in England as elsewhere in Christendom from time immemorial, and English clerics in the later Middle Ages never allowed English laymen to forget the fight to the death between Henry II and Archbishop Thomas Becket. Yet England, unlike areas of the Continent which much earlier had seen Albigensian and less radically deviant Waldensian beliefs entrenched among the laity, never experienced mass popular heresy until the second half of the fourteenth century – a fact that historians have found difficult to explain, though few have suggested that the outbreak of heresy in the reign of Richard II was in reaction to a particularly low level of spiritual life in the organized Church.

It is, nevertheless, true that laymen found much to criticize in the English Church towards the end of the fourteenth century, and nowhere more than in the Church's wealth. The Church owned great riches, yet these were very unequally distributed. Among its seventeen dioceses England had some of the best endowed bishoprics in all Europe : the archbishops of Canterbury and York, the bishops of Durham, Winchester, Ely, Lincoln, Bath and Wells and Exeter all had gross annual incomes at contemporary values of well over £1500, most over £2000, though the income of very small sees like Rochester was much more modest. Usually Popes appointed to these prize sees the candidates of the English Crown, with the result that the richest dioceses had come to be reserved for servants of the State. It has been calculated that throughout the fifteenth century (and the position does not seem to have been very different in the second half of the fourteenth) about half the bishops could not reside in their sees because their secular duties necessitated their attendance upon the royal government in London or upon diplomatic business on the Continent. Since, on the whole, the most extensive dioceses also had the largest revenues, the inhabitants of these sees became accustomed to their bishops being permanently or partially non-resident. In these cases the Church adapted itself to the usual absence of its bishop by building up a highly efficient judicial machine to which the bishop delegated his ecclesiastical administration and the general oversight of his flock, while his spiritual duties went to suffragan bishops, often insignificant friars, who needed to be paid little for performing the ordinations and consecrations which an episcopal official could not do.[2]

Some fourteen English Benedictine abbeys including Westminster, Glastonbury, Christchurch (Canterbury), St Albans, Reading, Bury St Edmunds and, in the north, St Mary's (York) and Durham had an income comparable with that of the richest English bishoprics, although unlike some Continental rulers English kings rarely tried to place their civil servants as abbots. In an attempt to secure the appointment of more suitable parish priests, a succession of popes in the high Middle Ages had encouraged laymen to give parochial livings previously under their control to religious houses: the result, quite contrary to their intentions, was that many abbeys derived a very substantial income from these appropriated rectories, leaving the vicars who served the parishes to exist on a mere pittance. By the end of the fourteenth century St Mary's Abbey at York had acquired some forty churches in the diocese of York alone, and in the early fifteenth century a not inconsiderable part of the gross income of rather over £2000 which Durham priory received annually came from its seventeen rectories and twenty-eight vicarages. The prior and convent of Durham did not make scandalous appointments to the livings they held, though the prior certainly felt some obligation to lay lords in the neighbourhood who wished him to advance clerics in their service. On the other hand, they do not appear to have recognized any particular duty to supplement the very meagre income of the curates who officiated in their parishes. Highly-placed clerics often lived at the expense of their humbler brethren, and increasingly in the second half of the fourteenth century lower clergy were choosing the less arduous but by no means richly rewarded life of a chantry priest rather than the responsibilities of a poorly paid appropriated parish.

Some ecclesiastics had long realized the dangers of worldly possessions: in the twelfth century Cistercians, inspired by a new form of St Benedict's rule, had gone out into the wilderness to establish new monasteries and had attracted massive lay support, while a century later the different orders of friars who made a cult of evangelical poverty captured the imagination of the laity. Even in the late fourteenth century, when York merchants made bequests to the Church, they regularly remembered in their wills the four orders of friars who had houses in the city, but rarely left anything to St Mary's Abbey or the equally well endowed Dean and Chapter of the Cathedral. Piety and charity followed the same pattern in late medieval London, and the London citizens also discriminated in favour of the mendicants at the expense of the possessioners. Austerity in religion continued to attract the laity: individual hermits found considerable support in their own locality, and the order most nearly akin to the hermit life, the Carthusians, could well be regarded as the 'new' order of the age. Between 1370 and 1415 gentlemen, noblemen and the King himself, in the person of Henry v, founded charterhouses at Beauvale, London, Hull, Coventry, Epworth, Mount Grace and Sheen.

For centuries laymen had influenced developments in the Church in this way, and the new movements which they patronized spread phenomenally while the old orders remained stationary. More novel in the fourteenth century was the rapid extension of literacy in lay society which gave an increasing number of laymen the capacity to intervene in intellectual matters once considered the particular province of the clergy. Some leading laymen, indeed, began to take it upon themselves to write theological and devotional books, and among these Henry, Duke of Lancaster seems to have been something of a pioneer. A diplomat and army leader, he produced in 1354 his *Livre de Seyntz Medicines*, a sophisticated spiritual treatise in which he first set out the seven wounds which afflict the Christian soul and then described the remedies offered by Christ, the divine physician, and his holy mother. Consciously designing his book for cultivated readers, he wrote in French, but felt it necessary to apologize for writing the French of an Englishman. Lancaster lived at the time of a cultural and language divide:

a generation later French had lost its dominance, even at the highest levels of society, so that Chaucer could compose in English and still aspire to please a courtly audience. For the first time since the Conquest all Englishmen enjoyed a common language, and the linguistic barriers between different orders in lay society had been broken. Nothing now prevented any layman who could read from having access to books in the vernacular.

This new homogeneity in English society, combined with the extension of literacy, popular enthusiasm for austere religious movements and the perennial jealousy of the wealth of the Church, all help to explain how the esoteric writings of an Oxford theologian could become the basis for an outburst of radical questioning of the Church which for a time found wide-scale support. John Wyclif spent virtually all his adult life from about 1350 at the university of Oxford, first as a student, then as a teacher, until he withdrew three years before his death in 1384 to the relative obscurity of Lutterworth in Leicestershire. Much admired for his philosophical and theological speculation (conducted according to academic propriety in Latin), Wyclif might never have been known outside academic circles but for the political exigencies of the 1370s caused by the senility of Edward III and by the succession in 1377 of his grandson, Richard II, too young to rule in his own right. In this time of weak royal government the King's uncle, John of Gaunt, rose to power, and Gaunt probably included Wyclif among his clerical dependants. For a while it suited the government, in conflict with the Papacy over clerical appointments, to have as its propagandist one who not only emphasized the practical independence of the English Church but went on to justify the possible confiscation by the State of the surplus, and corrupting, wealth of the Church. Arguments such as these proved immediately attractive to the Commons assembled in Parliament but understandably united the great churchmen against Wyclif. Since his attacks on the endowments of the Church and the powers of the Papacy came during the papal schism, he might yet have gone on to achieve advancement in State service had he not, as much as a philosopher as a theologian, proceeded to question the doctrine of transubstantiation which had been the official teaching of the Church since the Lateran Council of 1215. Gaunt would protect an iconoclast but not a self-proclaimed heretic, and pressure from his clerical opponents forced Wyclif to retire to his living in Lutterworth in 1381. There he produced, still in Latin, a stream of contentious works advocating a return to apostolic simplicity, contrasting the Church of Christ with the Church of Antichrist and, among much else, supporting the opening of the sacred scriptures to the laity.

Some twentieth-century historians, reacting against the hagiography of John Foxe in his *Book of Martyrs*, have been at pains to emphasize the division between the academic speculation of Wyclif and the teachings of his plebeian popularizers, and have denied that he could have intended his philosophical theses to be bandied about in the market place. Perhaps the distinction has been too sharply drawn, for there may well have been rather more of the evangelist in Wyclif than some have recently been willing to acknowledge. At least in the matter of the translation of the Bible Wyclif may not have been altogether unlike Erasmus who also saw all the advantages, and none of the dangers, of making the Bible available to the common people. At all events, within their master's lifetime Wyclif's own disciples, led by Purvey, began translating the Bible into English together with other of Wyclif's Latin works. By 1382 they had produced a literal, almost word for word, translation probably intended for priests with a poor command of Latin. A decade later they followed this with a far more polished and readable version which remained the only English translation until Tyndale brought out his New Testament in 1526.

The availability of the Bible in English and the increasing acceptance of written English as a cultural language conclusively removed the educational division between the clergy and the laity, as the orthodox clergy reluctantly and belatedly recognized. They could no longer maintain that the cleric was *literatus* and the layman *illiteratus*, or that the laity had not the knowledge to indulge in theological controversy. As early as 1382 William Smith, a humble Leicester layman, had become acquainted with some of Wyclif's teachings: he illustrates graphically the interaction of literacy and religious individualism which persisted in Lollardy well into the sixteenth century. Apparently only after he had become interested in religious matters and was already adult had Smith taught himself to read and write: then, with a Lollard chaplain, he began holding Lollard conventicles and kept a Lollard school. In 1389, in the course of his metropolitical visitation, Courtney came to Leicester, by then a notorious centre of heresy, and had the duty of pronouncing judgement upon Smith and several others brought before him as suspected heretics. The Archbishop singled

out Smith for his proselytizing activities, ordering him to hand
over to episcopal officers the English books he had been compiling
over the previous eight years based on the Bible and the Fathers.
It could well be that the preacher John Swetstock had the audacity
of such men as Smith in mind when in the reign of Henry v he
reiterated the platitude that no layman should meddle with the
scriptures or clerical business. He knew that Lollards had done so,
indeed that they had tried to intrude in the highest matters of
divinity, giving instruction upon the sacrament of the altar.
Lollards, he complained, would no longer accept the teaching of the
Church but in their wilfulness flew so high that they lost themselves in their rarefied surroundings. Even women possessed English
books and a smattering of theological knowledge, and hot-heads
had asked why women should not also preach like men. Over the
next two hundred years other frightened clerics regularly sounded
this alarm, but they could as well hold back the tide as they could
stem the growth of literacy among the laity.

The speed with which the second Lollard translation of the
Bible was published and distributed across England suggests a
considerable degree of organization within Lollardy, at least in its
earlier years. The careful correction of more than two hundred
copies of the whole or part of the Lollard Bible which still survive
indicates a scholarly control over Lollard book production, and
there may have been a book distribution centre on or near the
Latimer estates at Braybrook in Northamptonshire which sent out
copies of the Bible, English abstracts of Wyclif's Latin works, and
the Lollard sermon cycle. Through these writings, compiled between
about 1382 and 1415, Lollards could cling to a tenuous unity of
belief, in later years of persecution, after they had lost their
academic leadership; to this extent they can be described as a sect,
characterized first and foremost by their biblical fundamentalism,
and also by their critical attitude towards traditional teaching on
the sacraments, on the right of the clergy to temporal possessions
and on the supremacy of the Pope.

It now seems probable that influential lay patronage was responsible, at least in part, for the rapid spread of Lollard ideas and
books throughout England, and that Lollardy for something like
its first thirty years had the support and protection of devout
laymen of substantial means and with court connections. It may
indeed be more illuminating to consider orthodoxy and heresy as
shading imperceptibly the one into the other, and not to regard

them, as did contemporary churchmen, as clearly defined and opposed areas of belief. In this way Lollards in their Twelve Conclusions, as in their many other early writings, mirror with varying degrees of accuracy the longings, the uncertainties and the discontents of the laity in general. Perhaps in their radical theological speculation Lollards were least representative of most laymen, but in their desire to know the word of God as expressed in the Bible without any clerical mediation, their resentment of priestly superiority, their puritanical recoil at the wealth of the Church and their severe judgement upon the disparity between priestly profession and priestly attainment they touched upon matters of very general concern.

Wyclif's writings as popularized in English by his academic followers provided a storehouse of arguments where, at least in the early days before the State intervened with the imposition of the death sentence for heresy, interested laymen seem to have discovered sympathetic justifications for their latent aspirations and prejudices. Significantly, only one of the Twelve Conclusions of 1395 touched upon the mass and the crucial doctrine of transubstantiation – 'that the feigned miracle of the sacrament of bread induces all men but a few to idolatry'. Laymen seem to have been more eager to participate actively in the life of the Church than to overthrow its sacramental teaching, an eagerness particularly displayed in their enthusiasm to read and possess the Bible in English. At court Queen Anne of Bohemia with the approval of Archbishop Arundel had an English Bible (this must have been a Lollard translation since no other was available), and the two hundred or so copies of the whole or of parts of the Bible which have been traced back to the late fourteenth and early fifteenth centuries vary in quality from elaborate presentation volumes on which no expense had been spared to rough working copies. The chronicler Knighton grasped the immense difference which the accessibility of the Bible made to the position of the priesthood. 'The gospel that Christ gave to the clergy and doctors of the church . . . ,' he lamented, 'has become vulgar and more open to laymen and women who can read than it usually is to quite learned clergy of good intelligence. And so the pearl of the gospel is scattered abroad and trodden underfoot by swine.'[3]

With the new assurance that familiarity with the Bible gave them, some laymen proceeded to challenge other priestly privileges which they had long resented. In the ninth of the Twelve Conclusions Lollards condemned auricular confession, partly on the grounds that it enhanced a priest's pride and kept the people in subservience : another of the Conclusions declared that the 'priesthood which began in Rome . . . is not the priesthood which Christ ordained to his apostles'. From the Bible laymen now could draw telling parallels between true shepherds and hirelings and, while not deviating from orthodox sacramental teaching, could yet appreciate the Lollards' claim in the first of their Twelve Conclusions that 'faith, hope and charity began to fly out of our Church' when 'the Church of England began to dote in temporality after her stepmother the great Church of Rome, and churches were slain by appropriation to divers places'. Similarly the sixth Conclusion that 'all manner of curates both high and low should be fully excused of temporal office, and occupy themselves with their cures and nothing else' could scarcely fail to evoke a favourable response, even among quite moderate laymen.

Some laymen, again not necessarily unorthodox in theology, went considerably further and in several Parliaments of the late fourteenth and early fifteenth centuries called for the partial or even total disendowment of the Church. These demands reached their climax in the Parliament of 1410 when the Commons presented a bill to the King asking for the confiscation of the temporalities of bishops, abbots and priors. The lands taken over by the State, they considered, would enable Henry IV to create with sufficient maintenance in land 15 earls, 1500 knights, 6200 squires and 100 almshouses, and still leave the Crown with an additional annual income of £20,000 for the defence of the realm. The scheme had no chance of being taken seriously by a government which relied heavily upon the services of high ecclesiastics, but it demonstrates the level to which anti-clericalism could occasionally rise.

Laymen coupled their envy of the Church's wealth with a rather more edifying enthusiasm for morality and austerity. The call for a return to apostolic poverty which had resulted in much lay support for the friars in the thirteenth century still attracted many among the laity, but by 1400 they seem to have felt that these orders by themselves could not purify the Church. Radicals thought that if they forced the clergy to be poor they might become more moral and lead holier lives, and some Lollards maintained that laymen should withhold tithes from sinful clergy. They also believed that some of the sins of the flesh might be reduced if the

Church permitted clergy to marry and abolished all religious orders for women. Attacks upon the moral insufficiency of priests had always been a constituent of anti-clericalism; yet this emphasis on morality and simplicity in the late fourteenth century appears to have been more than just a convenient weapon with which to beat the clergy. Some laymen valued austerity for its own sake, stridently condemning ostentation and extravagance, and feared the seductive power of art in the Church. Lollards again reflected a more general preoccupation of the time in calling for a ban upon all unnecessary crafts which had formerly produced ornaments for churches, encouraging waste and curiosity, and for the destruction of roods and images, 'a book of error to the ignorant people'.

If laymen had confined their moral strictures to the clergy, the sincerity of their motives could be called in question, but some aimed much higher and tried to rescue their fellow-men from the snares of the world. Sir John Clanvow, a professional soldier like the Duke of Lancaster forty years earlier, resembled him even more closely by writing about 1390 a treatise in English on man's need to choose between the joys of heaven and the pains of hell.

> The gospel telleth that in a time when our Lord Jesu Christ was here upon earth, a man came to him and asked him if that few men should be saved. And Christ answered and said: 'The gate is wide and the way is broad that leadeth to loss; and many go in that way: and how strait is the gate and the way narrow that leadeth to the life; and few find that way.'

Just as two centuries later godly gentlemen in Elizabeth's reign had to endure being labelled Puritans for their support of scriptural truth, so Clanvow expected to be reviled as a Lollard for his devotional writing. He found solace in the knowledge that the meek of the earth gained nothing but opprobrium in this life.

> Such folk the world scorneth and holdeth them lollers and losels, fools and shameful wretches. But surely God holdeth them most wise and most worshipful . . . And therefore take we savour in those things . . . and reck we never though the world scorn us or hold us wretches. For the world scorneth Christ and held him a fool . . . And therefore follow we his traces and suffer we patiently the scorns of the world as he did.[4]

The Church never condemned Clanvow for heresy, and his horror of 'the foul stinking muck of this false, failing world' represented an attitude prevalent in the early fifteenth century among orthodox and unorthodox alike. Henry IV in his will, made unusually in English, dwelt upon his sinfulness. The ecclesiastic Philip Repton, once an academic follower of Wyclif but one who had sufficiently rehabilitated himself to be given the see of Lincoln, resigned from his episcopal duties in 1420 to live in retirement and ordered the utmost simplicity to be observed at his funeral. Another former university Lollard, Nicholas Hereford, left his office as Chancellor in Hereford Cathedral for the Coventry charterhouse in 1417. Even that hammer of the heretics, Archbishop Arundel, expatiated at untypical length on his sins in his will. At a very different level, Margery Kempe, the daughter of a mayor of King's Lynn, in her zeal to encourage a direct experience of Christianity and, incidentally, to propagate a moral reformation in society, dared to correct bishops in their palaces and to withstand the advice of her confessor. Had Lollardy not stimulated a mood which was already present, had there not been a body of laymen determined to seek God for themselves without waiting on priestly guidance, it would be difficult otherwise to account for its power to create a continuing lay tradition once the impact of its initial protest had passed.

While seemingly orthodox and unorthodox laymen shared much in common in the late fourteenth and early fifteenth centuries, it would be misleading to underestimate the extent of heretical doctrines concerning the sacraments current from an early date in popular Lollardy. The first attempts by Wyclif's academic followers to popularize his teachings in English met with an answering response from some townspeople. Philip Repton, then a Doctor of Divinity and a canon of the Leicester abbey of St Mary in the Meadows, may have brought Lollardy from Oxford to Leicester. It certainly quickly found support among the laity there. William Smith, the Leicester layman who helped in Lollard book production, has already been mentioned: he worked with William Swinderby who had formerly been a hermit in the woods outside the town. On his visitation of Leicester in 1389 Archbishop Arundel discovered that the Lollards had been proclaiming that 'any layman can preach and teach the gospel anywhere'. Three years later Northampton, under the encouragement of John Fox, mayor in 1392, was reputed as scandalous a centre of heresy as Leicester. Another lay evangelist, Thomas Compworth, had been active in

Northampton: an esquire, he came from Kidlington near Oxford and had been tried in 1385 for refusing to pay tithes to the rector of his parish.

Lollards of this type ignored the Church's division between priests and laymen. An Oxford scholar admitted in 1401 that he had said in his instruction to the laity that 'every man, holy and predestined to eternal life, even if he is a layman is a true minister and priest ordained by God to administer all the sacraments necessary for the salvation of man, although no bishop shall ever lay hands upon him': and some instances have been discovered when laymen seem to have acted upon this teaching. Walsingham, admittedly a biased chronicler, had heard a story of a layman, John Claydon, who had made his son (or in another version, even more shockingly, his daughter) a priest in order to celebrate mass in his house on the birth of his child. He also knew that Lollards were rumoured to be making their own priests in the diocese of Salisbury. Certainly in 1389 a Lollard, William Ramsbury, appeared before the Bishop of Salisbury at his manor of Sonning in Berkshire to renounce errors he had learnt from one Thomas Fishburn. He confessed that Fishburn had given him a 'priestly tonsure, and invested him with a certain habit, namely a tunic of russet with a mantle of the same cloth, giving him power both to preach and to celebrate masses'. Ramsbury asserted that he had believed that 'it is of greater merit for priests to go through the countryside with a Bible under their arm, preaching to the people, than to say matins, or celebrate masses, or perform other divine offices'. He claimed to have visited over twenty towns and villages in Wiltshire and Dorset where he had taught Lollard tenets in churches and church-yards, at private 'confabulations' and in inns, and also said that he had conducted masses according to a special Lollard order.[5]

Churchmen might well have succeeded in stamping out popular Lollardy of this kind at its first appearance, as under the leader-ship first of Archbishop Courtney and then of Archbishop Arundel they strove hard to do, if more powerful protection had not been forthcoming. Contemporary chroniclers spoke of a group of ten Lollard knights closely connected with the courts of Richard II and Henry IV; and recent studies have confirmed that there were other knights besides Clanvow seriously interested in new forms of lay participation in religion and so liable, as Clanvow foresaw, to denigration as Lollards. No evidence survives to confirm the sup-posed heretical tendencies of Sir John Trussell and Sir John Peachey,

two of the ten Lollard knights named by the chroniclers, though
Trussell owned lands in an area of Northamptonshire where
Swinderby went on preaching tours while Peachey's chief manor
lay in a part of Warwickshire also visited by Swinderby. But the
remaining eight knights, Sir John Oldcastle, Sir Lewis Clifford,
Sir Richard Sturry, Sir Thomas Latimer, Sir William Neville, Sir John
Clanvow, Sir John Montagu and Sir John Cheyne, had definite links
with the new lay movements in religion. With estates in counties
as widely separated as Hereford and Kent, these gentlemen had
been brought together by Crown service: almost all at some time
had pursued a military career and all were educated men. Montagu
wrote poetry and had connections with Chaucer; in 1388 Latimer
was accused of owning heretical books, and Clanvow's own
moralizing writing, shot through with biblical allusions, has already
been described. The protection of the Latimer family enabled
Robert Hook, a Lollard priest, to make converts at Braybrook in
Northamptonshire for something like twenty-five years before the
ecclesiastical authorities forced him to recant in 1425. Oldcastle
had his Lollard chaplain at Cooling in Kent and Montagu and
Neville both befriended Lollard priests. Knighton seems to have
been telling the literal truth when he alleged that knights like
Latimer imposed Lollard preachers upon their tenants.

Clerical writers understandably emphasized the anti-clerical, anti-
sacramental attitude of these eminent men, making much of incidents when knights and their servants kept their hoods on before
the holy sacrament. Yet such behaviour had its spiritual side. Some
of these men had a yearning for simplicity and a deep sense of
their own unworthiness before the majesty of God. Latimer, Clifford
and Cheyne all made their wills early in the fifteenth century,
writing in English probably with the conscious intention of disseminating their religious beliefs as widely as possible. To an
unprecedented degree all three emphasized their utter sinfulness,
their hatred of their mortal bodies and bodily sins, and renounced
all funeral pomp, but Cheyne, 'most unworthy and God's traitor',
most of all. Recommending himself 'wretched and sinful wholly
to the grace and to the great mercy of the blissful Trinity', he
ordered his 'wretched stinking carrion to be buried without the
chapel new made within the churchyard of the church of Beck-
ford', strictly charging his executors 'that on my stinking carrion
be neither laid cloth of gold ne of silk but russet cloth price the
yard fifteen pence'.[6]

These knights seem to have been more attracted by a severe morality than by theological speculation, to have sought direct contact with God for themselves and yet not openly to have attacked the orthodox teachings of the Church. This may partly explain why for so many years they could flaunt their activities and yet remain largely unchecked by Church or State. With the prevailing popularity of sermons and the growing demand for devotional literature in English, the dividing line between orthodoxy and heresy had in any case become increasingly difficult to draw, and, at least until the reign of Henry v when Lollardy had been irrefutably linked with treason, members of the governing classes presumed upon a considerable freedom to indulge their inclinations in religion. Others somewhat lower in landed society shared their tastes and had even fewer inhibitions about revealing their beliefs. Walter Brute, an associate of Swinderby, who described himself as 'a sinner, layman, husbandman and Christian', and who may have been an Oxford graduate as well, set out his views in two defiant treatises when he was being sought for heresy in the Welsh border country between 1391 and 1393. He made no attempt to conceal his Lollardy, denying transubstantiation, attacking the Pope as Antichrist, maintaining that laymen could lawfully withhold tithes from evil priests. Throughout his writings ran the theme that God did not reserve knowledge of his power and might for the eyes of the clergy alone.

> All these things have I written, to show that he that hath the key of David . . . doth . . . hide the mysteries, and hide the secrets of the scriptures from the wise, prudent and righteous; and otherwhiles at his pleasure revealeth the same to sinners, and lay persons, and simple souls, that he may have the honour and glory in all things.[7]

In the autumn of 1393 he submitted to the judgement of the doctors of the Church gathered at Hereford, making a highly ambiguous recantation of his beliefs. By this submission he regained his freedom and eventually met his death in the rebellion of Owen Glendower.

Orthodox churchmen recognized the potential political danger of Lollardy before Wyclif's disciples had even begun spreading his ideas in the vernacular, but the State seems to have been remarkably slow in supporting their action against heresy. This lack of concern persisted despite, or perhaps because of, shrill clerical protests. Immediately after the Peasants' Revolt of 1381 priests did their best to associate the attacks by peasants on ecclesiastical and secular property with Wyclif's teaching on lordship and dominion. If laymen now disputed the right of the Church to hold property, they argued, they would soon logically progress to question the property rights of lay lords. The government of the young King Richard refused to be forced into taking drastic measures and in 1382 merely consented to authorize sheriffs and other royal officials to arrest unlicensed preachers, in this way slightly strengthening the bishops' powers. In 1388 King and Parliament did sponsor the sending out of commissions, which included laymen as well as ecclesiastics, to seek out Lollardy, but they still seem to have been largely content to leave the control of heresy to churchmen.

One of the reasons for the State's hesitation may well have been the attraction, both to the government and to individual lay lords, of the idea of a partial disendowment of the Church. Proposals for the State to take over more of the possessions of the Church continued to be put forward in the Parliaments of Richard II despite clerical remonstrations. A precedent had already been established, since with the confiscation of alien priories under Edward III the State had carried out a limited form of dissolution, and laymen, including some of the Lollard knights, had invested in former monastic lands, paying rents below the market rate. When he had acquired a grant of the custody of Newent Priory Sir John Cheyne had even gained control of three appropriate rectories. It took a change of dynasty and the accompanying civil unrest for the State to concede that Lollards might constitute a threat to all owners of property whether ecclesiastical or lay.

The Parliament which passed the Act *De heretico comburendo* in 1401 had been summoned at a time when Henry IV's occupancy of the throne still seemed insecure, when he needed the full support of the Church hierarchy and could not afford to withstand clerical demands. So at last, some twenty years after the appearance of widespread popular heresy in England, a heretic could legally be condemned to death. The Act provided that heretics whose heresy had been proved in a church court and who refused to recant, or heretics who recanted and later returned to their heretical opinions, could be handed over to the civil power to be burnt. Ecclesiastical and civil offences could now in the last instance be punished with death, though some laymen in Parliament felt uneasy about this new departure and tried unsuccessfully in 1410 to amend the Act of 1401.

In fact throughout the reign of Henry IV and in the earlier part of the reign of his son the penalty of *De heretico comburendo* was very infrequently enforced. In 1409 Arundel condemned in London one of the earliest Lollard martyrs, John Badby, a tailor from Evesham, who may have come into contact with Lollardy in Bristol, and gave him to the secular authorities to be put to death as a relapsed heretic. Badby's offence had been to deny that the sacrament of the altar was the true body of Christ; witnesses recalled his rash declaration that 'John Rakier of Bristol had as much power and authority to make the like body of Christ, as any priest had'.[8] Until 1414 most of the handful of Lollards who suffered death for their beliefs seem to have come from a rather similar background to Badby's and it still was possible for the Government to disregard the political dangers of Lollardy. Sir John Oldcastle's revolt in 1414 completely changed the climate of opinion. It may very well be that desperation alone drove Old-castle to armed rebellion; he had for years been a trusted servant of Henry V and a member of his domestic circle, and no one then had disputed his loyalty. His attitude altered in 1413 when church-men challenged him as a Lollard in the presence of the King. His accusers went on to convict him of heresy, but he refused to recant and so they duly handed him over to the secular arm to be burnt. Such was his status that at this late stage the King intervened and ordered a stay of execution, hoping for a change of heart, but Oldcastle merely used the opportunity to contrive to escape from the Tower and sought refuge with a Lollard bookseller in Smith-field. Only apparently at this juncture did he contemplate over-throwing the existing government, installing himself as regent and imposing reform upon the Church by force of arms. His audacious plan to capture the royal family as they celebrated Christmas at Eltham stood little chance of success, and in fact waverers had betrayed it before Oldcastle gave the signal for the rising. The Lord Mayor of London was able to take a group of London Lollards by surprise, and soldiers loyal to the government had little trouble in routing those who converged on London from Oldcastle's estates in the Welsh Marches and Kent, and from Lollard communities in Bristol, in the Midlands, in the Chilterns and in Essex. Many of the rebels have been judged to be adventurers since so few were burnt as heretics, and social unrest undoubtedly contributed to the rising. The government, nevertheless, saw the revolt as a demonstration of the extent and political danger of popular heresy, and its crushing brought the relatively humane treatment of heretics to an end. From Oldcastle's capture and execution early in 1414 dates a much more severe campaign against heretics who now could all be considered potential traitors.

In some degree the government's fears may have brought their own fulfilment, for the harsher treatment of Lollards stimulated a further though in itself much less important revolt. In 1431 William Perkins, a weaver of Abingdon, and his companions planned again to overthrow the government and substitute an alternative Lollard government of Lollard lords financed by a partial disendowment of the Church. Again the treason came to light, and Perkins had been put to death at Abingdon before the Lollards could gather as intended at East Hendred in Berkshire. Yet this also seems to have been something more than a small local uprising. Perkins's assistants had spread propaganda leaflets in London, Oxford, Coventry, Northampton, Frome and Salisbury. John Russell, a woodman who had had connections with the London Lollard, Richard Gurmyn, burnt for heresy in 1415, provided a direct link between the revolts of Oldcastle and Perkins. The government in 1431 had expected Lollard disturbances in Leicester, Cambridgeshire and Kent, and imprisoned Sir John Cheyne and his brother from Buckinghamshire, a further link with 1414. The failure of Perkins's revolt finally drove Lollardy underground. There is no proof that Lollards subsequently engaged in civil unrest, and while more extreme Lollards may not have renounced their chiliastic expectations most seem to have retreated into quietism.

The State's view of Lollards after 1414 as subversive rebels has perhaps too much influenced some recent accounts of fifteenth-century Lollardy. It is certainly true that, after Oldcastle's revolt, Lollardy may indeed have lost virtually all its powerful lay patrons and, through burning, such academic leaders as had not already abandoned the movement, but it still retained sufficient vigour to make possible a later, surprising, second flowering. In the North of England Lollardy does seem to have been extirpated, and the Newcastle cell of priests and literate lay-people probably planted by the travelling evangelist Richard Wyche, possessing through him connections with other groups in Hereford, Bristol and London, did not long survive into the fifteenth century. In the South, however, the situation was very different. Lollardy remained entrenched in Bristol, and William Taylor, a priest and Master of Arts from Oxford, occasionally ministered to the Lollards there; around 1420 he was in the city, teaching that God alone should be worshipped, and condemning the invocation of the saints. He suffered death by burning in 1423. In 1429 William Emayn of Bristol withdrew a statement he had made that 'Master John Wyclif was holier and now is more in bliss and higher in heaven glorified than St Thomas of Canterbury, the glorious martyr'.[9]

Although for a time, immediately after Oldcastle's revolt, Bristol may well have overtaken London as a centre of Lollardy, orthodox churchmen never succeeded in eradicating heresy in the capital entirely. In 1414 Chicheley uncovered in London Lollards who seem to have acted as distributors for Lollard books. John Claydon, a London currier and a Lollard of twenty years' standing who had already been imprisoned for his beliefs for five years during Arundel's archiepiscopate, confessed to having heretical books in English, including the Wyclifite *Lantern of Light*. He had had books written and bound at his own costs and had been present at readings. Claydon was burnt as a relapsed heretic, and his associate, Richard Baker, may also have been put to death at this time. Other London Lollards abjured, including John Taylor of St Michael's, Quern, William James, MA, a physician who had long been in prison, and John Dwarf. This, however, did not end the authorities' fear of heresy in the city, and as it proved their fears had some justification. In 1434 a sign-writer was burnt on Tower Hill, another heretic suffered at Smithfield four years later, while Richard Wyche, whom some Londoners were subsequently accused of revering as a saint, met his death also on Tower Hill in 1440 (together with his servant). One other unnamed heretic died there eight years later.

Outside the great cities Lollardy still continued to take root in rural areas. In 1425 the Bishop of Norwich discovered a considerable amount of Lollardy in his diocese. A turner of Shilton had been asserting that the Pope and the Cardinals had no power to make laws and teaching that only Sunday should be kept holy. He condemned the worship of images, questioned the value of pilgrimages, and said tithes should not be paid to curates but divided among poor parishioners. Obviously he had been attracted largely by the social content of Lollardy, but a fellow Lollard, Richard Belward, belonged to a recognizably religious society. He was reported to have said, 'Truly, ye are fools that deny to learn the doctrine of my sect; for your neighbours who are of my sect

are able to confound and vanquish all other that are of your sect.'
The Bishop also heard 'that the said Richard keepeth schools of
Lollardy in the English tongue in the town of Ditchingham, and
a certain parchmentmaker bringeth him all the books containing
that doctrine from London'.[10]

There is evidence of gatherings for Bible reading in the diocese
of Salisbury where William Wakeham of Devizes led meetings of
weavers in Marlborough, and some Lollards in the diocese believed
in 1443 that 'holy Church Catholic is congregation of true men
which only shall be saved'.[11] In the same year in the Thames Valley
episcopal officers detected three priests from Bisham Priory, Cook-
ham and Wallingford of possessing the Gospels in English and
other Lollard books: they all abjured. At least one, Thomas Big-
nore, had been denouncing the Pope as Antichrist. From 1450
James Willis, a literate weaver who left Bristol and, after a term of
imprisonment in London, settled in Henley, revived heresy in the
Chilterns. After the exposure of a number of conventicles in
Norfolk and Suffolk between 1428 and 1431, Lollardy seems to
have remained dormant in East Anglia until 1457 when the Bishop
of Lincoln found a Lollard cell in Somersham in Huntingdonshire.
The Bishop's officers compiled a long list of heretical beliefs held
by Lollards there, and laid particular emphasis on two brothers,
William and Richard Sparke, who confessed to having attended a
large meeting of Lollards at which they had sworn on the Bible
to recruit as many to join their sect as they could, promising not
to reveal their names to any outsider until they had enough
members to destroy Antichrist and all his disciples.

Kent and the Midlands present a similar picture of Lollardy
in hiding between 1431 and 1460. The evangelist William White
had been very active in the Tenterden region before he escaped
to East Anglia, and for two years between 1434 and 1436 Richard
Wyche (who had probably taken Lollardy to Newcastle) held a
living near Ashford. In 1435 the new bishop of Rochester thought
it necessary to make enquiries into secret schools of heresy being
conducted by Lollards in his diocese, and three years after this
five men from Tenterden were burnt. In the 1450s the authorities
found anticlericalism particularly prevalent around Benenden,
Cranbrook and Tenterden and sporadically charged inhabitants of
the three towns with heresy. Far less has emerged about heresy
in the Midlands in this period. In 1431 the government suspected
Lollards from Coventry and Kenilworth of involvement in Perkins's

revolt, and some Lollards seem to have been executed. Other cases of Lollardy may have occurred in Staffordshire and Northamptonshire in the 1450s, but then all is silence for thirty years.

The apparent disappearance of widespread Lollardy between 1431 and 1460 (for which in any case the loss of the official records may partly be responsible) does not mean that either State or Church considered the problem of Lollardy had been solved. Indeed, these years mark the one attempt by a churchman to convert Lollards by 'doom of reason'. Reginald Pecock, a graduate of Oxford, had become master of Whittington College in London in 1431, and he continued to live in the city even after he obtained the Bishopric of St Asaph in 1444. The extent of Lollardy and anti-clericalism in London prompted him to write numerous books in English in the rather forlorn hope of winning heretics back to orthodoxy by means of logical argument. Pecock, like Swetstock and most of the clergy, had a keen appreciation of clerical prerogatives and did not doubt that the Lollards had overreached themselves by presuming to become their own interpreters of the scriptures. 'They would not fetch and learn their faith at the clergy of God's whole Church in earth,' he protested; rather, 'they would fetch and learn their faith at the Bible of holy scripture, in the manner as it shall hap them to understand it.' Pecock felt bitterly about the way in which misguided laymen ignored the teaching and biblical exposition of clerks learned in logic, moral philosophy and divinity, and insisted on going directly to the Bible. He knew from experience the misunderstandings this involved:

> I dare well say that so many opinions should arise in laymen's wits by occasion of texts in holy scripture about men's moral conversation, that all the world should be encumbered therewith, and men would agree together in keeping their service to God as dogs do in a market, when each of them tears the other's coat.[12]

Pecock's own books fared little better than the dogs fighting in the market place. His highly technical writings, expressed in ornate, latinate English, can have enjoyed little popular appeal, and conservative critics for their part strongly disapproved of his attempt to combat Lollardy by learning in this way since it involved a recognition of the educational attainments of some of the laity. His arrogance only fed the hostility of his clerical enemies, and from 1452, very soon after he had been promoted to the see of Chichester, his works came under attack. In 1457 Pecock, the antagonist of the Lollards, himself had to appear before an ecclesiastical court on a charge of heresy. By this date he had lost his protectors on the royal council: his political adversaries gave him the choice of abjuration, or degradation from his priestly orders and death as a heretic. He abjured, and though he was made to resign his see, he was permitted to end his days in relative comfort in Thorney Abbey. Pecock had had the misfortune to back the losing party in the State as well as in the Church, and undoubtedly part of the attack on him had been politically inspired; nevertheless, his fate provided an example of what could happen to clerics who tried to meet aspiring laymen on their own ground. No other English ecclesiastic courted the heretical laity with literary blandishments before the Reformation.

By 1460 the Church in England had been reduced to a checkmate. Some of the laity, at one stage representative of many sectors of society, had supported a movement designed drastically to reform the Church, and had failed. Equally, the clergy had attempted by persecution and fair words to dragoon the laity into subservience and orthodoxy, and had also failed. Churchmen could not divert a growing number of lay people from their interest in literacy and the independent thought that literacy fostered. While successive English governments during the years of dynastic uncertainty continued to rely on the moral support of the Church, and leading ecclesiastics continued to fill important offices in the State, the Church could expect protection from hostile attacks from the laity. As Edward IV and later Henry VII began to reassert the powers of the monarchy, however, very slowly the possibility of a Church more in tune with the wishes of some of the more assertive laymen began to revive. But this revival ultimately came too late for the victory of reformed Catholicism in England.

CHAPTER 2

LOLLARD REVIVAL AND
CONSERVATIVE REFORM

Between 1460 and 1520 articulate laymen continued to make as searching demands upon the organized Church in England as had their predecessors in the late fourteenth and the first part of the fifteenth centuries: in no way did their exacting view of the responsibilities of ecclesiastics both towards themselves as individuals and towards the Church as a whole diminish. In some parts of England there reappeared a surprisingly vigorous strain of Lollardy and this reveals in a heightened form the aspirations of some laymen. Others, doubtless the vast majority, remained theologically orthodox; yet, seemingly to meet their scarcely conscious promptings, a willingness to accept reform, in some cases an urgent call for reform, made itself felt in the Church. In the administration of dioceses, in the lives of parish priests, in some monasteries, in new foundations whose purpose was partly educational, changes, overall for the better, did take place between the accession of Edward IV and the reception of Lutheranism in England.

The reasons for the persistence of Lollardy in the later fifteenth century, almost a hundred years after it had lost its university leadership, have not yet been completely satisfactorily explained. To some extent a Lollard revival may have been an illusion created by contemporary churchmen who, after the chaotic last years of the reign of Henry VI, had a fresh opportunity to search for heretics under the more settled government of Edward IV. When they were in a position to visit their dioceses they again often found evidence of heresy and discontent. In addition, Edward IV, and later Henry VII, victors in civil war, were both engaged in building up new dynasties and relied on the moral and political support of their leading churchmen. They could not afford to ignore their susceptibilities as the Plantagenets had done, and may have actively encouraged heresy investigations as one means of securing internal stability. Some of the men condemned as Lollards by these ecclesiastical tribunals seem to have been little more than irreverent critics of the Church and its ministers, but equally clearly not all cases of Lollardy can be dismissed as the inventions of ultra-suspicious clerical minds. Whether there was an actual growth in the number of heretics towards the end of the fifteenth century must remain debatable; nevertheless an evangelical element certainly survived and perhaps even developed in Lollardy in this period and this manifested itself quite distinctly in certain parts of England.

From the incomplete knowledge at present available, the Chilterns seem to have been one of the main areas where Lollardy put down deep and lasting roots in the later fifteenth century. Lollard sympathies may well have lingered in the Thames valley from the time of Perkins's abortive rising, but the chief propagator of Lollard beliefs in the district was James Willis, the disciple of William Smith of Bristol, who left Bristol about 1450 and ultimately settled in Henley. Willis was burnt as a relapsed heretic in 1462, charged also with denying transubstantiation and with possessing Lollard books. Between 1462 and 1464 episcopal officials went on to expose his followers, who included John Polley of Henley, John Conwyrk, Thomas Scrivener and Geoffrey Simeon of Amersham, but the death of their leader failed to scotch the movement. Thomas White of Chesham soon emerged as another teacher and, according to information which came out of the 1464 persecution, the group seems to have been located in High Wycombe. With an intermission in persecution, clear evidence of Lollardy in the Chilterns vanishes for sixteen years; then at trials held in the early sixteenth century Lollards from the Chilterns reappear in some numbers, confessing, moreover, to having held their beliefs since 1480.

The Lollards in the Chilterns had easy communications with their fellows in Reading where ecclesiastics discovered several heretics in the 1480s and 1490s and a further Berkshire group at Wantage. All these communities owned Lollard books; they had the Gospels and Epistles in English, and perhaps some other books of the Bible. The Bishop of Salisbury began a major persecution in Berkshire in 1508 which resulted in two burnings and many abjurations. Bishop Smith of Lincoln carried out a similar campaign three years later and made a fresh onslaught on those parts of the Chilterns which lay in his diocese where he may have unmasked as many as sixty Lollards. Because of the very imperfect transmission of the records, information about all these episodes is fragmentary at best, but Foxe has preserved the detailed confessions of Lollards from the Chilterns brought to trial during the last great persecution of Bishop Longland in 1521. From this material

the spiritual life of the community can be pieced together retro-
spectively in very considerable detail; it gives some insight into
those aspirations for which some lay people were willing to risk
their lives at the turn of the fifteenth century.

Nicholas Durdant of Staines and his wife, Davy Durdant of
Akerwith together with their parents formed one Lollard family
cell. Robert Carder, a weaver of Iver, remembered how old Durdant
sitting at dinner had once ordered his boy to leave them, so that
he could not inform on them, and had then recited to the company
certain places out of St Paul and the Gospels. Joan Cocks, a
husbandman's wife, had come to Durdant, her master, and asked
him to teach her some knowledge of God's law. At the wedding
of Durdant's daughter, John Merryweather, his wife and son,
Isabel the wife of Thomas Harding, Hartop of Windsor, Joan
Barret, wife of John Barret of London, Henry Miller, Stilman and
Taylor had all joined the Durdant family in a barn to hear readings
from an Epistle of St Paul.

Robert Pope, who had lived in Amersham until the great abjuration of 1512 and then it seems fled to West Hendred, had obtained
a book of Epistles in English from Thomas Scrivener, probably a
relation of the William Scrivener of Amersham put to death for
heresy in 1511. Benet Ward of Beaconsfield had let him have a
book of the Ten Commandments and the Gospels of Matthew and
Mark, and had taught him five parts of the Eight Beatitudes.
Thomas Harding and his wife, John Scrivener and his wife, the
two Thomas Mans and their wives and Thomas Bernard had talked
with Pope about books of scripture and other matters of religion
concerning pilgrimages, images and the sacrament of the altar.
Ownership of books seems to have been widespread in the community; Richard Collins of Ging, a great reader, had Wyclif's
Wicket, a book of Luke and one of Paul and another of the
Apocalypse. Robert Pope supplied William Halliday of East Hendred
with the Acts of the Apostles, and Pope himself had borrowed
St John's Gospel from Richard Collins. Alice Sanders, wife of
Richard Sanders of Amersham, displayed a great keenness to
acquire English books, not matched by the necessary resources to
pay for them. On one occasion she gave Thomas Holmes 12*d*
towards an English book for her daughter which cost more than
a noble, and another time presented him with sixpence to buy an
English book priced at five marks.

The Collins family of Ging outdid the Durdants in their mission-

C.A.P.   B

ary activities, and Foxe supplies some details of their instruction
as well as of their reading. Richard Collins exhorted Robert Pope
not to worship images or go on pilgrimages. On the sacraments
he believed a man should confess himself to God alone, or to the
man he may have wronged, and he held that the sacrament of the
altar should be reverenced but was not very God. He taught from
Wyclif's *Wicket*, and had an exposition of the Apocalypse in
English, as well as *Our Lady's Matins*, a book of Solomon and
The Prick of Conscience. Alice, Richard Collins's wife, had won
a reputation equal to that of her husband. She had a good memory
and could recite much of the scriptures and other good books,
so that when a conventicle met in Burford the members sent for
her to recite the Ten Commandments and the Epistles of Peter and
James. Their daughter, Joan, had been brought up to follow in her
parents' footsteps. She had learnt the Ten Commandments, the
Seven Deadly Sins, the Seven Works of Mercy, the Five Wits Bodily
and Ghostly, the Eight Blessings, and five chapters of St James's
Epistle.

It would be hard to deny the very real piety of these Lollards
of the Chilterns and the Thames valley, nourished by the New
Testament in English and other Lollard works, by travelling
evangelists and by their own conventicles. In all the many confessions little of that crude anti-clericalism appeared which churchmen categorized as Lollardy in some other parts of England: these
Lollards made a point of speaking with respect of the Mass, but insisted that it was a remembrance of Christ's body, and not the very
body of Christ himself. The confessions illustrate the narrowness
of the distinction between orthodoxy and heresy. Richard Collins
owned copies of the apparently orthodox *Prick of Conscience* while
his daughter's teachings on the Seven Works of Mercy or the
Seven Deadly Sins would probably never have been questioned if
they had come from a priest. What, however, must have been
alarming to the ecclesiastics was the survival, even the growth, of
communities independent of the organized Church. Laymen like
Durdant and Collins proved to be quite capable of instructing their
fellows. Their friends spent money on Lollard books, and some,
who were illiterate, learnt to read with the express purpose of
reaching the kernel of the scriptures for themselves. Roger Dodds
of Burford was such a man; he persuaded the vicar of Windrush
to teach him his A B C so that he might attempt unaided to unravel
the mysteries of the Apocalypse.

The Lollards of the Chilterns and the Thames valley fail to conform to the stereotyped version of later Lollardy in another respect. While it remains difficult to assess the exact social distribution of these Lollard communities, almost certainly not all came from the lowest levels of society. Some Lollards had considerable sums to spend on books; the Bishop's officers heard that John Phip of Hughenden had burnt his books worth 100 marks when he feared that he was coming under suspicion. John Sawcourt alleged that Thomas Grove had given Dr Wilcocks £20 to avoid doing public penance, and he reported one Sanders of Amersham for defending 'known men', for buying out his penance and for carrying his Lollard badge in his purse instead of wearing it as the ecclesiastical court had ordered. Alice Sanders put pressure on her husband to dismiss one of his servants for abandoning his Lollard beliefs when the persecution grew hot; the Durdants, the Collinses and the Phips also seem to have been substantial households employing servants, and it may well be that some of them could claim yeoman status. Certainly it would be inaccurate to picture Lollardy as surviving in the Chilterns only among semi-rural communities of poor cloth workers, although Lollards did make full use of the commercial communications of the woollen and clothing industries in the South of England and the Midlands as a means of maintaining contact between communities.

James Willis, the weaver who had revived Lollardy in the Chilterns, had come from Bristol, where, in spite of persecution, Lollardy had persisted; though much less is known about it in Bristol than in the Chilterns. In August 1499, John Bouway the elder and John Bouway the younger of the parish of St Mary Redcliffe abjured their heretical opinions before the Bishop of Bath and Wells, and a little later in the year German Hay of Temple parish, John Walsh, it seems also of St Mary Redcliffe, William Lewis, weaver of St Thomas's parish in Bristol, renounced their Lollardy. In July 1499, William Hall, bottlemaker of Bristol, had denied that he had taught against pilgrimages and the veneration of saints. The Lollards taken in August and in the autumn admitted to having believed that the sacrament of the altar was not the body of Christ in flesh and blood and to have had fellowship and communed willingly with suspect men and women.

The sparse details in the register of the Bishop of Bath and Wells gave little indication of the nature of Bristol Lollardy: it could be taken to have been spiritually weak, but it may be very misleading to judge on such slight evidence. In the same year as the Bristol group of Lollards was discovered the Bishop of Salisbury's official examined two priests from the neighbouring diocese and recorded much more about their faith. John Whitehorn, parson of Coombe Bissett, displayed considerable skill in biblical exposition. He admitted having taught 'that Christ saying to his disciples, at his Maundy, "Take and eat, this is my body" etc. meant not of bread that he break there, but of God's word. "For the word is God, and God is the word," as in the beginning of St John's gospel. And, therefore, whosoever receive devoutly God's word, he receiveth the very body of Christ.' He had believed that there 'is no need to be shriven to a priest or to any other minister of the Church, but that it is enough to be aknowing to God and to be sorry for the sin, being in will to return no more to the sin'. He had condemned the worship of images, and questioned the value of pilgrimages. The Pope he regarded as Antichrist, for by his laws and dispensations he 'turneth up and down the laws that Christ left to the people'. At his ascension Christ bestowed his power to his apostles, and from them it passed to 'every good true Christian man and woman living virtuously as the apostles did, so that priests and bishops have no more authority than another layman that followeth the teaching and the good conversation of the apostles'. On the same occasion ecclesiastical officials condemned John Lidster, who had served in the parish of Sparfold, for holding heretical opinions similar to those of Whitehorn: at their common public abjuration Whitehorn had to deliver his heretical books to the flames.[1]

Lidster and Whitehorn were by no means the only clerks who had been propagating anti-hierarchical ideas from within the Church. In Coventry, also, priests found the simplicity of Lollardy attractive. A group of nine Coventry Lollards appeared before the Bishop of Coventry and Lichfield in 1486, but the size and importance of the community there did not fully emerge until 1511 when seventy-four people were examined on suspicion of heresy. One of the leading Coventry heretics, Robert Silkeby, knew John Bouway, one of the Bristol Lollards, and there were other indirect contacts with Bristol through John Johnson, a Birmingham Lollard. Like the Lollards in the Chilterns, the Coventry Lollards were well supplied with books; they possessed the Old Testament as well as the New and a volume of Tobit, and they held conventicles to hear readings from their books, some of which they had kept hidden for eighteen years. Women participated actively in the sect, and Alice Rowley in particular excelled in her readings. In Coventry Lollardy definitely seems to have penetrated the upper social levels in the town. Richard Cook, a member of the ruling oligarchy for a quarter of a century until his death in 1507, mayor in 1486 and 1503, member of Parliament for the town in 1491 and 1495, was incriminated posthumously in 1511. Cook had bequeathed two English Bibles in his will. The group contained two other mercers of similar standing to Cook and a physician, John Blumstone. William Wigston the younger of Leicester, married to Agnes Pysford, held office in Coventry during Cook's lifetime, and William Pysford the elder became mayor in 1501: two Lollards declared in 1511 that Mr Wigston and Mr Pysford had 'beautiful books' of heresy. It may well have been that men of this stature could have used their wealth and prestige to escape censure. In addition James Preston, a Doctor of Theology from Oxford and the vicar of St Michael's, Coventry, from 1488 until his death in 1507, had close connections with Pysford and Cook and, judging from the unusually austere terminology of his will, at least sympathized with some of the sentiments of the Lollards. The Bishop's officers picked up the rumour that another Coventry priest, Richard Shore, owned heretical books, while Dr Alcock of Ibstock had taken heretical books to a fellow priest, Mr Kent of Stanton, also in Leicestershire. The evidence so fully uncovered in 1511 indicates at the very least that among the higher clergy in the Coventry area there were priests who inclined towards Lollardy, and some among the leading citizens who wanted to have access to the Bible in the vernacular and who apparently supported Lollard criticisms of the Church.

The Coventry Lollards had links with Bristol, the Chilterns and London. Again it was London that provided the point of contact with a further vigorous Lollard community in East Anglia centred upon Colchester. Lollardy which had been fairly strong in the diocese of Norwich in the earlier part of the fifteenth century had apparently died out, and seems to have been re-established in Essex and Suffolk through the activities of proselytizers from outside the region, one of whom was Thomas Man who subsequently fled from Colchester to Newbury in Berkshire. Sweeting, burnt as a relapsed heretic in 1511, had come from Northampton to Essex and then served the Prior of St Osyth's for sixteen years. After his first abjuration he had obtained work as a holy water clerk at

Colchester and given readings from Lollard books to a little group
in the town. From these rather small beginnings the Vicar General
of the Bishop of London uncovered in 1528 a widespread network
of heresy stemming directly from the burnings and abjurations of
1511.

Although the episcopal officials came upon the Essex Lollard
communities so late, years after Lutheran ideas had penetrated the
English universities, these men still continued to observe traditional
Lollard practices. John Pykas spoke of Lollards in Colchester who
could recite by heart the Epistle of James, beginning 'James, the
true servant of God'. He himself had secretly discussed with John
Girling the meaning of Chapter 24 in Matthew where Christ had
said of Jerusalem 'If thou knowest, thou wouldst weep. For there
shall not a stone of thee be left upon a stone; for thou shalt be
destroyed.' This, he thought, foretold the eventual destruction of
the priests and the men of the Church because they punished
heretics. Pykas confessed to having taught others the Lord's Prayer
and the Ten Commandments in English and the Epistles of James
and John. He brought them to see that pilgrimages were not profitable for a man's soul, and that no honour or worship should be
given to the images in churches, but only to saints who were in
heaven. From Pykas's admission it emerges that some members, like
Alice Gardiner, had belonged to the group for twenty years. There
seems to have been substantial agreement in Colchester on the
sacraments, corresponding to the teaching of the Chiltern Lollards.
Mrs Girling, when questioned on the Mass, replied 'that the sacrament of the altar was but an host; and that the body of almighty
God was joined in the word; and the word of God was all one,
and might not be departed'.[2]

Between the Lollards of Essex and those of Kent there were
parallels but not the close contacts which might have been
expected. Lollardy may well have been indigenous in Kent since
the early fifteenth century, but a revival also seems to have occurred
there as in Essex, though perhaps beginning a little earlier. This
led to a similar exposure in 1511. Towards the end of the reign
of Edward IV one John Ive converted Agnes Grebill to heresy:
the Grebill family and William Carder, a weaver, then seem to
have been the main instigators of heresy in the Tenterden area.
In 1495 Joan Washingby of Coventry abjured at Maidstone. Apart
from this one example of a stranger apparently bringing in heretical
beliefs, the Kentish Lollards seem to have had fewer links with

communities outside the country than did other groups. By 1511 Lollardy appears to have been most strongly entrenched around Tenterden, Benenden and Canterbury. In that year Archbishop Warham sentenced William Carder, Agnes Grebill, now aged sixty, Robert Harrison, John Browne and Edward Walker to be burnt, while no less than thirty-four Lollards abjured. The ecclesiastical authorities extorted standardized confessions from these Kentish Lollards, with the result that it is not possible to assess the vitality of the movement there as it is in Essex. In their confessions they were assumed to have believed that the sacrament of the altar was not the very body of Christ, but only bread; to have denied the need of confession to a priest or of extreme unction; to have held that pilgrimages were not meritorious, that no worship should be paid to images of saints, and that God gave no more power to a priest than to a layman. Certain of the Lollards possessed heretical books. It may be that by regularizing the forms of confession in this way the Archbishop's officers in 1511 unduly played down the spiritual element in Kentish Lollardy and exaggerated its anti-clerical aspect.

Certainly it was the spiritual element that seems to have been uppermost in London Lollardy until it became merged into Protestantism. At various times towards the end of the fifteenth and early in the sixteenth century there are clear signs that London Lollards saw themselves in some sense as the organizing centre of Lollardy throughout southern England. Lollardy in London resembled Lollardy in Coventry in that it may have penetrated the governing class, but in a rather less spectacular way. Joan Boughton, aged eighty, burnt for heresy at Smithfield in 1494, was the mother of Lady Young, wife of a former lord mayor; Lady Young also appears to have shared her mother's fate. Joan Baker, tried in 1511, was the wife of a merchant tailor, and many offenders seem to have been city craftsmen. While the heresy of Richard Hunne must probably remain not proven, the evidence is fairly strong that he did own an English Bible with a Wyclifite prologue and in this respect at least he can be compared with the Pysford and the Wigston families in Coventry.

Within the city of London Lollardy seems to have been concentrated upon Coleman Street. The itinerant evangelist, Thomas Man, may have had a refuge in London; he certainly taught there on his journeys between the Lollard colonies in Colchester, Amersham and Newbury. He said himself that he had also spread Lollard ideas in Chelmsford, Stratford Langthorn, Uxbridge, Burnham, Henley-on-Thames and in Norfolk and Suffolk, and claimed that together with his wife he had converted six or seven hundred people to his opinions. Like any good pastor, he took pains to safeguard his flock and when persecution threatened in the Amersham area he helped five couples to flee to Norfolk and Suffolk to escape attention. Man was burnt as a relapsed heretic at Smithfield in 1518. John Hacker, an evangelist of a similar mould, though his travels did not take him so far afield, based himself on Coleman Street and seems indeed to have taken up Man's mantle after his martyrdom. He gained a reputation as a great reader and teacher in London and Essex from about 1520; he still taught the traditional Lollard doctrine that the sacrament of the altar was not the very body of God, but a remembrance of God who was in the heavens, and repudiated images and pilgrimages. In London Hacker held meetings for six years at one Russell's house in Bird's Alley, and had a reasonably good supply of books, *The Bayly*, *The Ten Commandments*, the gospel of St Matthew in English and *The Prick of Conscience*. One of his followers, John Sercot, a grocer of Coleman Street, paid the costs of a scribe called John to write out the Apocalypse in English in John Stacey's house in the same street. Together with Thomas Philip Hacker read a book of St Paul. From London Hacker went to Colchester where he left his copy of St Luke, and he passed on his Ten Commandments to the Lollard cell in Witney.

With the examples of evangelists like Man and Hacker, there can be little doubt that in some areas of England, in East Anglia, around Coventry, Bristol, in the Thames valley and the Chilterns, in Kent and in London, Lollardy survived as a living movement, with fairly coherent doctrines and with books, until the Protestant Reformation. It remained a heresy which could still win over some priests, and its enticements for independently-minded laymen need little demonstration. No one saw more clearly than John Tyball the attraction of Lollardy in the early sixteenth century. He had contacts with Lollards in Colchester, and through them with Hacker, but he claimed he became convinced of the truths of Lollardy by perusing the four evangelists in English, St John and certain Epistles of Peter and Paul: a chapter of St Paul to the Corinthians weighed especially with him. He then progressed to the belief that the sacrament of the altar was not the very body of Christ, but a remembrance of his passion, and that no priest had any power to consecrate the body of Christ. Taking literally the saying of St James, 'Show your sins one to another', he taught that it was as good for a man to confess himself to God alone, or else to any layman, as to a priest. He thought that the priest-hood was not necessary, for every layman might minister the sacraments of the Church as well as any priest. He shared the standard Lollard dislike of pilgrimages and of images in churches, but had reached this position for himself. He did not know whether the Pope or the Bishop had power to grant pardon; sometimes he thought they had, and sometimes thought they had not, 'because they had so much money for it'. Citing St Paul, 'Wear ye no gold, silver, nor pearls, ne precious stones', he considered it were better that mitres, crosses, rings and other precious stones should be given to poor and needy people than for churchmen to luxuriate in their riches.

Once grounded in his opinions, Tyball set to work to convert the incumbent of Steeple Bumpstead where he lived. For a time he debated with Richard Fox about the existence of purgatory; leaving him, he fell in with William Strynger and one Sir Arthur, other priests at Bumpstead, arguing that if he could bring a priest to accept his learning and heresies, he was 'sure and strong enough'. He failed to make any impression on them, but in the end he had more success with Fox when he showed him the books he had obtained from John Pykas in Colchester, the New Testament in English, the gospel of St Matthew and St Mark, a book expounding the *pater noster*, the *ave* and the *credo*, and certain of St Paul's Epistles. 'And so in process of time, by reasoning of things con-tained in the said books, and disputing and instructing, he brought Sir Richard Fox to his learning and opinions.' One articulate but humble layman (Tyball was probably a husbandman like most of the other Lollards of Steeple Bumpstead) had proved to his own satisfaction that his religious views could overcome the received ideas of his local priest.[3]

Tyball compounded his heresy of a nice mixture of religious idealism, scriptural fundamentalism and anti-clericalism. He exhi-bited in a somewhat extreme form traits which many orthodox laymen shared in the late fifteenth century. It cannot be denied that Lollardy provided a cloak under which some laymen could indulge their often temporary dislike and jealousy of the Church and the clergy, or that the Church, on the defensive, labelled as Lollards men who were merely expressing traditional anti-clericalism and whose outbursts, often mere drunken boasting, had little serious doctrinal content. The Bishop's officers suspected Richard Carder of belonging to the Lollard community in the Chilterns on the strength of his assertion that he could as well confess to a post, or to the altar, as to the vicar of Iver. Yet Carder's rash words seem to have been prompted as much as anything by his suspicions of his wife's intimacy with the vicar. Henry Phip's calling the rood the 'block almighty' can have been little more than a coarse joke, and Eleanor Higges's brag that she should burn the sacrament in the oven was mere bravado. More commonly Lollards linked abuse with some pious exhortations, however incongruous the conjunction may now appear. Stephen Swallow in 1489 admitted before the Archbishop of Canterbury to having said that 'the Pope is an old whore, sitting upon many waters, having a cup of poison in his hand. Also that the Pope is Antichrist, and all cardinals, archbishops, bishops, priests and religious men be the disciples of Antichrist . . . That the Church of Rome is the synagogue of Satan'; but even he had first stressed the need of every contrite man to make a sincere confession of his sins to God. That strain of almost mindless iconoclasm that has been noticed in the Chilterns and elsewhere in the mid-fifteenth century seems to have been an aberrant one. There are traces of it in the sixteenth century, but it cannot be considered a chief characteristic of late Lollardy.[4]

Lollards usually reserved their attacks for the upper reaches of the hierarchy of the Catholic Church and did not so often revile their particular parish priests. It may be that some like John Tyball or the Lollards in Coventry hoped to convert their clergy to their way of thinking: at least they knew at first hand the difficulties under which parish priests laboured. Some Lollards, again like Tyball, had grasped the economic realities in the late medieval Church; he wanted to divest bishops of their riches, but made no wild statements about the easy conditions in which parish priests lived. Perhaps only Lollards who could with equanimity contemplate the disendowment of the Church had a solution, albeit a drastic one, for the gross inequalities which had persisted unchecked. The Church still had vast revenues, but the great majority of parish incumbents continued to live on the verge of poverty. Rarely did a priest's remuneration coincide with the extent of his responsibilities: a tiny rural parish might happen by accident to have kept all its glebe land, a populous urban parish if appropriated frequently had a quite inadequate endowment. Part of the great problem of the insufficiency of the stipends of so many parish priests lay in the fact that by the end of the fifteenth century rather more than a third of all parochial livings in England had been appropriated to religious houses or religious corporations. Around 1500, it has been calculated, a parish incumbent needed an income of £15 a year if he employed a chaplain to help him in his work, or of £10 a year if he worked alone in his parish. This £10 covered his food, clothes and taxation which, through Convocation, Tudor governments were imposing more and more regularly upon the Church. With the beginning of the price rise in the 1520s, a priest with an income of £10 would have found himself hard-pressed to meet his obligations. Yet not all priests had even £10 a year. The *Valor Ecclesiasticus*, compiled for the government in 1535, suggests that three-quarters of parish livings were worth less than £15, half of all livings less than £10, and many less than £7 a year. Priests without a benefice, who served an incumbent as a chaplain, probably suffered most severely. Of nearly three hundred chaplains working in east Yorkshire in 1525 under thirty received more than £4 a year. Despite the resources of the Church, a large number of clergy in the reign of Henry VIII lived in conditions approaching poverty. It is hardly surprising that on occasions they sided with some of their parishioners against their ecclesiastical superiors.[5]

On the whole, however, and especially with the beginning of rapid inflation, the poverty of many of the lower clergy had the effect of increasing the antagonism of the laity towards the Church, particularly when beneficed clergy resorted to an over-zealous collection of tithes in order to obtain a relatively adequate income. Disputes over tithe collection in towns, where in any case the complications of the tithing system were far greater for an urban incumbent than for his rural colleague, seem to have intensified in the early sixteenth century, and perhaps most of all in London. With the increase of prices in the 1520s even the clergy's customary demands bore more heavily on lay people who equally had to contend with the rising cost of food and they bitterly resented any attempt to raise clerical dues. The laity opposed equally strongly the traditional remedy for clerical poverty, pluralism. One Lollard in the early sixteenth century, with pardonable exaggeration, said it was as lawful for a temporal man to have two wives as for a priest to have two benefices. The

Church, however, continued to license a man to hold two benefices with cure of souls simultaneously and justified the practice on the grounds that a single parochial benefice might well not provide an adequate income for a well-qualified cleric. A licensed pluralist, whether his non-residence was permitted because of poverty or because of demands by the Church or State for his service else-where, always had the responsibility of arranging for a substitute to carry out the parish work from which he was absent. By the end of the fifteenth century some parishioners at least felt that non-resident incumbents did not take these obligations seriously enough and had resorted to self-help. In 1473, for example, the laity of Masham in Yorkshire brought in a chaplain at their own cost because their absent vicar had not provided a replacement. At Thundersley in Essex, where the vicar scandalized the inhabi-tants by his behaviour with a certain mistress Jane when he came to the village and failed to make alternative arrangements for services when he did not, the parishioners hired chaplains, first on a day-to-day, then on a weekly basis at the rate of six shillings for fifteen days. The churchwardens of Braughing in Hertfordshire kept a careful record of when their vicar visited the parish and of the way in which he then performed his duties.

Paradoxically lay people shared some accountability for the very parochial absenteeism and the flight of the clergy from benefices with the cure of souls which they deplored. The multi-plicity of chantry foundations in the later Middle Ages made it possible for clergy, deterred by the obligations of a parish, to seek instead the often slightly better paid and certainly less onerous duties of a chantry chaplain. In the city of York alone at the time of the Reformation the Henrician commissioners found thirty-eight chantries still surviving in the Minster and a further thirty-nine distributed between nineteen different city parish churches and chapels: before the amalgamations of the early sixteenth century as many as one hundred and forty chantries may have existed within the city, more than half of which had been endowed by rich merchants. Belief in the efficacy of perpetual masses for certain named dead, to which this expenditure of wealth bore such eloquent witness, can be seen as yet another aspect of lay indivi-dualism of which Lollardy was but one expression. The very wealthy established perpetual chantries with priests offering prayers for their souls continuously; the less wealthy, unable to afford the very considerable financial outlay a chantry foundation involved, could still make bequests to chantries already in being for a similar return of prayers for their souls, while more humble lay people joined trade or parish guilds to ensure at least one requiem mass on their death. Although the spate of chantry foundations slackened in the late fifteenth century, more, it seems, because of difficult economic circumstances than through any widespread change in belief, a form of employment had been created which drew many of the lower clergy away from parish responsibilities. When laymen attacked parasitic priests, they could well have been attacking men whose offices they or their ancestors had created.

Critical lay attitudes may have alerted the higher clergy of the need for some action. Bishops and their officers increasingly tried to impose greater discipline upon unruly chantry priests: in York George Nevill, a future archbishop, and his brother, the Earl of Warwick, built a college in the 1460s specifically for the chantry priests from the Minster. Towards the end of the century, bishops paid more attention also to the problems of non-residence and pluralism in the parishes. Churchmen like Archbishop Bourchier and Cardinal Morton concerned themselves particularly with the evils which could result in a parish through the parson's absence. When they carried out ecclesiastical visitations their administrators regularly enquired about absence without licence, and it could be that by the early sixteenth century unlicensed non-residence was declining. Nevertheless, when the Bishop of Norwich's official visited 489 parishes in the diocese in 1499 he found 48 incumbents absent. In 1511 37 vicars and rectors did not reside in the diocese of Canterbury out of a total of 266 parishes. A visitation of the diocese of Lincoln in 1518 showed that a quarter of the incumbents were not living in their parishes. Such evidence suggests that the Church was responding in a piecemeal way to an abuse, but it probably would have needed far more vigorous action to have won the co-operation of the laity. Pious admonitions, even fairly effective administrative action, could not remedy the inequalities of remuneration in the ecclesiastical establishment.

The generous endowment of certain high offices in the Church also continued to contribute to the dereliction of duty, just as did the poverty of the majority of parochial livings. As in the past the Crown used rich bishoprics to reward its leading servants but there are signs that these bishops by the end of the fifteenth century were taking their pastoral duties much more seriously. For William Smith translation to the see of Lincoln in 1495 crowned his career

as an industrious servant of the Tudor interest. Advanced by the
Lady Margaret (the mother of Henry VII) he had held office in the
royal Chancery, then become a member of the Council in the
Marches of Wales and ultimately its president, until he retired in
1512. Despite his necessary residence in the Welsh Marches, Smith
worried about his absences from Lincoln and managed to visit his
cathedral four times between 1501 and 1510 and hold eleven
ordinations in an episccpate lasting nineteen years. Bishop Atwater,
who came to Lincoln in 1514 when already an old man, did not
have high government office and so could devote himself almost
exclusively to his diocese. In the five years he was bishop, the
last five years of his life in fact, he seems to have visited every
archdeaconry in the diocese and conducted visitations of at least
one hundred and three deaneries and religious houses. Here was
a pastor actively trying to know his immense diocese. At Rochester,
a much smaller diocese, between 1504 and 1535 John Fisher built
up a reputation as a model pastoral bishop. At York, on the other
hand, some of the worst abuses of the Middle Ages continued:
Wolsey, a flagrant pluralist, never visited his diocese and gave pride
of place to his service of the King. Despite his example, most of
the early Tudor episcopate did seem to have a higher appreciation
of their responsibilities to the Church than did the bishops of the
generation of Reginald Pecock, although their conscientiousness
and diligence, within limits, were still not sufficient to silence
radical lay criticism of lordly prelates.

In another sphere the Church had begun to respond to the
implied criticisms of the laity. More highly educated men were
being admitted to livings. Of the 198 men presented to benefices
in the diocese of Lincoln between 1421 and 1431 only seven were
graduates. In the twenty-five years between 1495 and 1520, however, their number rose spectacularly to 261, out of a total of 1429.
Representing something like an eight per cent increase over the
century, this seems to have been a rising trend. During Bishop
Tunstall's tenure of the see of London (1522–30) about a third of
those in possession of livings had university degrees: in the city
of London out of 52 incumbents six were Doctors of Theology or
Law, 33 Masters of Arts. Because of its uniquely favourable opportunities for advancement, London always enjoyed more than its
fair share of the highly-educated clergy, but even in the more
typical diocese of Norwich out of 1454 men presented to benefices
between 1503 and 1528 256 were graduates, or just over one-sixth.

A university degree by the end of the fifteenth century almost invariably acted as a passport to high office or at least to a comfortable series of ecclesiastical livings. Yet the increase of university educated men among the clergy probably did not improve the Church to anything like the extent expected by the rather naïve enthusiasts for education. For it was graduate clergy who proved to be most liable to non-residence, since these were the men needed for secular or ecclesiastical administration. Although they may well have picked up some rudiments of theology during the long period necessary to acquire their MA degree, most graduates until well into the sixteenth century studied not theology but canon and civil law. This was an excellent training for episcopal officials, holding church courts, carrying out visitations, administering the temporalities of the see, but not for pastors of souls. A new type of theological learning more appropriate to the needs of some of the more forward laity in the parishes was indeed just beginning to penetrate the universities, but the doctrines of continental Protestantism reached England too early for it to have any general revivifying effect.

In spite of the advent of printing, and the publication of scholarly editions of Latin and Greek authors, the lower clergy at the beginning of the sixteenth century showed little sign of enthusiasm for the 'new learning' beloved of Colet and More. Of the clerics in the Norwich diocese, for example, who died between 1500 and 1550 and made wills only a fifth included books among their possessions – though it is highly likely that a larger proportion may well have owned one or two books but did not think of mentioning them. Of the known book owners only nine were university graduates. In the main they had service books, practical aids to preaching, and copies of the *Golden Legend*, that mine of information for lives of the saints. A very few clergy possessed commentaries on the Vulgate, but these were still medieval commentaries by Haymo of Faversham and Nicholas de Lyra. The exceptional cleric with historical interests continued to turn to Geoffrey of Monmouth; another left a book on rhetoric by Alanus de Insulis, while a Bachelor of Sacred Theology had kept perhaps from his undergraduate days a commentary on Aristotle's philosophy by Averroes. Only one priest revealed any interest in the classics: he bequeathed several books of Virgil and some Terence and Ovid. More than anything else the survey demonstrates the conservatism of the Norwich clergy. Neither illiterate nor incompetent, they remained quite untouched by the new trends appearing in the universities in the latter part of the fifteenth century.[6]

In their conservatism these clerics most probably reflected the attitudes of the majority of their parishioners. Caxton and Wynkyn de Worde, the first English printers, discovered an apparently unlimited market for edifying saints' lives and traditional devotional treatises. Laymen might revere the austerity of the Carthusians and the Observant Franciscans and yet themselves indulge in highly elaborate religious ceremonies and ostentatious display. Henry VI, Edward IV, Henry VII and Henry VIII all patronized the construction of the royal chapel at Cambridge whose ornamentation developed into a massive tribute to the Tudor dynasty. At a socially somewhat lower level in the nearby county of Suffolk, the rebuilding of the parish churches of Long Melford and Lavenham took the form of an open acknowledgement in stone of the munificence of the earls of Oxford, the rich clothier family of Spring, and other wealthy inhabitants. Under the benevolent eye of the civic corporation, not unaware of the pecuniary advantage to city traders, crowds flocked to York at Corpus Christi time to watch the mystery plays staged by the city guilds. These cycles of plays and the rebuilding of churches had parellels all over England. Lay people seem to have had an insatiable appetite for the spectacular and magnificent in religious as in secular life. Yet some laymen, and particularly some of the better educated, had been turning away from such extravagance. They placed a new emphasis on the written and spoken word, and particularly on the kind of preaching which, under the influence of the exponents of the new learning, was becoming more of a direct exposition of the New Testament than a pietistic homily on the lives of the saints. Significantly, when Lollards found anything to praise in the English Church in the early sixteenth century they lighted upon this new style of preaching. From the Chilterns Lollards went up to London to hear Colet preach at St Paul's, while a few years later Essex Lollards made an excursion to Ipswich in order to profit from Bilney's evangelical teaching.

The innate conservatism of the mass of English lower clergy and laity created problems which the Christian humanists of the late fifteenth and early sixteenth centuries never seem to have fully understood. In aspiring to reform the Church through reforming the education of the clergy they did not foresee that some enter-

prising laymen might respond to their innovations more readily
than the generality of the clergy. At the outset men like Colet,
Linacre, More, and above all Erasmus overestimated the appeal of
the new learning. Even in the universities until almost the middle
of the sixteenth century the majority of the teachers and students
remained loyal to late medieval scholasticism: an interest in
classical Latin developed only slowly, and an interest in learning
Greek more slowly still. At both Oxford and Cambridge a number
of colleges had been founded during the fifteenth century: among
others, Lincoln, All Souls and Magdalen at Oxford; King's, Queens',
St Catharine's and Jesus at Cambridge. In most of these foundations,
however, traditional late medieval piety seems to have been a
more pressing motive than any appreciation of learning for its
own sake. First, as at the royal foundation of King's, came participation by masters and scholars alike in the regular round of inter-
cessions for their founder and his progenitors; only after they had
fulfilled their religious obligations might they engage in scholarly
activities. A change in emphasis, however, can be detected at the
turn of the century. Bishop Alcock, by closing down the ancient
but almost defunct nunnery of St Rhadegund and using its endowment to create Jesus College, showed his belief in the value of
university learning. At Oxford Wolsey imitated Alcock on a much
greater scale and dissolved the monastery of St Frideswidel, taking
its revenues and those of other smaller monastic houses which he
had also dissolved to found Cardinal's College, subsequently renamed Christ Church after Henry VIII became its new patron on
Wolsey's fall. With the support of the Lady Margaret at Cambridge
Fisher established Christ's College and St John's, both specifically
designed to teach the new learning and to reinvigorate the spiritual
and intellectual life of the Church, and at Oxford in 1517 Bishop
Fox created his trilingual college of Corpus Christi with a similar
reforming intent. In time these foundations did engender zeal for
reformed learning and a reformed Church, but the movement came
too late to transform the Catholic Church in England.

The expansion of the universities towards the end of the fifteenth
century, while primarily intended to bring about a more scriptur-
ally educated upper clergy, had the secondary consequence of
widening lay opportunities in higher education. Some of the new
colleges like Magdalen at Oxford had their attendant grammar
schools, and many founders provided scholarships to take promising
boys from a particular town or county to their colleges. Sir Thomas

More was anything but a typical Oxford student – few young men
not destined for the Church stayed so long at the university or
carried their interest in humanist learning as far as he did – but
he became a shining example of the sort of scholarship a layman
could achieve. Not many laymen who went to the university to
acquire a humanistic education in the generation after More also
retained like him an abiding loyalty to the Catholic Church; they
progressed instead to demanding much more drastic change.

Given the inspiration of the new humanist propaganda, two
areas within the Church establishment cried out for reform – the
cathedral and collegiate foundations outside Oxford and Cambridge,
and the monasteries. In secular cathedrals and collegiate churches
the forces of intense conservatism and the interest of the State
proved too strong, but in the monasteries some reforms were
achieved which might have marked the beginning of a more searching reorganization. Cathedral corporations and, to a lesser extent,
collegiate churches were the source of a massive supply of sinecure
posts, difficult to justify on the grounds of ecclesiastical usefulness.
York Minster, for example, had 36 prebends varying in value from
£136 to a little under £3 a year which entailed upon their holders
no obligation of residence whatsoever since the duties which once
had belonged to the canons had been performed for centuries by
the vicars choral. Lincoln Cathedral had even more prebends,
though less well endowed, and in all the non-monastic cathedrals
there was a large amount of patronage at the bestowal of the
bishop. The State, however, did not allow the bishop to exercise
his patronage undisturbed and frequently, as at York, the richest
canonries went to important ecclesiastics in the government. For
this very reason successive governments had an interest in seeing
that the system continued unchanged. Individual prebendaries like
Colet, when Dean of St Paul's, or William Melton, as Chancellor
of York, may by their own examples have tried to bring new life
into cathedrals and to make them into centres of preaching and
learning, but few followed their lead. Since one of the motives of
founders of collegiate churches seems to have been to increase the
amount of patronage at their command, the transformation of
collegiate churches would have been even more difficult to accomplish, especially as some of these foundations had been made
comparatively recently; as with Lord Cromwell at Tattershall, the
founder or his kin were often still living and so could ensure in
person that the priests in their colleges continued to offer up their

cycle of prayers, though even in these collegiate churches it had become customary to set aside the residence requirement. Lollards who disputed the value of prayers for the dead might well question the purpose of these lavish cathedral and collegiate establishments and argue that their revenues should be deployed to greater advantage elsewhere.

Those among the laity and clergy who were critical of the state of monasticism in the fifteenth and early sixteenth centuries had rather more success in securing mild remedies. Some bishops, as has already been mentioned, founded colleges at the universities by dissolving a small number of ill-endowed houses which had failed to attract monastic recruits. Though drastic, and carrying important implications for the future, such actions were not of great moment at the time. Those who wanted change within monasticism, however, while cherishing the institution, preferred to reform by example. Just as in the late fourteenth century leading noblemen took a special interest in establishing the Carthusians in England, so in the late fifteenth century first the Yorkists and then the Tudors encouraged a rather similarly severe religious order, the Observant Franciscans. Edward iv set up the first Observant house at Greenwich in 1482; Henry vii obtained papal permission to transfer Franciscan friaries at Canterbury and Newcastle upon Tyne to the Observants; and in 1499 an English province of Observant Friars was created, soon joined by two new houses, Richmond, founded in 1500, and Newark, founded in 1507. With their reputation for austerity, and their siting near the royal palaces of Greenwich and Sheen, the Observant Franciscans served the families of both Henry vii and Henry viii as confessors, preachers and counsellors. The Carthusians, meanwhile, continued to evoke lay admiration, and the London Charterhouse, to which More felt particularly drawn, reached a new level of popularity among the citizens in the early sixteenth century on account of its piety and scholarship.

In their bequests and gifts laymen discriminated between the monastic institutions with contemporary reputations for sanctity like the Carthusians and the older and more wealthy religious orders. Envy of the possessioners still persisted, though it was usually contained beneath the surface: the government had taken considerable alarm when a London Carmelite friar in 1461 had rashly reopened the dispute over the poverty of Christ and implied that all churchmen should renounce their endowments and live

off pure alms like the friars. Their apprehension was abundantly
justified, for in addition to stirring up the ancient jealousies between
the monks and the friars he succeeded all too easily in reawakening
the old resentment of the Church's wealth among the London
populace. Even so, laymen do not generally seem to have thought
of monasticism as such as being outmoded, and there was no
shortage of recruits to the monasteries. By the accession of
Henry VIII in 1509 there were some 12,000 men and women in
religious orders in England, a new peak after the catastrophic fall
caused by the recurrent outbreaks of plague in the later fourteenth
century. Few Benedictine or Cistercian recruits rose so high in
popular estimation as the Carthusians, but on the whole they seem
to have led sober if not unduly exacting lives. Even Erasmus, that
constant critic of monasticism, would have found it difficult to
fault Richard Whytford or his fellow monk, Richard Reynolds,
skilled in Latin, Greek and Hebrew. More quickly than among the
parochial clergy, humanism was gaining acceptance in some monasteries, particularly those large enough to send their young monks
to the universities. Evesham nourished a scholar monk and
enthusiast for the new learning in Robert Joseph, and Reading
Abbey provided a flourishing school for the townspeople with a
modern humanist schoolmaster who taught Greek.

Clearly, improvements were being effected in the English Church
in the later fifteenth and early sixteenth centuries. More graduates
went into the Church; the learning of the parish clergy in most
respects seems to have been adequate; more incumbents appear
to have resided in their parishes; more bishops paid attention to
their pastoral duties. Some monasteries kept abreast of humanist
changes in education, while others achieved a new reputation
for sanctity. Too frequently historians have overlooked these real
gains in the late medieval Church through their overriding need
to discover explanations for the acceptance of the Protestant
Reformation in England later in the sixteenth century. Even so,
for laymen jealous of the privileges of the clergy, laymen who
wanted access to the scriptures without priestly mediation, these
changes seemed far too little and came too late. Lollards did not
long remain satisfied with the Christian humanism of Dean Colet:
they went on to Robert Barnes, the Cambridge Protestant, who
could supply them with a new translation of the Bible which they
could read in English for themselves.

CHAPTER 3

THE HENRICIAN REFORMATION: PROTESTANTISM, ANTI-CLERICALISM AND THE ROYAL SUPREMACY

In one fundamental respect the Henrician Reformation must still be seen as a naked act of State, the imposition of the will of one man, the Monarch, upon an entire nation. Ideas for positive, if conservative, Church reform had indeed been discussed in England long before the accession of Henry VIII. Lutheranism had penetrated into the country from the Continent for almost a decade before the Reformation Parliament first assembled, and had found some receptive auditors, especially in the universities. The laity had indulged in criticism of the clergy from time immemorial and this anti-clericalism seems to have been increasing in virulence. Particularly in the south of England, Lollardy had survived and attracted new adherents. Yet until the Crown, first for dynastic and political and later also for economic reasons, considered it necessary to separate the English Church from Catholic Christendom no single agency existed capable of uniting these disparate elements. The few educated English Catholics who remained loyal to the papacy after Henry VIII severed the links with Rome looked upon the new national Church as a schismatic Church. This English Church also failed to satisfy the high expectations of some Protestant clerics and forward lay people. Both groups watched with foreboding as by action after action the King demonstrated the triumph of the Monarchy over the Church. The recognition of the prince's supremacy in all matters spiritual and temporal signified a revolutionary defeat for the clergy in England from which they never subsequently recovered. A layman had won control over the Church as an institution, but he had no intention of sharing his newly acquired power with the laity in general.

The universities from which More and his friends had hoped that a stream of educated, moral priests would come to purify the English Church, ironically, though perhaps not surprisingly, proved to be the places where Lutheran reforming ideas first took root. By the accession of Henry VIII both English universities contained small groups of young scholars drawn to humanist studies. From

1511 to 1514 Erasmus taught Greek at Cambridge, and newly-founded colleges there such as St John's and Christ's were placing increasing emphasis on the study of biblical languages, Greek and Hebrew, as well as Latin, an example followed a little later in the decade at Corpus Christi at Oxford. As a result of this scholarly interest in the ancient languages when at last in 1516 Erasmus's much publicized translation of the New Testament from Greek into classical Latin came from the press it at once found a ready market among English academic readers. Thomas Bilney confessed to his friends some years later that he had bought the translation primarily to savour its latinity: he only gradually discovered in its pages the evangelical message which altered the whole direction of his life. Whatever may have been their conscious motivation, in these early years of Henry VIII's reign some scholars do appear to have been studying the Bible in a different way. It proved to be a relatively small step to move from reading and expounding the Bible from the literal, philological and historical standpoint, as Colet had done, to examining the new inspiration of Luther.

The career of Thomas Bilney illustrates how some young scholars, immersed in Christian humanism, could absorb some Lutheran teachings at the universities without, apparently, making any conscious decision to break away from the Catholic Church. Bilney probably came up to Cambridge when very young, in about 1510, and after completing the undergraduate arts course went on to read canon and civil law at Trinity Hall. In 1519, two years after Luther had posted his theses upon the church door at Wittenberg, he received ordination from the Bishop of Ely. It is impossible to say whether Bilney reached his belief in justification by faith directly from reading St Paul or through knowledge of the teachings of Luther. Certainly some of his friends like Latimer, whom Bilney won over to his way of thinking, stopped attacking Luther about this time and subsequently became explicit Protestants. Bilney never went as far as this, despite the suspicions of the Church authorities, but persevered in the tradition of Colet, condemning superstitions and corruptions in the Church, but not departing from the traditional teaching on papal headship or the crucial doctrine of transubstantiation. Nevertheless he antagonized the higher clergy by his evangelical preaching. Licensed to preach only in the diocese of Ely, he determined to preach, unlicensed, in his native diocese of Norwich, and stirred up considerable controversy there by his attacks on image worship. At a time when churchmen were having to contend with an apparent revival of Lollardy among the populace, as well as with the infiltration of Lutheran ideas at the universities, they dared not tolerate Bilney's preaching mission. Wolsey summoned him twice to London, and in 1527 Tunstall, who had taken over his examination, forced him to recant Lutheran beliefs he probably did not hold. After a year's imprisonment the Bishop allowed him to return to Cambridge, but back in his university his remorse knew no bounds for having betrayed his deepest convictions. At length he could keep quiet no longer and in conscious imitation of Christ's example decided to go up to Jerusalem. In 1531 he set out, again unlicensed, on another preaching tour of Norfolk and Suffolk, making his purpose quite clear by distributing copies of Tyndale's English translation of the New Testament to his hearers. The Bishop of Norwich replied by ordering his arrest. The ecclesiastical judges had little choice but to sentence him as a relapsed heretic and then to hand him over to the civil authorities for burning: he died at Norwich in August 1531.

Few university men lived and died in the equivocal position of Bilney, neither a conservative Catholic nor an explicit Protestant. Tyndale, who graduated as an MA at Oxford in 1515 and so was slightly Bilney's senior, progressed much further than he did and ended his life a convinced Protestant, much influenced by Luther, though scarcely an orthodox Lutheran. The humanist desire to open the scriptures to the people which had so attracted Bilney Tyndale made his life's work. He tried, without success, soon after he left the university to get Tunstall's patronage for his project of translating the Bible into English, but he did gain some practical support among the London merchant community. A few years later London Church officials brought a charge against Humphrey Monmouth, a substantial merchant of All Saints, Barking, of helping Tyndale and Roy, an apostate Observant friar, to go to Germany to study Luther's sect and of providing them with exhibitions so that they could make a translation of the Bible. Tyndale arrived in Germany in 1524 and matriculated at the university of Wittenberg. From Wittenberg he went to Cologne where he got part of his translation of St Matthew's Gospel printed and then, at Worms in 1526, he saw the publication of his complete translation of the New Testament. Monmouth, so the authorities discovered in 1528, organized the importing and distribution of the New Testament in England immediately after it had been printed abroad.

While working on his translation of the New Testament, Tyndale seems to have remained completely under's Luther's influence, incorporating much of Luther's own writings in his annotations and introductions to particular books. After he had published his New Testament, he wrote *The Parable of Wicked Mammon* and *The Obedience of a Christian Man*, books of Protestant propaganda designed to strengthen lay hostility towards the unreformed Church in England and to encourage the secular government, under the guidance of the King, to go forward to reformation. Tyndale next learnt Hebrew in order to read the Old Testament in its original language, and in 1530 settled in Antwerp where he spent the remainder of his life until his violent death in 1536 at the hands of imperial officers. He never finished his translation of the Old Testament, but substantial portions were later incorporated into the Matthews (or Bishops') Bible published by royal authority in England in 1537. During his work on the Old Testament Tyndale became more and more interested in the idea of law, and of the covenant between God and man, legally binding upon both. Increasingly in his last years he dwelt upon morality rather than on theology and, moving away from the doctrine of justification by faith alone, emphasized the covenant, works which grew out of the covenant and the rewards it conferred. In these later writings Tyndale substantially affected the development of one tradition within English Protestantism.

The theological thinking of John Frith, for a time one of Tyndale's helpers, moved in a very different direction. Frith, an early member of Wolsey's new college at Oxford, joined Tyndale on the Continent in 1528 but returned to England three years later, despite the danger, to take up a pastoral ministry. In his literary contests with Sir Thomas More he defended to the end Luther's teaching on justification by faith, but refused to entertain any suggestion of the idea of double justification, that good works in some sense demonstrated a man's election before men, the position which Tyndale eventually reached. Frith also very decidedly did not share Tyndale's optimism that reform would come in England through the activity of the godly prince, the father in Israel to whom his subjects owed their allegiance both in body and soul. Avoiding political entanglements, Frith concentrated on theology and in his writings on the sacraments drew considerably upon Oecolampadius's work. Frith seems to have been the first undisputedly Protestant English writer to be put to death: he was burned at

Smithfield in 1533.

Frith and Tyndale in their eclecticism and willingness to go on from the doctrines of Luther to find truths in the theology of other Continental Protestant leaders represent a certain openness and a disposition to discriminate between reformed ideas which characterized early English Protestants both at home and abroad. This also was the case with Robert Barnes, Prior of the Augustinian Friary at Cambridge, who began his career as a reformer in the tradition of Colet and Bilney, denouncing the abuses in the Church in a series of sermons at St Edward's Church in Cambridge in 1525. On account of his preaching Wolsey summoned him to London and had him imprisoned in the Fleet. While there, he was visited by the Steeple Bumpstead Lollards eager to obtain a copy of Tyndale's translation of the New Testament. Barnes later escaped, making his way to Wittenberg and for a time accepting Luther's teaching fully. However, like Tyndale, he began to waver when the possibility arose of reformation being brought about by the Crown in England. Barnes never abandoned his belief in justification by faith alone, but he did modify his views sufficiently to allow the King some sovereignty over the spiritual realm, though insisting that the King himself remained under the sovereignty of the word of God. Luther, no admirer of Henry VIII, considered that Barnes, by changing his attitude on the rightful extent of royal authority, had fallen a prey to the blandishments of the powers of this world.

Until the Vice-Chancellor silenced him in 1526 and Wolsey had him removed to London Barnes, by the very force of his personality, seems to have been one of the leaders of a little band of reforming theologians who met at the White Horse in St Edward's parish in Cambridge. Luther's works had certainly been available for some time in both universities: already in 1520 an Oxford bookseller had been offering some for sale and in the same year at Cambridge the Vice-Chancellor had ordered a ceremonial burning of Lutheran books. Official bans, however, could not check theological speculation and from early in this decade the first generation of English academic Protestants began to discuss reform. Besides Barnes, the biblical translators Tyndale, Roy and Coverdale, theologians such as Cranmer, Frith, Latimer, Ridley, Rowland Taylor, the Marian martyr, and Matthew Parker, Elizabeth's first archbishop, were among others, later eminent for their Protestant leadership, who resided in Cambridge at the time of the White

Horse meetings. In spite of the early sale of Protestant books, active Protestantism seems to have established itself at Oxford much more slowly, and when it did appear the university authorities blamed Cambridge for the infection. By 1526 Thomas Garret, an Oxford graduate who had gone on to study in Cambridge, had returned to his old university and was selling Tyndale's New Testament and other heretical books there. A small Protestant cell seems to have formed in Oxford around Garret which included among its numbers Anthony Dalaber and John Clark, a Cambridge man whom Wolsey had recently brought to his new college. The commissary of the Bishop of Lincoln exposed these heretics in 1527: Garret and Dalaber recanted, Clark and two others died in prison, while John Frith fled to the Continent.

Outside the universities Lutheranism does not seem to have spread very rapidly in the 1520s; it appealed to some intellectuals among the clergy, but only to a small minority, to some gentlemen, especially those who had been to the university or were connected with the Court, and also made some headway among the London merchant community. It may well be that Luther's theology appeared too abstruse for lay people still able in some areas to satisfy their longing for practical reform in Lollardy. Whatever the explanation, when in 1528 the Vicar General of the Bishop of London made a visitation with the express intention of exposing heretical ideas, those arraigned among the clergy revealed a fairly detailed acquaintance with Lutheranism while the lay heretics almost without exception expressed traditional Lollard views, condemning the Mass, criticizing pilgrimages and image worship, and showing hostility generally against the clergy as a caste. The form of the visitation is in itself significant of the relative popular appeal of Lollardy and Lutheranism. Only after he had heard very detailed disclosures about the Colchester Lollards and their links with other Lollard communities in Essex and London did the Vicar General come upon evidence of a tentative interest in Lutheranism among some London clergy. Sebastian Harries, curate of the parish church of Kensington, admitted possessing Tyndale's New Testament and *Unio Dissidentium*, a collection of biblical passages and extracts from the Fathers published in 1527 at Antwerp in support of the reformers' cause. The rector of All Saints, Honey Lane, London, Robert Forman, STP, also stood convicted of secretly keeping Lutheran books after the bishops had issued fresh prohibitions on their possession in 1526. Forman gave away little, but subsequent information made it clear that he was probably one of the chief agents for the distribution in England of Protestant books printed on the Continent. A book pedlar, called Robert Necton, told the court that since Easter that year he had bought no less than eighteen English New Testaments, twenty-six copies of the *Oeconomica Christiana* and two copies of *Unio Dissidentium* from Forman's servant. Another London cleric, Vicar Constantine, had helped him obtain further supplies of Lutheran books, and he had then embarked on a sales campaign in Lollard areas of East Anglia. Some clergy had proved eager purchasers: Sir William Forboshore, a singing man of Stowmarket, bought five New Testaments for seven or eight groats apiece; a priest of Pickenham Wade in Norfolk took *Oeconomica Christiana* and *Unio Dissidentium* as well as a New Testament, and yet another priest, Richard Baysell, had paid him 3s 4d for two unbound copies of the New Testament the previous Christmas. Necton in fact must have sold books on a fairly large scale for he went on to disclose that a Dutchman from the Continent had offered him at the end of 1527 three hundred English New Testaments priced at 9d each.

Although some clerics bought books by Luther and his disciples, it was Tyndale's New Testament which found the most immediate sale, and particularly with the laity. Some London merchants under the aegis of Monmouth had helped sponsor the translation financially and others, once it had been published, used their business acumen to aid its distribution in England. A number of men Necton mentioned by name as purchasers of his New Testaments were themselves merchants or involved in trade, and, despite all their attempts, the episcopal authorities failed to prevent the circulation of the New Testament and other Protestant books, especially, it seems, in old Lollard districts. When Tewkesbury, a leather seller of St Michael Quern, in London, came before Tunstall in 1529 on a charge of reading Tyndale's New Testament he admitted to the Bishop that he had been studying the scriptures for the past seventeen years, which suggests that he must have previously had access to Lollard translations. Tewkesbury abjured in 1529, but was recaptured two years later and burnt in 1532 for heresy, one of the first laymen with some knowledge of Protestantism so to die. By the 1530s rather more evidence exists for the ownership of Protestant books among more humble Londoners in spite of the continuing official prohibitions. Laurence Staple, a serving man, confessed to having a New Testament and other English books, and of having delivered some books to Bilney. These men, moreover, not only read themselves but also encouraged others to read. One of the charges against Staple was that he had urged one Henry Thomson to learn to read in order to gain access to the New Testament for himself. Episcopal officials discovered that another serving man, John Hewer, had read the New Testament in English and kept some of Frith's books after the royal proclamation banning their possession, and that Walter King, a servant, had similarly offended. In addition to the New Testament he had acquired the *Sum of the Scripture*, a Primer and a Psalter and hidden them in Worcester. It was this comparatively rapid dispersal of Protestant books through various levels of lay society which particularly concerned the ecclesiastical authorities: if the enthusiasm for Bible reading had been confined to the gentry the bishops' task of attempting to retain control over the religious opinions of the laity would have been far less difficult.

This demand for the Bible in English and other contraband Protestant books reveals the more constructive aspect of lay attitudes towards religion and the Church in the late 1520s. Yet even clandestine Bible reading could have destructive implications, for some laymen seem to have wanted to possess the Bible in the vernacular at least partly to undermine the traditional authority of conservative priests. Jealousy and fear of the clergy appear to have been especially strong at this time and confrontations between clergy and laity to have been increasing, since the more some laymen tried to obtain forbidden books the more they laid themselves open to heretical proceedings and ultimately to the death penalty. The government of Henry VIII did not create this anti-clericalism, but it did succeed in harnessing it for its own purposes which gradually emerged as being the assumption of total control over the English Church. Yet the nationalization of the Church by the State which took place in the 1530s and which in one respect demonstrated the supremacy of the lay monarch over the clerical estate did not bring about the victory over the backward clergy that many Protestants wanted. As the King and Parliament were passing momentous acts to establish an independent English Church, some educated lay people as well as clerics began to realize that the replacing of the Pope by the Monarch in no sense automatically led to a reformation of religion.

The actions of the Commons when apparently left to their own initiative soon after the assembling of the first session of the

Reformation Parliament in the autumn of 1529 demonstrate the kind of administrative reform in the Church which attracted many gentlemen. Essentially they seem to have been eager to improve and safeguard their position as laymen against the privileged clergy, but they did not call for radical change. Very early in this session the Commons introduced a bill to limit the granting of probate of wills, an occasion when virtually all laymen of substance at some time or other came into contact with ecclesiastical courts. They then went on to consider a bill restricting the mortuaries a priest could demand, obviously referring to the affair of Richard Hunne and the mortuary for his dead baby which had aroused such bitter hatred against the clergy in the city of London. Most importantly they brought in a bill against pluralism, absenteeism and non-residence in the Church. This bill, which became the Act against Pluralities of 1529, allowed existing pluralists to retain up to four benefices, but provided that in future any cleric receiving a second benefice with cure of souls should have to vacate the first, and forbade incumbents to leave their livings for more than two months at a time. The Act permitted exceptions for a whole range of chaplains and dignitaries in the service of the State, but these exceptions had to be sanctioned by Parliament: it tried to invalidate in advance any attempt the papacy might make to circumvent the Act's provisions.

In the 1529 session of Parliament, the Commons voiced in no uncertain terms their discontent over the operation of Church courts which eventually emerged in 1532 as the Supplication against the Ordinaries. They protested against the power of Convocation to make ecclesiastical laws binding upon the whole realm and against the delays and expense involved in the operation of the courts. A renewed fear of heresy proceedings, from which no layman, whatever his social status, was immune, may have added fresh intensity to the Commons' traditional dislike for any form of clerical inquisition. Yet this criticism of the Church by the Commons still falls into the long series of attacks made for centuries on the juridical powers of the Church and can scarcely be seen as an unprecedented attempt to overthrow the Church's ancient authority. At this stage members of Parliament seemed to have aimed at limited and moderate administrative reformation, not at destruction.

The necessity for a revolutionary separation of the English Church from Rome originated not in this somewhat conservative

House of Commons, however hostile it may have been to the clerical estate, but with the King and his advisers. As Henry VIII came to see that he could not solve the dynastic problem of the succession to the throne with the concurrence of the papacy, he and his advisers increasingly realized that a solution could be found only if the King freed himself from papal overlordship. To most lay people, whether conservative Catholics or Protestant sympathizers, the papal supremacy seems to have meant very little: it appeared remote and very rarely impinged upon their lives. Whereas the royal advisers knew they could count upon the enthusiastic support of the Commons whenever the matter of clerical privileges was raised, they needed to build up a propaganda campaign against Rome, in the process much exaggerating the extent to which English bullion left the realm to subsidize an Italian papal state, in order to direct nationalist feeling against the continuance of papal government in England. Henry VIII at least seems to have convinced himself of the inadmissibility of the Pope's authority in England by arguments of this sort. From starting as a somewhat extravagant supporter of the papacy against Luther, Henry slowly became the papacy's implacable foe as Clement VII, under the influence of the emperor Charles V, refused to annul Henry's marriage with Katherine of Aragon. Step by step Henry reached the conclusion that the papacy's claims to jurisdiction in England had never been legitimate, and that he, like the eastern emperors in the wake of Constantine, enjoyed by divine institution imperial powers over all his subjects, clerical and lay alike. Initially some Protestant writers readily supported this change in royal thinking, though for rather different reasons from Henry's desire for release from his Queen. In the *Obedience of the Christian Man*, which Anne Boleyn herself was said to have presented to the King, Tyndale wrote the first whole-hearted defence of the godly prince. Setting Henry, as a king approved by God, in a line of descent from the monarchs of the Old Testament, Tyndale maintained that his subjects owed him their entire allegiance, both of body and soul. Henry, in his turn, had the moral duty of reclaiming his rightful place as the head of the Christian community of which the papacy centuries earlier had wrongfully deprived him.

It is of the greatest significance for the progress of religious change in England that Henry required Parliament to recognize the authority of the Monarch over the Church, an authority which had existed ever since the conversion of England to Christianity

but had subsequently been unwarrantably denied by an illegal
ecclesiastical potentate. In no sense, however, did the King ask
Parliament to confer new powers upon the Crown. By his belief
in the imperial power of a divinely appointed king – which
virtually abolished the old divisions of Church and State – Henry
may have hidden the revolutionary nature of his proceedings even
from himself. For many of his subjects the religious revolution
countenanced step by step by Parliament was probably at least
partly disguised by its very gradualism. The complete separation
took five years to effect. There was no one instance when England
remained in full communion with the see of Rome and another
when the tie could be seen to have been cut irretrievably. Instead,
the break happened by stages, each apparently reversable. The
Commons' attack on the clergy in 1529 had been reformist rather
than destructive, but in later sessions of this Parliament the mood
of the laity changed or was made to change. The Crown used
the threats implicit in the Commons' Supplication against the
Ordinaries of 1532 to bring Convocation to admit that it was
incapable of passing any legislation without the express consent
of the monarch. Until 1533 the King and his councillors probably
looked on parliamentary bills and the harrying of the clergy in
Convocation largely as a means of putting pressure upon the
papacy to extort the dissolution of Henry's marriage. Even as late
as 1533 the Pope sent regular instruments from Rome for the
consecration of Thomas Cranmer, Henry's candidate for the archbishopric of Canterbury on Warham's death. Then, in the course
of 1533, the acts were introduced into Parliament which led by
degrees to the severance of the English Church from Rome. First
Parliament passed the Act in Restraint of Appeals. This prohibited
the taking of ecclesiastical appeals outside the jurisdiction of the
English courts and so made it possible for Henry's case for a
divorce, which Katherine had had transferred to Rome, to be tried
and concluded by Cranmer in England. In the first session of 1534
the Act of Dispensations gave to the Crown the Pope's right to
grant dispensations from the law of the Church. The Act for the
Submission of the Clergy confirmed Convocation's surrender to the
Crown of 1532, while the Heresy Act declared that denial of the
papal supremacy no longer constituted heresy. By the Act of
Succession which vested the succession to the throne in the issue
of Henry and Anne Boyeln, the King's subjects could be required
to acknowledge by oath the legality of the marriage. The climax

of this spate of law making came in the second parliamentary
session of 1534 when in the Act of Supremacy Parliament recognized Henry as supreme head of the English Church on earth.
A national English Church had taken the place of two English
provinces subject to the see of Rome.

Few Englishmen, and exceedingly few laymen, followed More,
Bishop Fisher and the London Carthusians in choosing to die rather
than to acknowledge the lawfulness of the break with Rome.
Nevertheless, even among the laity unease soon appeared over the
way in which Henry went on to exercise his supremacy over the
national Church, and nowhere more keenly than over the King's
attitude to the Church's wealth. For the last century and a half,
to judge from expressions of opinion in Parliament, laymen had
envied the wealth of the Church and some had considered that its
riches should be drastically curtailed. The Act of First Fruits and
Tenths of 1534, therefore, which gave the Crown new powers to
tax all livings in the Church in itself does not seem to have been
unpopular with the laity. This Act permitted the King to take a
year's income from the incumbent of every newly-acquired benefice
and a tenth of its annual value thereafter, bringing him a sum in
the region of £40,000 a year, a far greater amount than the Pope
had ever derived from the English Church. Yet even when Lollardy
had had its widest appeal, idealists had never intended that the
Church should be deprived of its surplus wealth solely to benefit
the State, and with the spread of Protestantism had come a new
concern for improving the way of life of the whole nation. Laymen
who now wanted the monarch to rid the Church of the excesses
of monasticism confidently expected that revenues from the
monasteries would be diverted to Protestant good works, particularly to the setting up of schools and colleges, the creation of
generous funds for the relief of the poor and sick, and above all
to the strengthening of the Church at the parish level. The
commonwealth men who thought in this way looked to Thomas
Cromwell to realize their aspirations, sending him the most diverse
schemes to revivify society, and in the mid-1530s visionaries could
still hope that some of their ambitious plans might be achieved.
Sir Francis Bigod, an educated Yorkshire gentleman, although
essentially an individualist, shared these general expectations to the
full. Once Wolsey's ward, Bigod had become a convinced Protestant; he had studied at the university and later befriended Protestant ministers, at one time having Thomas Garret as his chaplain

and associating with William Jerome who later died for his faith. As a Protestant he believed that monasteries, the supposed stronghold of papalism in England, should be destroyed but in the interest of parishes up and down the country. He felt particularly strongly about the number of parish churches appropriated to monasteries and published, probably in 1535, *A Treatise concerning Impropriations of Benefices.* Here he asked pertinently, 'How can the people have any faith in God without preaching?' Preaching, he argued, was impossible in many parts of England because the impropriators had robbed the ministers of their living. He therefore concluded that the State had a clear duty to deprive the monasteries of vast impropriations in order to restore them to the parishes from which they originally came. Only in this way could the ministers of the gospel be adequately rewarded and Protestantism be extensively preached.

When Cromwell undertook his great survey of the revenues of the English Church which resulted in the *Valor Ecclesiasticus* of 1535 there may well have been other forward laymen like Bigod, as there certainly were clergy, who expected that surplus ecclesiastical revenues would soon be diverted to new spiritual and social purposes. To these men the Act of 1536 must have been a considerable disappointment. It allowed the King to dissolve monastic houses with revenues of less than £200 a year but largely on the grounds that these communities had been so small that their inhabitants, through sin and inefficiency, had contrived to consume and spoil their endowments. In order, therefore, to prevent future waste and maintenance of sin Parliament simply decided that the lands of these houses should now come to the King and his heirs in perpetuity. The Act made no provision for any of the revenues to be returned to the local communities, and those with eyes to see realized to their dismay that the proposed partial dissolution was to be carried out not, as they had intended, for the good of the nation as a whole but for the benefit of the King and his government.

The novel extent of the intervention of the central government in the regions caused by preparations for dissolving the lesser monasteries probably formed a major reason for the most significant outburst of political and social unrest of the reign. The Pilgrimage of Grace, or more accurately the series of loosely linked uprisings subsumed under this name, affected almost all the north of England in the autumn and winter of 1536–7 and at its height may have involved some 40,000 armed men. If the Emperor Charles v had played a more active part in the crisis, above all if Reginald Pole had returned to England to lead the northern rebels in person, it is conceivable that in 1536 the Tudor dynasty might have been overthrown in the name of religion. Inflation, the prospect of dearth through bad harvests, conflict between lords and tenants over forms of land holding all undoubtedly contributed to unrest in the north in 1536, but both the almost accidental rising in Lincolnshire in October and the much more serious subsequent rebellion centred on Yorkshire and Durham demonstrated how quickly men throughout the county had grasped that change determined upon by the King in Parliament might drastically alter the whole tenor of their lives. Apprehensive clergy and lay people, fearful of losing what spiritual possessions they had, made common cause against what they saw as an over-intrusive State. Too much governmentally inspired activity in Lincolnshire in the autumn seems to have precipitated the first rising: simultaneously parliamentary commissioners were collecting a subsidy in the county, episcopal commissioners enforcing religious articles upon the clergy for a somewhat over-punctilious Bishop of Lincoln, while royal officials were gathering information in advance of dissolving some of the smaller monasteries in the county. Some eight hundred priests who had come together in Louth in October to meet the Bishop's commissary were literally afraid for their livelihood. As one priest said, 'They will deprive us of our benefices because they would have the first fruits, but rather than I will pay the first fruits again I had liever lose benefice and all!' Others believed that the State might confiscate a priest's stipend on the pretext of his having insufficient learning to fulfil his religious duties adequately. In Lincolnshire clerics succeeded in infecting the laity with their fears: the government, they argued, which now harried them would next attempt to take over those ecclesiastical possessions in which laymen felt they had a particular interest, church plate, church furnishings, even perhaps some parish churches. Rumours of what might be about to happen brought together a considerable number of local priests and people. Dislike of doctrinal change took second place to this hostility to the State's intervention in Lincolnshire church affairs, but a group of rebellious priests, led by Thomas Kendall, did criticize the very concept of the royal supremacy and condemned erroneous teachings about Our Lady and purgatory.

The Pilgrimage of Grace proper only began in Yorkshire after the Lincolnshire rising had virtually collapsed. Though on a much larger scale and far more dangerous, it resembled the Lincolnshire revolt closely in that rumour and the activity of priests and monks seem to have done much to precipitate the rising. Whatever their economic grievances, and some rebels complained vociferously about the high entry fines levied by grasping landlords, they chose to rally behind a standard showing the five wounds of Christ and considered they were defending the Church against illegal usurpation. In Robert Aske the Yorkshire rebels produced a leader far more articulate than any who had emerged in Lincolnshire: he and at least some of his followers could look beyond merely local matters. They called upon the government to suppress Protestant doctrinal innovations: indeed, at Pontefract they repudiated somewhat indiscriminately the heresies of Luther, Wyclif, Hus, Melanchthon, Oecolampadius and Bucer and writings such as the Augsburg Confession, Melanchthon's *Apology*, and the works of Tyndale, Barnes, Marshall and St German. Attacking by name such laymen as Cromwell, Audley and Sir Richard Rich and churchmen who shared the views of Cranmer, Latimer, Hilsey and Barlow, they tried to protect themselves behind the ancient fiction of the King being misled by evil councillors. Some rebels seem genuinely to have questioned whether a layman could indeed be head of the Church: in the heat of the rising a monk of Furness was heard to shout, 'There should be no lay knave head of the Church.' Yet in their concern for their monasteries the northern rebels displayed the same provincialism as that of the Lincolnshire men. They anticipated that if the State confiscated the monasteries, their place in society would be filled by extortionate, absentee landlords and the wealth of the north drained to the south. Some monks deliberately exploited these fears. Fantastic rumours about the financial implications of the royal supremacy spread from mouth to mouth, that the Government was intending to levy taxes on baptisms, marriages and burials, on cows and sheep, even on poor men who had presumed to eat white meat and white bread above their station. Aske, who did not allow himself to be deflected by this localism, still seemed more concerned to deny the Crown's supremacy over the Church, and with it the supreme governor's right to levy first fruits and tenths, than to restore the Pope's supremacy over the English Church. The spiritual benefits of the Church which the northerners most cherished but feared they would lose, if the King closed the monasteries and then went on, as they had heard he might, to dissolve some parish churches, were prayers for the dead and the present availability of the sacraments. The Pilgrimage of Grace did not uncover a widespread attachment to the teachings of the pre-Tridentine church but it indicated that many northerners thought that the policies of King and Parliament over the previous seven years would deprive them of the meagre privileges, temporal and spiritual, they had until then enjoyed.[1]

The northern pilgrims, though so overwhelmingly conservative in their religious sympathies, managed to recruit at least one committed northern Protestant. This came about not altogether illogically, since in their fear of the consequences of the exercise of the royal supremacy far-sighted Catholics and Protestants shared indeed some common ground. Sir Francis Bigod, who had supported the royal supremacy in his book of 1535 when the Crown seemed to be in the process of confiscating the lands of the Church in order to bring about a redistribution of wealth among churchmen, subsequently developed serious reservations. He wrote a new treatise (which he did not live to try to publish) 'against the title of supreme head, the statute of suppression [of the monasteries] and the taking away of the liberties of the church'. While in no sense deviating from his Protestantism, he threw in his lot with the pilgrims with the intention now of defending the newly liberated Church against the State as he had earlier tried to free it from a corrupt papacy. 'That the king should have cure both of your body and soul is plain false,' he is alleged to have told the commons of the East Riding, 'for it is against the gospel of Christ, and that will I justify even to my death.' The government had paid no heed to Bigod's scheme for providing for a teaching clergy out of the endowments of the monasteries, and he for his part had abandoned all hope of gaining a truly Protestant reformation on the basis of the royal supremacy.[2]

The Pilgrimage of Grace brought home to Henry VIII, and probably even more to Cromwell, the political dangers consequent upon religious change, even though this change was being effected through the Crown's collaboration with Parliament. The rebellion did not halt the process of the dissolution of the monasteries but Cromwell strove even more actively after the rebellion than before to keep himself fully informed of any stirrings of unrest anywhere in England. Government propaganda, and the preaching of dependable Protestants, could to some extent counter unfounded rumours of the King's designs upon the Church, and it may be that the threat of anarchy revealed by the northern rebellion shocked many of the laity in authority locally into acquiescing in the government's plans. Certainly the pace of religious change did not abate after 1536 and by far the greater part of the immense transfer of property involved in the dissolution of the monasteries occurred after that date. Practically no area of England escaped a visitation from royal officers, for the government did not stop, as many of the pilgrims had quite accurately anticipated, at confiscating the poorer monasteries. By persuasion and, if that failed, by the Act of Parliament of 1539, all monasteries without exception fell to the Crown. Considering the extent to which royal officers intruded upon local interests during the dissolution of the monasteries, it is remarkable that so little active opposition resulted. A few abbots, like those of Reading, Colchester and Glastonbury, intrigued against the King's supremacy and died on account of their temerity, but no fresh revolt occurred in any sense comparable with the Pilgrimage of Grace.

At a time when the King's usual income from land did not exceed £40,000 a year, the dissolution of the monasteries brought to the Crown an additional net annual income of over £136,000. The King also acquired monastic plate, bullion and jewels, as well as the benefices formerly appropriated to monasteries which may have amounted to two-fifths of all benefices in England. Henry showed little willingness to dispense much of this immense extra income in the ways the commonwealthmen had hoped. In reply to the elaborate schemes to establish a host of new bishoprics in England, so that in future bishops could be true fathers in God to their flocks rather than lordly prelates, the King agreed to the creation of six new dioceses, Chester, Peterborough, Oxford, Bristol, Gloucester and Westminster, though the latter did not long survive. In marked contrast with the implementation of the Reformation in some German states and imperial cities, Henry put aside very little of his monastic gains for educational foundations or projects to benefit the poor. Admittedly he created Regius Professorships at the two universities, and established Trinity College at Cambridge in addition to making some other more minor grants, but he did little else. This proved cold comfort for the idealists who had expected that the monastic lands would at the very least have maintained

. . . godly preachers
Which might well have led
The people aright
That now go astray
And have fed the poor
That famish every day.[3]

In the long run, however, the attitude of the influential laity
mattered more to the Crown than that of the Protestant idealists.
Slowly in the late 1530s, rapidly after the death of Cromwell as
Henry began again to pursue a more belligerent foreign policy and
his need of ready cash soared, the King allowed the sale of more
and more former monastic land so that the ultimate beneficiaries
of this greatest change in landownership since the Norman
Conquest were the nobility and gentry. Perhaps partly accidentally,
the most powerful laymen in England gained an entrenched interest
in the abolition of monasticism and, by implication, in the maintenance of the royal supremacy.

In contrast with the creation of the royal supremacy, the
confiscation of the monastic lands and the more severe taxation of
the secular clergy when the initiative always remained with the
King in Parliament, the propagation of Protestant ideas in England
in the 1530s rested almost entirely with sympathetic clergy and
laity, with the rather fitful protection of royal servants such as
Cromwell. Yet particularly in the south of England, allegiance to
Protestantism had been growing. An inquisition taken for the
Bishop of London in 1541 gives some impression of how some
enterprising clergy had been trying to spread Protestantism in the
city in the previous decade. Some parish incumbents had done
little more than express their distrust of ceremonies. The parson
and curate of St Antholins, for example, had not used the old
ceremonies in making holy water, or kept processions on Saturdays.
John Hardyman, the parson of St Martin's Iremonger Lane, had
spoken out rather more explicitly, condemning confession as a
confusion and a deformation and exhorting his flock against the
'butcherly' ceremonies of the Church. He quite clearly had absorbed
some Lutheran teaching. 'What a mischief is this,' his accusers
recalled him saying, 'to esteem the sacraments to be of such
virtue? For in so doing they take the glory of God from him.'
Others remembered that he had taught that 'Faith in Christ is

sufficient without any other sacraments to justify'. Obviously in a capital city the parish clergy had come into contact with a great variety of beliefs. Wilcox, a Scottish friar, had been attacking in his sermons confession, holy water, prayer to saints and for the souls of the departed, and the very existence of purgatory, and had defended the marriage of priests. Another Scot, Alexander Seton, chaplain to the Duke of Suffolk, had preached at St Anthony's that Christ alone brought man justification before God. At St Katherine's, Thomas Lancaster, a priest, had embarked on a career as a hawker of bibles, as Vicar Constantine and Mr Forman had done a decade earlier: he was imprisoned in the Counter for his activities in bringing prohibited books into the country. In some parishes university men had been preaching, like Dr John Taylor who had said at St Bride's Fleet Street, 'that it is as profitable to a man to hear Mass and see the sacrament, as to kiss Judas's mouth, who kissed Christ, our saviour'. Elsewhere less able men had taught less coherently. John Birch, priest of the church in St Botolph's Lane, had gained notoriety as 'a busy reasoner in certain opinions which agreed not with the Pope's Church'. These clerics in this atmosphere of theological *laisser faire* remained no more wedded to Luther's teachings than did their more academic colleagues, but freely adopted those doctrines of other continental reformers which seemed appropriate to the English situation. Thomas Cappes, priest of St Mary Magdalen in Old Fish Street, did not show any appreciation of Luther's complex teaching of the presence of Christ in the sacrament, but came near to the Zwinglian position (or indeed to the old beliefs of London Lollards) when he instructed his parishioners 'that the sacrament of the altar was but a memory and a remembrance of the Lord's death'.

If sympathetic ecclesiastics at the universities and parish priests felt at liberty to discriminate between different systems of continental Protestantism, it is not surprising that those of the laity drawn to Protestantism displayed an even greater eclecticism. In one very real sense the 1530s marked the emancipation of the laity since then, for the first time, they could legally read and possess the Bible in the vernacular. Convocation, apparently disregarding its earlier fears of the consequence of casting pearls before swine, had in 1534 actually petitioned the King to allow an English translation of the Bible. In the following year Coverdale's translation was fairly freely available, and in 1536 Cromwell, acting as the King's deputy, issued his first injunction that all priests should obtain a copy of the Bible in English; in 1538 he put further pressure on bishops to encourage priests to provide an English Bible in every parish. A year later, just before Cromwell fell, there appeared in 1539 the Great Bible, the translation officially approved by the government incorporating much of Tyndale's and Coverdale's work. But such a change in government policy did not change the attitude of conservative clergy towards the general availability of the Bible. They still prophesied dire effects for the nation if laymen had free access to the scriptures, as is dramatically illustrated by an incident which happened at Windsor recorded by John Foxe. Robert Testwood was both a musician and an advocate of the new learning and he had recently, with some difficulty since some of the older canons seem to have been prejudiced against him, acquired a place in the collegiate church. Soon after his admission a chantry priest, Mr Ely, an old Bachelor of Divinity, 'began to rail against laymen who took upon them to meddle with the scriptures, and to be better learned (knowing no more but the English tongue) than they that had been students in the universities of Oxford and Cambridge all the days of their lives'. To this Testwood self-confidently retorted, 'I think it be no hurt for laymen, as I am, to read and to know the scriptures . . .' Some years later Testwood's independent thinking cost him his life. In 1544, after the government had reacted against the propagating of Lutheran teaching, he and two other Windsor singing men were put to death for holding heretical opinions concerning the sacrament of the altar, and their fellow musician, Marbeck, who had not only embarked upon compiling a concordance of the Bible but had also been copying out an epistle of Calvin, escaped solely through the intervention of Sir William Barrington.

The laity inclined to Protestantism particularly relished reformed preaching. In London in the parish of St Clement without Temple Bar, Gerard Frise had said in the presence of witnesses 'that a sermon preached is better than the sacrament of the altar, and that he had rather go to hear a sermon than to hear a mass'. In Aldermanbury in 1541 eight parishioners were brought before the Bishop for supporting Barnes and other preachers, and in the parish of St Matthews William Ellis and his wife appeared in court on a similar charge. Another group of Londoners, which included the goodman of the Saracen's Head in Friday Street and Thomas Gardiner and his three apprentices, had to answer the accusation that they had gathered together secretly in the evening and introduced ill preachers among the people. Some of the uninformed populace were indeed discussing the Bible in ale houses; the apprehensions of the conservatives of a decade earlier proved to have been fully justified.

At least in London a considerable number of lay people seem to have been indulging in religious speculation, in expounding passages from the Bible and even preaching. By 1541 in the parish of St Benet Fink, Robert Plat and his wife were known as 'great reasoners in scripture, saying that they had it of the Spirit and that confession availeth nothing'; Plat admitted to being illiterate. Another layman who could neither read nor write, John Harry-daunce, a bricklayer of Whitechapel, had been preaching in season and out of season from the window of his house and drawing crowds to hear him. When examined about his activities he said that for thirty years he had tried to learn the scriptures. In St Nicholas in the Flesh, Shambles, one Brisley's wife came before the Bishop's officers for 'busy reasoning on the new learning, and not keeping the church'. The same officials found Mistress Castle of St Andrews in Holborn 'a meddler and a reader of the scripture in the church'. In St Botolph's without Aldgate Margaret Ambsworth, like Lollard women earlier, had failed to reverence the holy sacrament at sacring time; her neighbours knew her well for her instruction of maids and for 'being a great doctress'. Mistress Elizabeth Stretham had borne witness more sedately to her religious convictions: she had received in her house in Milk Street in St Mary Magdalen's parish a whole galaxy of eminent Protestant preachers, including Latimer, Barnes, Garret and Jerome.[4]

The extent to which these London lay people had adopted as their own the leading tenets of continental Protestantism varied immensely. Mrs Stretham may well have been a willing pupil of her Protestant guests, but the Plats and Harrydaunce showed little sign of waiting for clerical guidance; indeed, they came near to the idea of individual illumination and acted quite outside the formal parish structure. These Londoners seem to have been in the process of grafting Protestant beliefs on to ideas derived from Lollardy. The same amalgamation of old and new teachings seems to have been taking place elsewhere in southern England, the Chilterns and East Anglia, and perhaps in other Lollard areas in Kent and in the Midlands around Coventry. In Hughenden, very much Lollard country, local men heard from Nicholas Field of London, recently returned from Germany, the already acceptable teaching 'that the sacrament of the altar was not, as it was pretended, the flesh, blood and bone of Christ, but a sacrament, that is a typical signification of his holy body'. The Lollards of Essex enthusiastically welcomed the new translation of the Bible, responded eagerly to the evangelical preaching, agreed with the attacks on ceremonies, confession and purgatory, but seemingly did not sympathize with Luther's and later Calvin's teaching on the sacraments or their belief in predestination and the total depravity of man. One Suffolk man in 1536 called before an ecclesiastical court for disseminating heresy, actually identified his teacher. William Broman said he had learnt from Dr Barret 'that the blessed sacrament of the altar is but a figure, and a remembrance of the passion of Christ'. From Bale he had taken the idea 'that Christ would dwell in no church that was made of lime and stones by men's hands, but only in heaven above, and in men's hearts in earth'. The parson of Hothfield had instructed him not to put his trust in the host when it was lifted up, but to remember the passion of Christ and put his whole trust in that. Without this specific acknowledgement of his mentors, Broman could easily have been taken for a conventional Lollard: in fact he may have imbibed some Zwinglian doctrines through Bale.[5]

Again and again in the 1530s venturesome lay people had speculated about the sacraments and nowhere more so than in London. Thomas Trentham of St Giles without Cripplegate thought 'the sacrament was a good thing, but it was not as men took it, very God'. Thomas Plummer of Matthew's said enigmatically, 'that the blessed sacrament was to him that doth take it, so; and to him that doth not, it was not so'. A plumber of St Bride's, Christopher Dray, had explicitly reached the memorialist interpretation of the sacrament. He considered that the sacrament of the altar 'was not offered up for remission of sins; and that the body of Christ was not there, but only by representation and signification of the thing'. There were lay people at this early date who displayed an informed knowledge of such key Protestant beliefs as justification by faith and predestination, but they were much more unusual and probably came from a higher, and more educated, sector of society. In Norwich in 1539 Robert Watson, later the town clerk, took offence at the conservative preaching of Bishop Rugge who had implied in a sermon that man possessed a measure of free will which, through God's assistance, might contribute to the working of grace. Watson insisted in the Bishop's presence that 'a natural man destitute of the spirit of God cannot receive the grace of God when it is offered by the gospel'. He had clearly absorbed some of the continental Protestant emphasis on the powerlessness of an un-regenerate man to help himself. Protestant teaching must have been current in Norwich for some time since a considerable body of citizens openly sided with Watson against their Bishop.[6]

Such was also the case in Bristol and the adjoining county of Gloucester. Latimer had the support of the Mayor of Bristol when he began preaching in various Bristol city churches but he soon encountered the opposition of many local clergy who incited clashes between rival parties of Protestants and conservatives. Particularly after 1536 the corporation realized how easily indigenous civic unrest could express itself in religious radicalism. Nevertheless the ruling group still upheld the Henrician changes in religion. Both in Bristol and in Gloucestershire a strain of Lollardy seems to have persisted. Bell, Latimer's successor as Bishop of Worcester, discovered in 1539 a conventicle whose members, drawn from different parishes, had been meeting at James Knolles's mill at Upleadon and had discussed there various religious issues including the eucharist. They had questioned confession to priests, and the sacraments; some thought the eucharist but a sign of Christ and one man had allegedly been heard to say, 'Our Saviour Christ Jesus received not flesh and blood of the Virgin Mary and that he was never flesh and blood.' These Upleadon men may conceivably have heard and approved of some of the more extreme ideas of continental Anabaptism, but their views could equally well have derived from a version of popular Lollardy.[7]

In Gloucestershire what could have been a long-standing popular tradition of discontent with the unreformed Church combined with an informed desire for Protestant reform among some of the gentry. Tyndale had been a tutor in the house of Sir John Walsh at Little Sodbury and went on preaching tours from there before he fled to the Continent. In 1533 the family next offered protection to John Erly, another energetic Protestant evangelist. James Bainham, gentleman, burnt in London for heresy in 1532, came from Gloucestershire, and William Tracy of Toddington, who left the famous Protestant preamble to his will which caused the ecclesiastical authorities to order his posthumous burning, may also have been influenced by Tyndale. Tracy's son, Richard, became a convinced Lutheran and in 1544 published, as Sir Francis Bigod had done a decade before, a *Supplication to . . . King Henry the*

Eight in which he petitioned for a systematic reform of the Church. He, too, longed to see a preaching ministry established throughout England, called upon the government to desist from employing bishops as ambassadors to foreign princes and to encourage them instead to become pastors of souls, and suggested the abolition of all chantry priests, canons and cathedral prebendaries.

As a result of the protection afforded to Protestant clergy from a very early date by such Gloucestershire gentlemen, Latimer found when he became Bishop of Worcester that there already existed a Protestant base on which he could build. In his four years as bishop he gathered round him a group of Protestant preachers and worked to spread a knowledge of the scriptures among the people with the result that Protestantism began to flourish among some of the Gloucestershire clergy. James Ash and his curates made Staunton into a recognized centre of Protestantism, while at Winchcombe some of the monks from the abbey followed the Lutheran teaching of the parish priest, Anthony Saunders. Thomas Garret, rector of Hartlebury, preached against purgatory, and the vicar of Coaley, subsequently found in possession of works by Luther, Bucer and Zwingli, condemned masses for the dead. The curate of Wooton-under-Edge went further, daring to attack ceremonies which Henry VIII had not yet abrogated, and at Tidenham the vicar set an example to his parishioners by smashing the painted windows in the church and destroying a calvary there.

Yet even in Gloucestershire under the direction of Latimer, it was the negative aspects of Protestantism which still continued to dominate the imagination of the ordinary people. As elsewhere in England, the populace at large, when attracted to Protestantism at all, seems to have been much more attracted by its anti-authoritarian, anti-sacramental and iconoclastic aspects. As might be expected at a time when the government itself, disregarding entirely the susceptibilities of the more conservative clergy, was leading the way in pulling down monasteries and shrines, particularly shrines associated with saints like Thomas Becket who had opposed the secular State, some of the laity felt free to take the initiative to deride, attack and destroy. The behaviour of Eleanor Godfrey of Great Marlow can scarcely have contributed to the edification of her neighbours. According to Foxe, she had jeered at Thomas Collerd, a religious conservative, who like a 'pope-holy hypocrite' used to kneel behind the children at mass time in Marlow church and, when the priest crossed his head with a saucer, would do the same. Equally there was little of spiritual value in William Hart's outburst at Great Brickhill: 'Thinkest thou that God Almighty will abide over a knave priest's head?'

Londoners, especially, did not miss a chance to flaunt their apparent emancipation from clerical control. When he saw a priest preparing for mass, William Clinch, of St John the Baptist Wallbrook, called out, 'Ye shall see a priest now go to masking,' a pun his fellow parishioners repeated with relish. An apprentice from St Mildred's Bread Street asserted that he would as soon listen to the crying of dogs as hear priests singing matins or even-song. In St Margaret's parish, it was later alleged, Richard Bugges fed holy bread to a bitch. Henry Patenson and Anthony Barber of St Giles without Cripplegate had encouraged their boys and the common singers of the parish to sing ribald songs against the sacraments and ceremonies of the Church, while Shermons, the keeper of Carpenter's Hall in Christchurch parish, had allowed an interlude to be performed in which priests were mocked and called knaves. The Londoners' latent anti-clericalism came most forcibly to the surface in an incident which happened in St Botolph With-out. Foxe, not troubling to conceal his bias, relates how one Giles Harrison, being in a place without Algate, merrily jested with a certain company of neighbours. When some of them said, ' "Let us go to the Mass." "I say, tarry," said he. And so taking a piece of bread in his hands, lifted it up over his head. And likewise taking a cup of wine, and bowing down his head, made therewith a cross over the cup, and so taking the said cup in both his hands, lifted it over his head, saying these words, "Have ye not heard Mass now?" '

For Londoners and others, however, destructive words and symbolic actions were not enough, and they turned to spontaneous destruction of images and looting of churches, though these incidents may only have been a pale imitation of the iconoclasm which occurred on the Continent. Image breaking seems to have appeared early in East Anglia. In 1532 some Dedham men and Robert Debnam of East Bergholt went to Dovercourt ten miles away and smashed the rood there: three of them were sub-sequently hanged for felony. In the same year bands of rioters broke down the image of the crucifix on the highway at Cogges-hall, the images of St Petronel in Hawksleigh church, the St Christopher by Sudbury and the St Petronel in the chapel by Ipswich together with the cross at Stoke Park. Elsewhere in Lollard country, in West Wycombe, one William Webbe showed his contempt of images by setting the statue of a headless bear in the 'tabernacle of St Roke'. Perhaps one of the most unsavoury incidents happened at Portsmouth. A mob in the parish church pulled down an image of St John which had stood by the high altar and broke a table of alabaster before moving on to the image of the crucified Christ. This they mutilated, boring out one of its eyes and piercing its side. Gardiner, reporting the outrage, admittedly not without ulterior motive, called the multitude 'Lollards, who denying images, thought therewithall the crafts of painting and graving to be generally superfluous and naught, and against God's laws'.[8]

Henry VIII would no more tolerate mob action in the name of Protestantism than he had at the time of the northern rebellion countenanced uprisings on behalf of conservative Catholicism. Cromwell had tried with some success to channel and guide popular enthusiasm but on his fall a conservative reaction set in. The King attempted to reassert traditional Catholic orthodoxy, though of necessity a Catholicism without the Pope. By the Act of Six Articles of 1539 Parliament not only restated Catholic doctrine on disputed points but conferred upon episcopal courts new powers to initiate trials for heresy. The King, the traditional bishops, even, apparently, the governing classes as represented in Parliament, preferred some form of clerical inquisition and an ordered society to possible social anarchy. The Act of Six Articles, though not enforced so severely as Protestants feared, led to a number of burnings, all the more significant in that the victims numbered influential clergy and laity. On the same day in July 1540 Robert Barnes, Thomas Garret, curate of Honey Lane, London, and William Jerome, vicar of Stepney, died at Smithfield and their deaths were followed by the burning at Salisbury, York and perhaps in the Chilterns of some seven virtually unknown lay people whose main offence seems to have been to have spoken against the sacrament. The burnings began again in 1546 and this time the heresy hunt touched the royal court. The trial of Anne Askew, the daughter of Sir William Askew of Stallingborough in Lincolnshire and sister of Edward Askew, one of the King's gentlemen pensioners, may at least partly have been a political manœuvre to discredit Queen Katherine Parr. Torture failed to bring Anne Askew to incriminate the Queen, or Ladies Suffolk, Sussex, Hertford, Denny or Fitzwilliam, though she freely confessed her rejection of transubstantiation. In her own account of her trials, deliberately designed to confirm her fellow Protestants in their faith (and later published by Bale), she revealed the intimate knowledge of the scriptures which became the hall-mark of subsequent generations of godly lay people. Anne Askew died at Smithfield in June 1546 with a priest, John Belenian, a tailor, and John Lascells, gentleman of the court.

There persecution halted. Henry did not withdraw his protection from Cranmer or from other advanced churchmen though he must have been aware of their deviance from Catholic doctrinal ortho-doxy. Even more significantly for the future he allowed his son to be educated by Protestant sympathizers. It may be that in his last years Henry realized that his successor might be forced to recognize some form of Protestantism to ensure the continuation of the royal supremacy over the English Church. In a speech to his last Parliament in December 1545 he made plain the extent of his authority as supreme governor. He first admonished both the clergy and the temporality in turn, the clergy for preaching against each other and causing dissension, the laity for not showing proper respect to the clergy and for taking undue powers of judgement upon themselves. Then addressing himself to the laity, the King proceeded to elaborate on their failings:

> You rail on bishops, speak slanderously of priests, and rebuke and taunt preachers, both contrary to good order and christian fraternity. If you know surely that a bishop or preacher erreth, or teacheth perverse doctrine, come and declare it to some of our council, or to us . . . and be not judges yourselves of your own fantastical opinions . . . And although you be permitted to read holy scripture, and to have the word of God in your mother tongue, you must understand, that it is licensed you so to do, only to inform your own conscience, and to instruct your children and family, and not to dispute and make scripture a railing and a taunting stock against priests and preachers, as many light persons do. I am very sorry to know and hear how unreverently that most precious jewel the word of God is disputed, rhymed, sung and jangled in every alehouse and tavern, contrary to the true meaning and doctrine of the same.[9]

Through the co-operation of Parliament Henry VIII had attained an unprecedented authority over the English Church. As his speech indicated, he saw clergy and laity as equally at his command, and, as all his actions declared, he intended to rule his country in religious matters through bishops who held a similar view of the royal supremacy to his own. Yet years before Henry's death some Englishmen had questioned on religious grounds whether their King could exercise such power over their spiritual salvation. No informed Catholics loyal to the papacy would concede that a layman, however mighty, could be head of the Church, while the experience of the previous twenty years was already beginning to convince the traditionally minded that Catholic orthodoxy could not be maintained without re-establishing the connection with Rome. To committed Protestants no human ruler could grant (and by implication withhold) the scriptures to the people as Henry suggested it lay within his capacity to do; already the supreme governor seemed to be aspiring to interpose his authority between the individual and God, thus taking away what to lay people seemed to be one of the greatest attractions of Protestantism. By the sheer brute force of his personality Henry succeeded while he lived in quelling debate upon the royal supremacy, but none of his three children after his death envisaged the royal supremacy in the same exalted form as their father. The laity as represented in Parliament had recognized the power of the Monarch in the Church: it proved impossible for Protestant monarchs subsequently to prevent them participating far more actively in determining the religion of the nation.

CHAPTER 4

PROTESTANT ADVANCE AND
POPULAR REACTION

The rule of the boy King Edward VI certainly fulfilled the prophecy that no land would prosper where a child was king. His six and a half years' reign permanently modified the monarch's exercise of the royal supremacy over the English Church. After the death of Henry VIII no other English ruler succeeded in governing the Church from a half papal, half regal standpoint as he had done. Because of Edward's youth his authority had to be employed on his behalf by political and ecclesiastical advisers, and the Crown never recovered the power it had thus to delegate to leading laymen. The years between 1547 and 1553 mark both the almost unhindered advance of Protestantism in England, a time of great idealism when the Protestant churchmen in England came nearest to bringing the reformed English Church into full harmony with reformed continental Protestantism, and a time of crude materialism when the State no longer even tried to disguise its annexation of the Church, and the Church's remaining riches appeared to be available to all comers. In the regions continuing political uncertainty and pressing economic difficulties sparked off fresh revolts in the name of religion, and religious conservatives struggled with religious progressives. In the midst of the unrest some Protestant churchmen attempted to bring magisterial Protestantism to the people more systematically than they had ever been allowed to before; but they soon discovered that they had to contend not only with Catholic survivalism but also with Protestant radicalism for already in some advanced areas there were people whose beliefs had outpaced those of the leaders of Church and of State. Rapid religious change presented new problems of social control which none of Edward's governments every fully mastered.

In the last two decades of Henry VIII's reign the authority of the Pope had been renounced, monasteries had been destroyed, certain superstitious practices such as pilgrimages and the veneration of saints discouraged, and the Bible made available in the vernacular, but the King had permitted his churchmen sympathetic to Protestantism to do little openly to define either the doctrine or the worship of the national Church. It seemed at first on Edward's accession that Cranmer, as Archbishop of Canterbury, and his small band of fellow Protestants might be given a free hand in reforming the Church: in fact, Edward's successive governments always retained ultimate command over Church affairs. In the first Parliament of the reign which met in November 1547 Protector Somerset sponsored the repeal of the Act of Six Articles and introduced an act which enabled the laity to receive communion in both kinds. The result was a spate of unrestrained Protestant preaching at court, in London and wherever else Protestantly inclined clergy had access to pulpits. Church leaders and politicians alike realized the necessity of providing a prayer book in English which could guide and restrain the Protestant radicalism particularly evident in London and some other southern towns.

As an interim measure the Government ordered the communion to be available to the laity in bread and wine at Easter 1548 and prayers in English to be inserted in the Latin Mass, while throughout the year Cranmer consulted his fellow bishops on the nature of the eucharist and on the proposed English service book. Cranmer's soundings revealed the conservatism of the majority of the bishops; at this date only a very few, who included Ridley, Holbeach and Goodrich, had yet adopted a Protestant interpretation of the sacrament of the altar, and the First Prayer Book approved by Parliament in January 1549 took full account of this conservatism. Essentially still a translation into English of the Latin liturgy, it substituted in a muted form the idea of the Mass as a thanksgiving and a memorial of Christ's death for the concept of the eucharistic sacrifice. The Prayer Book became mandatory for use throughout England from Whit Sunday 1549. Perhaps to most congregations the most novel feature of this Prayer Book was its language since all the services were now in the vernacular. Conservative priests could still contrive to interpret the Prayer Book in a Catholic sense without much difficulty. 'The public celebration of the Lord's Supper is very far from the order and institution of our Lord,' the convinced Protestant and Henrician exile, John Hooper, wrote to his Swiss Protestant friend, Heinrich Bullinger, 'although it is administered in both kinds, yet in some places the supper is celebrated three times a day.' Priests had simply renamed what had formerly been the Mass of the apostles or the Mass of the virgin, the communion of the apostles, the communion of the virgin, and so on. 'They still retain their vestments and candles before the altars; in the churches they always chant the hours and other hymns relating to the Lord's Supper, but in our own language. And that popery may not be lost, the mass priests, although they are compelled to discontinue the use of the Latin language, yet more carefully observe the same tone and manner of chanting to which they were heretofore accustomed in the papacy.'[1]

In his letters to the Swiss churchmen Hooper reluctantly recognized some of the limitations upon the establishing of a fully Protestant Church in England. Under Somerset the State no longer prevented the free expression of Protestant doctrine as had been the case with the government of Henry VIII in his latter years, but the conservatism of the majority of English parish priests remained a major obstacle. Until the universities could produce a new generation of Protestant ministers, the Archbishop of Canterbury and his Protestant colleagues had no choice but to depend at best upon an imperfectly converted clerical estate, some members of which, as the rebellions in the West Country and the Midlands demonstrated, could still effectively stir up their congregations against even these relatively moderate changes. Conservatism and resentment against any intervention by a distant government in London characterize these revolts as they did the Pilgrimage of Grace. The Edwardian revolts occurred at a time of serious agrarian discontent which trouble-makers undoubtedly exploited, but again, like the Pilgrimage of Grace, it seems improbable that the outbreaks were precipitated exclusively by economic grievances. There were murmurings against the Crown's religious policy in Cornwall in 1548 and then early in 1549 unrest appeared in Wiltshire and Somerset, though mainly directed against enclosure of commons. In Hampshire, however, religious susceptibilities had come to the fore, and malcontents in Winchester boasted that they would have the help of priests in the Cathedral close. Then in June and July 1549 full-scale revolt erupted in Cornwall and Devon. Incited by the clergy, the commons assembled behind banners bearing symbols of the holy sacrament. In their articles they re-affirmed the old belief that the bread and wine became the very body and blood of Christ in the Mass, and called upon the government to allow the Mass to be celebrated as in times past without any layman communicating with the priest. They went on to ask for the holy sacrament to be reserved in churches as it used to be, for holy bread and holy water to be distributed again and for priests to return to singing, or saying, God's service in the choir. They concluded by condemning Cranmer's new Prayer Book out of hand, comparing it disparagingly to a Christmas play, and demanding that celibacy should be kept for all priests, and that the act of Six Articles be restored.

The First Prayer Book of Edward VI, clearly at least the occasion for the western rising of 1549, seems also to have inspired similar, though less serious, disturbances in Oxfordshire, Buckinghamshire and Yorkshire, again led by clerics. Protector Somerset was convinced that the Buckinghamshire and Oxfordshire risings had been instigated by sundry priests for religious reasons, and the gentlemen who went to restore order threatened to hang rebel priests from their own steeples as a means of enforcing the peace. Yet not all those who revolted in 1549 turned to the old religion to give respectability to their cause or to the old priests for guidance. The Norfolk rebels did not justify their actions in Catholic terms, as Somerset's government expected, but as followers of Protestant commonwealthmen; in fact, they used the recently issued Prayer Book in their camp and persuaded Matthew Parker and other indubitably Protestant ministers to preach to them under the cloak of reformation.

The risings of 1549, though nowhere as threatening to national stability as the Pilgrimage of Grace, did bring home to the government the volatile nature of English society, and the frequent preaching which Protestant leaders considered a means for restoring control may indeed for some time have made the situation more inflammatory. Those who protested on Mousehold Heath in the summer of 1549 against the enclosure of Norfolk commons and other forms of exploitation by great lay landlords had been given cause for thinking that the spread of Protestantism would usher in a new era of social justice. The leading Protestant preachers, among them Hugh Latimer, Thomas Lever, Robert Crowley, John Hooper, Miles Coverdale, had raised expectations in their sermons from the beginning of the reign that the reforms which had not come about under Henry VIII might now be implemented under their new, godly King. Both in their preaching and writing they entreated the government to divert some of the secularized lands of the Church to Protestant good works such as founding schools where children might be nurtured in true religion, setting up hospitals for the young, the aged and the sick, and granting relief to the deserving poor. No one thundered more awesomely than Latimer, the son of a Leicestershire yeoman farmer. These preachers may have encouraged Somerset to order an enquiry into illegal enclosure and inclined him towards leniency to the poor in general, and they may even have brought Northumberland to make some provisions for the refounding of schools formerly attached to chantries, but they discovered in time to their chagrin that the claims of social justice moved the ostensibly Protestant governments of Edward VI little more than they had that of Henry VIII.

Cranmer did not figure prominently among those clerics who campaigned to improve social conditions and he seems to have had a rather different order of priorities than a commonwealthman like Latimer, convinced advocates of Protestantism though they both were. Cranmer, one of the least insular of the Archbishops of Canterbury who led the English Church after the break with Rome, put first the necessity of bringing the English Church into full communion with the continental Protestant churches, while Latimer, less of a theologian, left the definition of dogma to others and went ahead preaching Protestantism to the people. Throughout Edward's reign Cranmer cherished the ambition of achieving a reconciliation between the German and Swiss branches of Protestantism. Very soon after the death of Henry VIII he made overtures to the great continental Protestant divines, then under threat in Germany after the triumph of the Emperor Charles V over the Protestant princes at the battle of Mühlberg. He hoped to persuade them to take refuge in England so that the English Church might benefit from their teaching, and sent invitations to Martin Bucer, a fellow worker for union between the Zwinglians and the Lutherans and one of the most outstanding Protestant leaders, his friends Fagius and Peter Martyr from Strassburg, Ochino from Augsburg, Peter Alexander from the Netherlands, the Pole, John à Lasco, the superintendent of the beleaguered Zwinglian church in Emden, Dryander, a Spanish Lutheran, Tremellio, an Italian Jew, and Poullain, Calvin's successor as pastor of the French church in Strassburg. They accepted Cranmer's summons and subsequently wielded considerable influence over the theological development of the English Church. The only Protestant leader of commanding stature who refused even to visit England was Melanchthon.

Cranmer took great pains to place his much honoured foreign visitors in the universities and in London where their ministry could have the most immediate impact. Peter Martyr, who arrived in England in December 1547, received the Regius Professorship

of Divinity at Oxford early in the next year. In his Oxford lectures
his unequivocally Protestant interpretation of the eucharist caused
a sensation, as, at a different level, did the presence of his wife
at Christ Church. Martyr in his turn drew a little colony of foreign
Protestant refugees to Oxford which included Augustine Bernher,
later Latimer's faithful servant during the Marian persecution, and
a nephew of Froschover, the printer. As might have been expected,
this sudden manifestation of Protestantism at a university where,
until the death of Henry VIII, any public teaching of Protestantism
had met with considerable hostility provoked a violent reaction.
English Catholic apologists, Smyth, Tresham and Chedsey, tried
to stage a disputation with Martyr and his inoffensive wife had
to face a stream of obscenities from the Oxford populace. At
Cambridge the transition from Henrician Catholicism to open Protestantism progressed more gradually: the university had in any
case by 1547 a much stronger strain of indigenous Protestantism
among its more senior members and in Bucer a much less rebarba-
tive professor. When Bucer reached England rather later than
Martyr in 1549, the Regius Professor of Divinity at Cambridge
retired in his favour, and Bucer, though already a sick man, quickly
attracted numbers of Cambridge academics to his type of mediating
Protestantism. He died in Cambridge in February 1551 having made
Matthew Parker, Edwin Sandys and Edmund Grindal his executors;
in different degrees in their subsequent careers as bishops in the
Elizabethan Church they passed on Bucer's aspirations for a Christian commonwealth to a new generation of English Protestants.

   Besides teaching at the universities Martyr, Bucer and their
companions spent lengthy periods as guests in Cranmer's household, and Cranmer personally discussed with them the exact
Protestant interpretation of the eucharist, then so hotly debated
between Lutherans and Zwinglians. In John à Lasco, Superintendent
of the Strangers' Church in London, Cranmer had a skilled exponent
of Zwinglianism who certainly influenced Martyr's view of the
sacrament and possibly also Bucer's, but there was no comparable
continental theologian at hand to defend the more conservative
Protestant account of the eucharist. Indeed, the refusal of any
major Lutheran leader to visit England between 1547 and 1553
meant that at the very moment the Archbishop was devising the
formularies of faith for the English Church he could call only
upon the 'purest' stream of continental Protestantism. Theologians
still dispute Cranmer's final position in the eucharistic controversy,

but the presence of these foreign Protestant clerics in England in Edward's reign certainly ensured that Lutheranism subsequently had little place in the English Church.

Cranmer and other convinced Protestants on the episcopal bench may well have moved beyond the doctrine implied in the First Edwardian Prayer Book even before Parliament prescribed its use in the early summer of 1549 in the first Act of Uniformity. Their reservations must have increased, as Hooper's certainly did, when Gardiner demonstrated from his cell in the Tower that the Catholic doctrine of transubstantiation could still be read into the English communion service. In 1549 England was in the process of becoming, but had not definitively become, a Protestant nation. Early in that year Parliament had permitted priests to marry, a notable step in lessening the division between the clergy and the laity, but, partly because of popular unrest, little further progress was made in implementing Protestant change until after Somerset's fall in October. Northumberland's assumption of power drastically altered the political situation. Since his government depended for its survival on the defeat of the conservative interest, it acted at once to remove the Henrician Catholic bishops still remaining in office. Gardiner and Bonner lost their sees of Winchester and London and Ridley took responsibility for the crucial diocese of London. Here he soon made his opinions felt by ordering altars to be changed into communion tables and by banishing all other traces of popery from the parish churches. More single-minded even than Ridley, Hooper, the bishop elect of Gloucester, tried unsuccessfully to abolish the use of vestments in the Church. For him vestments not only recalled the Catholic past but also gave outward expression to the separation of clergy and laity. From among the foreign reformers only à Lasco supported Hooper's belief that the retention of such garments constituted a grave stumbling block to the godly, and rather than forgo the service he so ardently wanted to give as a Protestant bishop, Hooper in the end very unwillingly agreed to be consecrated wearing the hated vestments. With his elevation, the episcopal bench leaned even further in the direction of explicit Protestant change.

Urged on by Northumberland, in 1550 Cranmer undertook a further revision of the English Prayer Book, much influenced in his work by Bucer who submitted to him detailed criticism of all aspects of the 1549 book. The resultant Second Prayer Book of Edward vi effected a conscious break with the Catholic past: a congregational communion replaced a sacrificial Mass, the very word Mass disappeared, and the minister officiated in a surplice rather than in the former mass vestments. Yet decidedly Protestant though it was, and revised with the aid of foreign scholars, this Second Prayer Book remained an essentially English compilation. In it Cranmer succeeded in maintaining something of a middle position between the traditionalism of the 1549 book and the straight Zwinglianism which it seems the extreme wing of English reformers, under the leadership of Hooper, would have preferred him to adopt.

Parliament passed the second Act of Uniformity, which gave approval to this Second Prayer Book, in April 1552 but did not order its use until the following November. Consequently many parishes had less than a year's experience of the new Prayer Book before Mary's accession allowed conservatives to set it aside. Yet in Yorkshire a parish priest, Robert Parkyn, saw enough of the 1552 book to exclaim against the abominable heresy he considered it contained. The substitution in the communion service of loaf bread for the wafer and the giving of bread into laymen's hands particularly offended him. In the new service priests could no longer adore the sacrament: indeed, they had now to instruct their congregations that Christ's true body was not in the host but in heaven. Parkyn perceived how the book implicitly denied all the former Catholic teaching on the sacraments: it permitted baptisms only to be performed on Sundays, made no provision for the administration of extreme unction, or for dirges for the newly dead, and contained no reference to purgatory.

With the Forty-Two Articles brought out in 1553, the Prayer Book of 1552 which incorporated the reformed order for the consecration of bishops, priests and deacons of 1550 completed Cranmer's achievement in devising liturgies and codifying doctrine for the English Church. Like the Prayer Book, the Articles contained doctrine more advanced than Lutheranism and inclined towards a Zwinglian-Calvinist consensus without fully accepting it; they also revealed an almost obsessive fear of Anabaptism. When Edward VI died in July 1553 Cranmer still had not finished the revision of the old canon law necessary in order to adapt it to the needs of a Protestant establishment, and the English Church never subsequently acquired a specifically Protestant form of discipline.

The churchmen had produced a Protestant Prayer Book and

confession of faith, but they could not impose them without the close co-operation of the State. The implementation of Protestantism in England in the reign of Edward VI was a profoundly Erastian process and favoured churchmen could procede only so far as lay politicians would allow. Even in the sphere of liturgy, where Cranmer probably enjoyed more independence than in any other, the Edwardian Council kept the upper hand. Months after Cranmer had drawn up the Second Prayer Book, and Parliament had approved its contents, Knox, preaching before the King in September 1552, criticized the requirement that the people should continue to receive communion kneeling. This, he thought, would give the uninstructed the opportunity of worshipping the elements as they had done in Catholic times. The Council tried to persuade Cranmer to delete the provision but he refused to alter a book already sanctioned by Parliament. So, on its own authority, the Council inserted a statement, the 'black rubric', explaining that kneeling during the communion service in no way implied adoration of the host or the presence of Christ's natural body. Cranmer, Ridley and Latimer, Hooper and Knox, all in their different ways religious idealists, might propagate religious truths as they saw them, but their teachings never gained the whole-hearted support of the politicians in power.

The leading Edwardian churchmen strove valiantly in times of unrest and great uncertainty to cast down popery in order to build up Protestantism, but their masters could scarcely afford the same idealism. The politicians' first consideration had to be to keep and if possible strengthen the basis of their power, and particularly in years of rapid inflation power meant wealth. Simultaneously with the doctrinal advance of Protestantism went an accelerating onslaught on what remained of the institutional independence and property of the old Church. No longer pretending to maintain the fiction of episcopal election, Somerset's government under the provisions of the 1547 Act appointed bishops by letters patent to hold office during pleasure. Procedures begun when Henry VIII assumed the supremacy over the English Church continued: royal visitations of the Church took precedence over visitations by the archbishops or the diocesan bishops. Churchmen could act decisively only as long as their actions coincided with the intentions of the government of the day. This did not involve any theoretical change in the nature of the royal supremacy over the Church but the balance shifted, and powers which Henry VIII had exercised in person now, under a minority, fell to a group of councillors. Again, Edwardian politicians devised no new plans for confiscating the Church's wealth, but wealth which Henry had intended should benefit the Crown during his son's minority came more and more to be turned to the benefit of the politicians in office.

The last Parliament of Henry VIII had approved his scheme for the dissolution of the chantries but he had not lived long enough for the plans to be carried out. The first Parliament of Edward VI, therefore, confirmed the scheme and gave royal commissioners authority to take for the Crown the endowments of all chantries and guilds designed to maintain superstitious practices, though foundations which existed primarily to support schools or relieve the poor or infirm escaped. The wealth involved in the confiscation was small compared to that which the Crown had acquired from the dissolution of the monasteries but this act probably affected the generality of lay people even more closely. There can have been few parishes of any substance not required to forfeit property which parishioners felt to be more truly theirs than ever the more remote monastic foundations had been. The worst fears of the Lincolnshire rebels of 1536 were in process of being realized. Next the parish churches came under the government's scrutiny and in the last year of Edward's reign commissioners took from cathedrals and parish churches all ornaments and vestments beyond the minimum laid down in the 1552 Prayer Book. From the rich Cathedral of York alone commissioners seized for the King's use dozens of sets of vestments in the liturgical colours of red, blue, green, white and black, jewelled crosses, mitres, staffs, reliquaries and vessels of silver and gold, while the reports from the counties show that not even the humblest parish church escaped sending up to London its surplus, and often tawdry, vestments and communion plate.

By 1553 all foundations to provide prayers for the dead had gone, by far the greater part of the Church's goods given by the pious to maintain the elaborate ceremonial of late medieval Catholicism had been taken away, and the lands of the bishops, the most significant accumulation of wealth still partly under churchmen's control, stood under attack. Here, again, Edwardian politicians merely followed the examples set by Henry VIII, but with a subtle change of emphasis. During the last years of Henry's reign some bishops, and these included both the Archbishops of Canterbury and York, had been forced to surrender many of their ancient episcopal manors to the Crown and to accept in exchange parcels of impropriate rectories which had come to the King on the dissolution of the monasteries. Successive Edwardian governments continued this process, and in some cases scarcely even preserved the appearance of an exchange, however unequal. Holbeach took possession of the see of Lincoln in 1547 only after he had agreed to a disadvantageous exchange of episcopal lands with the Crown and to an outright grant of manors to Somerset which together reduced his income by more than half. The government suppressed the newly founded see of Westminster as no longer necessary and reabsorbed its endowments. Under Northumberland some attempt seems to have been made to implement the scheme of transforming the bishops into salaried officials which had first been suggested by some radical thinkers associated with Cromwell's entourage. When Ponet became Bishop of the previously very rich diocese of Winchester the government made him surrender his lands in return for an annual income of 2000 marks, and in the next year a similar bargain was exacted from Hooper as Bishop of Gloucester. By Edward's last months Northumberland had progressed far with his plan to break up the lavishly endowed diocese of Durham and to replace it with two smaller bishoprics with bishops on fixed stipends. In contrast with the last decade of Henry VIII's reign when royal servants on the King's behalf kept a tight control over the process of confiscation of ecclesiastical lands and arranged for sales at realistic prices, Edward VI as monarch benefited less, but his servants more. It was, in fact, the Edwardian governments and not Henry VIII which were responsible for squandering monastic lands either by selling them to favoured noblemen and gentlemen at very advantageous rates or even by giving them to highly placed royal servants. The two most powerful Edwardian politicians, first Somerset and then Northumberland, profited at the expense of both Church and Crown. In 1548 the Bishop of Bath and Wells owned twenty-four episcopal manors, but by the time of Somerset's disgrace he had lost all except seven and a large proportion of this property had fallen into the hands of the Seymour family, its friends and dependants. Northumberland in turn expected to gain handsomely from the break-up of the see of Durham and would have done so if the dismantling process had not been halted by the King's death. Had Edward VI lived longer more bishoprics might well have received the attentions of his land-hungry servants, and it is scarcely likely that the still substantial endowments of the cathedral chapters of the old foundation would have been left untouched. Only the accession of Mary prevented further spoliation of the Church.

The behaviour of Edwardian politicians was imitated by laymen lower in society and, when opportunity offered, they also tried to enrich themselves indiscriminately at the cost of the Church or monarch. Churchwardens secretly sold the treasures of their churches before the Edwardian commissioners reached their parishes to take them in the King's name. Although the traditionally minded inhabitants of York had gone on making bequests to chantries right up to the year when Henry VIII had made the breach with Rome, the civic leaders still did not hesitate to take financial advantage of the religious changes. After a parliamentary amalgamation of some of the poorest parishes in the city, carried out at the city's prompting, members of the corporation bought up some of the twelve surplus churches at absurdly low prices; the mayor in 1550 got the best bargain, paying 10s for a redundant church. Windfalls like this must have been available in many localities, and the central government probably never heard about them; even when there were few gains to be had the wilder elements in the population seem to have gone on destroying monuments of the Catholic past for destruction's sake alone.

Despite this appetite among all sections of the laity for personal enrichment at the expense of the Church, the idealism of some of the Protestant church leaders could evoke an answering response from some of the laity. Thomas Hancock, an enthusiastic Protestant preacher, in his own account of his ministry at Poole in Dorset acknowledged that the godly in the town had invited him to serve there at a time when the local Protestant party had already attained some power. At the beginning of Edward's reign Poole enjoyed considerable prosperity but when its economy declined backsliders began to appear. As he was preaching one Sunday Hancock spoke out against idolatry and covetousness and denied the real presence of Christ in the sacrament. 'Whereat old Thomas White, a great rich merchant, and a ringleader of the papists, rose out of his seat and went out of the church, saying, "Come from him, good people. He came from the devil, and teacheth unto you devilish doctrine." John Nothrel, alias Spicer, followed him out, exclaiming, "It [the sacrament] shall be God, when thou shalt be but a knave." ' At All Saints tide in the same year White, Nothrel and one William Haviland approached a priest in Poole and asked him to say a dirge for all souls. Hancock forbade him to do it. 'Then did all three with one mouth call me knave and my wife strumpet.' They went so far as to threaten Hancock with violence in his own church, but the mayor, Morgan Reed, an 'honest, good man', pulled him to safety into the church choir and, shutting the chancel gates against White and his party, ordered them to keep the peace. Even then it took the mayor some time to quell the uproar. Because of the incident Hancock appealed to Somerset for protection who passed on the case to Cecil and he wrote reproving the town for its unruliness. From then onwards until the death of Edward vi peace reigned, and Hancock preached the word of God without open hindrance.[2]

Horror at doctrinal innovations among some of the laity at Poole and genuine attachment to old religious practices, such as praying for the dead, seem to have reinforced already existing divisions within the governing group of the town, and as long as the central government remained Protestant the local Protestants, too, kept the upper hand. This sort of strife between rival lay factions seems to have been quite common in towns in the mid-sixteenth century as Protestantism spread. When, as at Hull, the central government had a representative in residence in the person of the governor of the castle, or as at Berwick the town consisted of little more than the military garrison, Protestant preachers, in this instance both Scotsmen, John Rough and John Knox, encountered minimal opposition. Through their labours Hull and Berwick together with Newcastle had become notable centres of Protestantism by 1553. In towns less exposed to governmental influence preachers had often to rely solely on their own powers of persuasion, but even in the unpromising field of Lancashire where priests and people still overwhelmingly adhered to the practices of the old religion Protestantism made some impact upon the towns in the Manchester area.

The development of Protestantism in south Lancashire is particularly interesting since it can be traced directly to the activity of local scholars who had studied at the universities in the 1540s and early 1550s and now felt called to propagate the gospel in their native county. None of the Edwardian Protestant apostles of Lancashire, who included John Bradford, George Marsh and the subsequent turncoat, Henry Pendleton, held a living there, indeed, the increasingly valuable livings in the county continued to be monopolized by pluralists who did not reside but left their pastoral work to conservative and ill-educated assistant priests. Pendleton had been a member of Brasenose, the college of the martyrologist, John Foxe, and of fellow Lancastrians, the brothers Alexander and Laurence Nowell. Bradford and Marsh had both received their higher education at Cambridge, Bradford coming to the university via the Inns of Court where he had fallen under the sway of Latimer and Sampson, while Marsh, a farmer, who like Bradford had turned to academic studies relatively late in life, had not entered Christ's College until 1551. All three men on their own initiative engaged in missionary preaching in Lancashire before Edward vi's death. Pendleton was a vehement advocate of Protestantism in Manchester in the last years of his reign. John Bradford's family also lived in Manchester, and he first directed his attention there. By letters from London and by frequent visits between 1550 and 1553 he managed to plant Protestant cells in Manchester, Bolton, Wigan, Liverpool and the surrounding areas in south Lancashire. Marsh, a curate first in London and then in Leicestershire, took part in a preaching tour of Lancashire in 1552 or 1553 and the two Lever and three Pilkington brothers, yet more Lancastrians converted to Protestantism at Cambridge, probably came back to Bolton to preach. As a result of their labours there emerged a group of committed and articulate lay Protestants, unusually well instructed concerning the teachings of the Edwardian reformers, well versed in the Bible and the Book of Common Prayer and even familiar with some of the most recent works of continental reformers such as Melanchthon and Bucer supplied to them by Bradford from London. Informed converts might be won, as the Lancastrian evangelists proved, in some of the most backward regions of England; but though the harvest might be great, the labourers still were few.

The difference between a remote county such as Lancashire and more prosperous and populous regions in the South lay not so much in the general religious conservatism which faced most reformers throughout England, but in the additional problem of Protestant radicalism. To their consternation university Protestants discovered early in Edward's reign that unorthodox, sometimes clearly heretical, ideas had already become entrenched among some of the advanced laity. Soon after his return to England in 1549 from Zurich, John Hooper reported to Bullinger on the states of mind he had encountered among those to whom he had been lecturing in London. Some of his hearers held heretical opinions about the incarnation of Christ, others believed in the perfectability of a man reconciled to God, yet others maintained that a man, having once received the Holy Ghost, was irretrievably damned if he later fell away. From beliefs current in London he went on to give a shrewd, if somewhat exaggerated, analysis of the different types of religious anarchy prevalent in the nation at large:

> How dangerously our England is afflicted by heresies of this kind, God only knows . . . There are some who deny that man is endued with a soul different from that of a beast, and subject to decay. Alas, not only are those heresies reviving among us which were formerly dead and buried, but new ones are springing up every day. There are such libertines and wretches who are daring enough in their conventicles not only to deny that Christ is the Messiah and saviour of the world, but also to call that blessed seed a mischievous fellow and deceiver of the world. On the other hand, a great portion of the kingdom so adheres to the popish faction, as altogether to set at nought God and the lawful authority of magistrates; so that I am greatly afraid of a rebellion and civil discord.[3]

Hooper saw his mission as the bringing of Protestant order to this disorderly laity and two years later his opportunity came on his promotion to the episcopate.

Northumberland's government appointed Hooper as Bishop of Gloucester in 1550 though, because of his reluctance to be consecrated wearing the traditional vestments, he did not enter into possession of the see until early in 1551. A year later he received the adjoining diocese of Worcester to run in combination with Gloucester and so had the chance of imposing his religious ideals over a large area of the West Midlands. When Bishop of Worcester for two and a half years between 1536 and 1539 Hugh Latimer had indeed attempted to act as a preaching pastor, but Hooper seems to have been the first Protestant bishop in England to try to transform the old office of a Catholic prelate into that of a godly superintendent in a thoroughly reformed Church. In his visitation of the Gloucester diocese in 1551 Hooper was somewhat overwhelmed by the conservatism and sheer ignorance of his parish clergy. He found that nearly a third of them failed to achieve an elementary educational standard; they could not repeat the Ten Commandments or cite events in the Gospels to support assertions of belief made in the Creed. In his injunctions Hooper solemnly enjoined upon them the need to study and arranged for the continuing instruction of the clergy through regular gatherings. He urged on all the necessity for frequent preaching while commanding the abolition of all traces of Romish practices. A little later he summoned suspect clergy before him and made them take an oath explicitly denying the real presence in the sacrament. Even in his relations with his clergy Hooper showed more energy than most of his fellow bishops but he differed most signally from them in his attitude to the laity. Hooper did not, as most bishops had normally been content to do, leave the instruction of the laity to the parochial clergy, but examined some of the laity himself on their knowledge of the Creed, the Commandments and the Lord's Prayer. He imposed penances on ignorant laymen like John Trigg of Dursley who in August 1551 had to explain to his neighbours that the cause of his public humiliation was 'because I cannot say one of the commandments of Almighty God, but I am more like an ethnic than a christian man'. A frequent preacher – sometimes his Swiss wife feared he would make himself ill by his constant preaching – Hooper not only fulfilled the ideal of a reformed bishop as a pastor of his flock but also attempted to attain to that other requirement of the continental reformers, even less often observed, the strict imposition of discipline. Working within the confining restrictions of the unreformed canon law and the old episcopal courts which had come into being to administer it, he contrived to overcome earlier conservatism and inertia by the simple, but revolutionary, expedient of sitting as judge in his own courts. Taking back authority from the officials to whom for centuries bishops had customarily delegated their legal powers, Hooper himself tried cases between laymen disputing the settlement of a will, attempted to reconcile estranged husbands and wives, and corrected those who had slandered their neighbours. His concern over the laity went hand in hand with his pastoral care for his clergy and he sat equally frequently to hear cases which involved their doctrine, morals or behaviour. His unprecedented activity won him a eulogy from Foxe who regarded him as 'a spectacle to all bishops who shall ever hereafter succeed him, not only in that place but in whatsoever diocese through the whole of England':

No father in his household, no gardener in his garden, nor husbandman in his vineyard, was more or better occupied than he is in his diocese amongst his flock, going about his towns and villages in teaching and preaching to the people there.[4]

Hooper blazed a trail as a reformed bishop even without the assistance of many educated, zealous Protestant clergy. Yet just as some reformed bishops were realizing that their prime duty lay in more or less continuous residence in their dioceses, so some educated Protestant clergy who would also previously have used their talents in ecclesiastical or secular administration began to hear the call to a parochial ministry. One such was Rowland Taylor. A Northumbrian, Taylor had studied at Cambridge during the exciting years of the 1520s and, as he later said, had been converted to reformed religion by reading *Unio Dissidentium* and the sermons of Hugh Latimer. He had then become a doctor of both laws and joined Cranmer's household, and yet, when presented to the living of Hadleigh in Suffolk, he actually decided to live in his parish. He ministered there throughout the reign of Edward VI and gained golden opinions for his devotion to the spiritual and temporal welfare of his parishioners. The effect of the ministry of a man of Taylor's intellectual eminence emerged soon after Mary's accession; when first Taylor and later his clerical successor had been removed from Hadleigh on account of their Protestantism, a layman, John Alcock, came forward: Foxe describes him as a woad setter, yet learned in the Holy Scriptures. Until imprisoned by the Marian authorities he used the [Second] Prayer Book of Edward VI in the parish church, read prayers in English and gave the people godly lessons and exhortations out of the chapters he had read to them. Even from prison Alcock continued his evangelism, writing two epistles to the people of Hadleigh, rebuking them for turning away from the grace of Christ, and warning them against the ministrations of hireling priests. If such able and conscientious Protestant ministers as Taylor could be brought into the parishes, as was indeed beginning to happen in Edward's reign, then laymen like Alcock might respond actively to the attractions of continental Protestantism.

Nevertheless, Hooper had been right to be troubled about diversities of belief among the radical laity and he was untypical of most Protestant leaders only in the amount of attention he gave to the subject. Despite more than six years' exposure to fairly frequent preaching on the tenets of the continental reformers, Protestant laymen in parts of southern England continued to cling to a wide variety of doctrines at the time of Edward's death. Whereas the theological debates between English Protestant leaders and their foreign guests had concentrated upon the nature of Christ's spiritual presence in the eucharist, some laymen, while violently rejecting the popish Mass, were far less preoccupied with the sacraments, and turned increasingly to the issues of preaching and study of the word. By 1550 Calvin's teachings had penetrated widely in England and especially his teaching on predestination derived from Luther's works. This proved to be the one doctrine of the magisterial reformers which some of the English laity could not stomach. Reports reached the Privy Council in 1550 of a group of Kentish men from around Maidstone and Faversham who had been affirming that 'the doctrine of predestination was meter for devils than for christian men'. Their leader, Henry Harte, had taught publicly 'that there is no man so chosen or predestinate, but that he may condemn himself; neither is there any so reprobate but that he may, if he will, keep the commandments and be saved'. He had also boasted that 'his faith was not grounded upon learned men, for all errors were brought in by learned men'. Humphrey Middleton, one of Harte's followers, phrased the concept of universal salvation in a different way: since Adam was elected to salvation, and since all men, being then in Adam's loins, were also predestined to salvation, therefore there could be none predestined to reprobation. Before the end of 1550 this group migrated as a body to Essex where persecuted Lollards from the Chilterns had previously found refuge. Late in January 1551 Thomas Upchard of Bocking was brought before the Privy Council on a charge of receiving the Kentish men in his house at Christmas-time and of having fallen with them 'in argument of things of the scripture, specially whether it were necessary to stand or kneel, bare head or covered, at prayer'. The privy councillors clearly showed far less anxiety over what had been discussed than in the fact that some sixty people had assembled in an illegal conventicle. In the next month some of the chief members of the group appeared in London for further examination and divulged that several of their number 'had refused the communion above two years upon very superstitious and erroneous purposes, with divers other evil opinions worthy of great punishment'. Some were imprisoned, others bound over to be conformable in the future, but this did not end unorthodox teachings among the laity.[5]

Historians have hotly debated whether this group was Anabaptist in inspiration. Since contemporaries all too readily labelled any unorthodox popular religious assembly Anabaptist, and since only scanty evidence survives about this particular group, the issue must remain undecided. However, neither Harte's book, *A Godly, New and Short Treatise*, which he published in 1548, nor the reports of his teachings contain any mention of re-baptism or pay any particular attention to baptism at all. Throughout Mary's reign his disciples reiterated their conviction that all men possessed free will:

> Christ saith, 'He that loveth me, keepeth my commandments.' And Christ came not to break the law, but to fulfil it. And will we say we are not able to keep it? . . . Saint James saith, 'Whosoever shall keep the whole law, and yet fail in one point, he is guilty in all' . . . God hath given unto man a more principal gift than he hath done to the unreasonable creature, which doth all things by nature . . . but to man [he has given] to do all things out of his free will.[6]

Harte was evidently an educated man, and Cole, one of his adherents, was a Maidstone schoolmaster for a time, but it seems more probable from their towns of origin, from the nature of their opinions, their biblical fundamentalism and devotion to St James's Epistles, that they had developed out of the Kentish Lollard tradition rather than been directly influenced by continental Anabaptism. How much popular support this apparently tiny but articulate group of Protestant deviationists ever raised outside their own localities in Kent and Essex and, after their imprisonment there, in London it is impossible now to judge. Yet it is likely that in those areas where Lollardy had persisted well into the 1530s lay enthusiasts accepted fully only those Protestant teachings which coincided with their already received religious attitudes. A one time Lollard who, at the risk of persecution, had emancipated himself from the authority of his Catholic priest would have been unlikely to abase himself without a struggle before a new Protestant clericalism.

Edward vi had succeeded to the throne at a time when, for a variety of reasons little connected with religion, society was in a state of turmoil which new religious divisions between Catholics and Protestants only served to exacerbate. During his short reign

Parliament imposed upon the nation a thoroughly Protestant Church system of doctrine and liturgy, but it failed to supply a new Protestant form of discipline. Protestant divines, in alliance with those of their continental colleagues who had taken refuge in England, tried hard to turn the system approved by Parliament into a reality, but they had less than a year between the adoption of the second Edwardian Prayer Book in November 1552 and the death of the King in the following July. Pockets of informed Protestantism had certainly been planted in many towns and in some counties, particularly where a convinced Protestant bishop, or an active and educated local Protestant minister had control of Church affairs, but nothing resembling a religious uniformity had come into being. A larger number of lay people than ever before, from leading government officials to very minor property owners, had a greater personal interest in maintaining the dispersal of former Church lands, though they had not necessarily adapted their religious views to harmonize with their economic concerns. Probably in 1553 the majority of priests and people remained conservative, while the gulf separating the Protestantism of the university-trained clerics and their congregations from some types of popular Protestantism may even have been widening. When, after the failure of Northumberland's ten-day attempt to preserve his power under the puppet Queen Jane, Mary Tudor gained her inheritance, she had some reason for still supposing that she could restore the English Church and nation to the old papal allegiance through nothing more formidable than the action of the monarch in an acquiescent Parliament.

CHAPTER 5

CATHOLIC RESTORATION AND
PROTESTANT RESISTANCE

The process of the restoration of Catholicism between 1553 and
1558 demonstrates the growing strength of the laity in the English
Church perhaps more clearly than at any other period in the
sixteenth century. From the first Queen Mary made no attempt to
hide her overriding desire to bring back the form of Catholicism she
had known and loved in the days before her father had summoned
the Reformation Parliament. The laity as represented in the frequent Parliaments Mary held, countenanced the return of this
traditional pattern of services and ceremonial without too much
unease, after a struggle and with very much greater reluctance
allowed the re-enactment of the heresy laws, but absolutely refused
to make any restitution of former monastic lands to the Church.
Although some of the Catholic churchmen led by Cardinal Pole
clearly recognized the need for cautious reform within English
Catholicism, the changes which they sought evoked little enthusiasm even among those of the laity who willingly accepted the
old forms of worship. By contrast Protestant resistance in certain
parts of England was increasingly supported by laymen from very
varied sectors of society, not least because Mary's marriage to
Philip of Spain brought political opposition and religious protest
together in a heady brand of English nationalism. The clerics and
laymen who suffered religious persecution, either risking death by
maintaining Protestantism at home in secret or going into exile
for the sake of their religion, decisively affected the subsequent
development of the English Church.

Mary's triumph in preventing the diversion of the succession
from what most English people considered the senior legitimate
descendant of Henry VIII at one and the same time discredited
convinced Protestants and enhanced the Queen's plans for a total
Catholic restoration. Foxe made some acute comments on the
situation soon after Mary's accession when he tried a few years
later to account for this general reversal in popular attitudes.

In November [1553] the people, and especially the churchmen,

perceiving the queen so eagerly set upon her old religion, they
likewise for their parts, to show themselves no less forward to
serve the queen's appetite (as the manner is of the multitude,
commonly to frame themselves after the humour of the prince
and time present) began in their choirs to set up the pageant of
St Katherine, and of St Nicholas, and of their processions in
Latin, after all their old solemnity with their gay gardeviance
[gear] and grey amices.[1]

If the Queen had not insisted from the beginning on linking the
Catholic restoration with a Spanish marriage the religious history
of her reign might have been very different. Certainly in her first
Parliament which assembled in October 1553 Mary fairly successfully mastered the opposition in the Commons to the repeal of the
Edwardian Act of Uniformity. With this withdrawal of authorization both for the Second and for the more conservative First Prayer
Book of Edward vi the religious situation had officially reverted to
the state it had been in at the end of the reign of Henry viii.
Members of Parliament would tolerate, though in some cases unwillingly, the form of worship favoured by the Queen but resisted
the granting of any new powers to the conservative clergy. For this
reason they would not re-impose the heresy laws repealed by
Edward's first Parliament and without them no thorough religious
reaction could be enforced. This Parliament showed where its
primary concern lay when it sent a deputation to Mary to petition
against her proposed marriage to Philip, a marriage to which the
Queen had already privately committed herself.

Mary's second Parliament, meeting in the spring of 1554,
displayed no less hostility to any form of clerical revival than its
predecessor. Gardiner, who had regained his bishopric of Winchester and had been appointed Lord Chancellor in the first month
of the reign, did his best to get the Henrician heresy laws and the
Act of Six Articles brought back. Parliament refused again to
accept any new form of clerical supervision: Paget, the leader of
a faction in the Privy Council against Gardiner and the apparent
attempt at clerical resurgence, may have co-ordinated the opposition in Parliament. The government, so recently threatened by
Wyatt's rebellion in late January which had underlined the extent
of the hostility to Mary's marriage, dared not push the Queen's
religious policy further until her marriage had been safely accomplished. In fact, the wedding of Philip and Mary took place in July

1554 without the popular disturbance expected by the government
and in the few months of quietness which followed, before popular
hatred of all things Spanish became predominant, the Queen
summoned Parliament for the third time. The meeting of this
Parliament in November 1554 coincided with the much delayed
return to England of Cardinal Pole whom the Emperor had
prevented from crossing the Channel until the Spanish match had
been performed. After the fullest assurances which emanated from
the Papacy itself that the secularization of the monastic and
chantry lands would not be reversed, Parliament finally consented
to the re-enactment of the old laws against heresy, passed new
treason laws and repealed all the anti-papal and anti-clerical laws
made since the beginning of the Reformation Parliament. In a
dramatic and moving ceremony on 30 November 1554 Pole
absolved the nation from schism and brought England again into
full communion with the holy see. In the heat of the moment
Parliament had been persuaded to sue for this reconciliation and
its proceedings mark the apparent completeness of the Catholic
reaction: from January 1555 heresy could be fought in England
once more with the support of both the ecclesiastical and secular
arm. Yet the heresy trials held with increasing frequency from
the beginning of 1555, show the essential shallowness of this
national reunion with Rome. At best the persecutions were stolidly
accepted, at worst they generated active hostility to the government. Mary's next Parliament, called in October 1555, openly
criticized the government's policies, resentful of the persecutions
which spared no sector of society, and it refused to pass a government bill designed to confiscate the lands of those who had gone
into exile on account of their religion. As Mary's reign proceeded,
the Commons as a body may have felt no deep adherence to
Protestant doctrine, but they clearly were no less antagonistic to
clerical pretensions and no less nationalistic and anti-Roman than
the Commons of the Reformation Parliament had been.

The Queen probably did not look much further than this formal
reconciliation, assuming that once England had returned to Rome
Catholicism would revive under its own spiritual impetus. Above
all, Mary seems to have wanted to erase religious memories of the
past twenty-five years, and to restore the Church to the condition
it had enjoyed in her youth. Some of Mary's earliest actions as
queen indicate her priorities: immediately after the repeal in her
first Parliament of the Edwardian Act of 1549 which had permitted

clerical marriage she sent out a royal proclamation in December
1553 forbidding married priests to officiate any longer in the
Church. Throughout 1554 and into 1555 episcopal officials, in
obedience to the Queen's wishes, went to work all over England
to remove married clergy from their benefices. In Essex as many
as a third of the clergy in the county lost their livings for this
reason, and even in the backward diocese of York perhaps a tenth
of the clergy were so deprived. Most of these priests do not seem
to have been convinced Protestants for they set their wives aside
and, after performing penance, accepted other livings. Yet their
treatment, considerably more severe than the penalty reserved for
clerics who had committed adultery, can only have served to lower
even further the reputation of these priests in their own localities.
Before they could take up a new cure many had to go through an
ordeal like the former vicar of Whenby in Yorkshire who at
offertory time at high Mass, wearing a surplice and carrying a
lighted candle, was required to declare to his old parishioners:
'Masters, I have been seduced and deceived, thinking that I might
lawfully marry, but now knowing the truth, I perceive I **have** done
unlawfully so to marry and am sorry therefore, desiring you not to
be offended with me.' In the short run this widespread humiliation
of conformist clergy had the effect, quite contrary to Mary's intentions, of lessening the prestige of the local clergy in the eyes of
the laity.[2]

Some of the Queen's clerical advisers, however, were more
discriminating and envisaged rather more than a simple return to
conditions as they had been before 1529. Cardinal Pole in particular
worked for a renewal of Catholicism, although this former harsh
critic of the Roman Church proved in action to be the most
conservative and hesitant of reformers. In December 1555, a year
after the full restoration of Catholicism, he called a national synod
at Westminster of bishops and representatives of the lower clergy
of both English provinces. In a censorious opening speech Pole laid
the blame for the religious changes of the previous twenty-five
years on the clergy themselves. If they had been better instructed
in their faith and less ignorant, he implied, more willing to make
a stand for their principles, and less covetous, the Protestant
innovations might never have been carried through. He planned
that the decrees which the synod went on to pass would strengthen
the quality of English Catholicism for the future. The synod, like
so many sessions of Convocation and indeed of Parliament before it,

exhorted all pastors once again to reside among their parishioners; now, however, residence imposed upon priests and bishops alike a fresh obligation to refute false doctrine and to instruct their flocks in true religion. The synod tried to extend censorship by prohibiting the printing or sale of heretical books, but recognized that Bible reading had taken root among the laity and could no longer be forbidden entirely. In an attempt to counteract the effect of the Protestant Bible, it commissioned a Catholic translation of the New Testament as well as a book of Catholic homilies and a Catholic catechism. Perhaps among the most constructive of the synod's decrees was the one which encouraged the founding of diocesan schools and colleges from which in the future bishops would be able to recruit educated candidates for the priesthood, an anticipation of the seminaries subsequently approved by the Council of Trent.

Much of Pole's scheme for Catholic revival, as the individual decrees of the synod of Westminster reveal, depended upon priestly action, and its weakness lay in the scarcity of priests who could provide this example of Catholic orthodoxy, frugality and chastity. Pole's episcopal bench did indeed largely sustain his ideals. Some bishops had already suffered imprisonment and deprivation under Edward for their beliefs and these received restitution under Mary. Gardiner returned to Winchester, Bonner to London, Heath to Worcester, though he did not remain there long before being promoted in 1555 to the archbishopric of York. These men, as far as their secular duties allowed, strove conscientiously to act as pastoral bishops. Pole made an equally reputable choice of new men to fill the gaps in the episcopate caused by the removal of the Protestants; all the Marian bishops who survived after Elizabeth's accession proved to be men of principle, refusing to forswear their allegiance to the Pope, or to recognize again a secular head of the English Church. Pole even attracted to England some who had had experience of Catholic reformation on the Continent. Thomas Goldwell, who had been in exile like Pole for his religious convictions, and had joined the new Italian order of the Theatines, accepted the bishopric of St Asaph. Pole also attempted, though without success, to bring monks from the reformed Benedictine Monastery of Monte Cassino to Westminster when that monastery was refounded. Yet his caution never left him and he refused in 1555 the offer of Ignatius Loyola to train Jesuits to work in England, the one new order which might most speedily have invigorated academic Catholicism.

Pole, however, did grasp the crucial importance of the universities in supplying orthodox higher clergy for the future. By the
time he became Chancellor of both Oxford and Cambridge
Cranmer's distinguished foreign Protestant visitors had gone back
to the Continent, and he took pains to fill their places with English
Catholic scholars, though he could find no continental Catholic
theologians of the calibre of Bucer, Martyr or Fagius to bring to
England. At his legatine visitations at Oxford and Cambridge he
gave the restoration of orthodoxy pride of place and showed little
interest in changing the academic curriculum. Perhaps Pole's limited
success in this endeavour simply resulted from lack of time. The
Queen relied on his counsel in London, and this meant that both
his visitations of the universities had to be carried out by deputies.
In this respect Mary's backward-looking policy of preferring her
leading ecclesiastics to high office in the State in the long run
worked against the achievement of her own most cherished aims,
for it prevented some of her most able bishops, men like Gardiner
and Heath, from ever residing for any length of time in their
dioceses, an abuse which good Catholic reformers had been
condemning for at least fifty years.

An attempt, nonetheless, was made to compensate for the small
numbers of reforming Catholic ecclesiastics at the universities by
a handful of Catholic laymen. For though churchmen paid little
attention to the decrees of the synod of Westminster calling upon
them to devote a considerable part of their stipends to education
and other forms of charity, education remained a cause to which
laymen eagerly responded. Sir Thomas Pope, a member of Mary's
Privy Council, in 1555 founded Trinity College, Oxford, on the site
of Durham College, and his friend, the London merchant, Sir
Thomas White, quickly followed his example by endowing another
college in Oxford dedicated to St John the Baptist and designed
particularly for the teaching of divinity, as well as philosophy and
the arts. When White died in 1567 Edmund Campion delivered
his funeral oration, and Trinity subsequently became notorious
for the number of its recusant scholars and fellows early in Elizabeth's reign. By the mid-sixteenth century higher ecclesiastics and
some leading Catholic laymen had recognized the importance of
academic learning in the defence of the faith.

Similarly Pole's aim of establishing diocesan seminaries did not
proceed very far, but it was not neglected entirely. At York the

dean and chapter, perhaps prompted by Archbishop Heath, referred specifically to the decrees of the synod of Westminster when they founded a grammar school for fifty boys in the spring of 1557. They, moreover, quite consciously intended that the school should combat heresy, teach orthodox doctrine and, it seems, produce recruits for the priesthood. Their foundation deed declared their aim to be the propagation of the Christian religion, 'by which in the Church militant shepherds may everywhere be preferred who with the sword of the spirit, that is the word of God, may be able to drive away and put to flight the rapacious wolves, that is, devilish men ill-understanding the Catholic faith, from the sheep-folds of the sheep entrusted to them'. They hoped they might best achieve their object 'if the giddy and ignorant youth is kept in tight reins by the work of schoolmasters, and having been exercised alike in letters and learning as in sound morality may afterwards pass into the broad field of sacred and canonical literature and emerge learned'.[3]

Time was the essence of this scheme for the dissemination of informed Catholicism, and time Pole did not have. As the examples of White and Pope indicate, it might have won the active support of more laymen and bred a new generation of committed Catholic laymen and better qualified priests. Lack of time, however, can scarcely be seen as the chief reason for the failure of another vehicle for the revival of Catholicism in England, the restoration of monasticism. Mary and Pole never disguised their belief that the dissolution of the monasteries and the confiscation of monastic lands by the State had been sacrilegious. From early in Mary's reign Pope Julius III had been far more ready to accept the accomplished fact than had the Queen, and Pole, even after the reconciliation with Rome, continued to imply that lay owners of former ecclesiastical lands only possessed their property on sufferance. Recognizing their inability to compel lay owners to restore lands to the Church, Mary and Pole hoped to bring them by example to make some reparation. Certainly the Queen, to the consternation of Parliament and her more far-sighted economic advisers, did her utmost to restore monastic lands still held by the Crown. Early in 1555 she gave back Westminster Abbey together with an annual endowment of about £2000, a little over half its pre-Reformation income, to a band of sixteen Benedictine monks led by Feckenham. All the founding monks of Westminster were over forty years old, and while its abbey soon attracted recruits,

most óf these, too, were mature former monks, Cistercians and
Austin canons as well as Benedictines, a nucleus of whom had
studied together at Durham College at Oxford twenty or so years
previously. Pole's attempt to introduce greater austerity into this
community had little effect, and throughout its short life the
revived monastery resembled more a secular cathedral chapter than
a Benedictine community of the reformed Cassinese type. Significantly the refoundation of Westminster aroused little lay interest,
and no single lay owner of monastic land felt moved to imitate
the Queen's generosity. The Observant Franciscans did return to
Greenwich, again on Mary's initiative, the site having remained in
Crown hands; the same royal bounty enabled some Bridgettine nuns
to return to Syon, a company of Carthusians to settle at Sheen
and some Dominican friars to re-establish themselves at St Bartholomew's, Smithfield. This constituted the total of the monastic
foundations during Mary's reign, all of them the result of the
Queen's initiative and that of some of her leading churchmen.
There is singularly little evidence at this period that even convinced
traditional Catholic laymen any longer looked upon monasteries as
a bulwark of Catholic orthodoxy.

The Queen's concern for the secular clergy who had suffered at
the hands of the Crown and royal councillors since 1529 equally
failed to awake any significant lay response. Mary, long uneasy
about receiving spiritual revenues which she considered rightfully
belonged to the Church, by the Act of 1555 renounced first fruits
and tenths paid by the clergy to the Crown since 1534 and also
revenues from impropriate livings which had come to the Crown
on the dissolution of the monasteries; she then returned this money
to the Church through the mediation of the Archbishop of Canterbury. Pole had still to use part of this windfall to pay the pensions
of former monks and nuns, but the surplus helped him finance a
very necessary scheme for improving impoverished livings throughout England. Having first obtained information from his bishops
on the numbers of poor benefices in their dioceses, Pole made
allocations from the fund diocese by diocese and required each
bishop, once outstanding obligations had been met, to make
contributions to clergy holding impropriate livings. In 1557 he
released clergy in benefices of less than 20 marks in value from
paying any tenths on their income and the following year removed
this payment from all clergy, whatever their income. Even so, he
still needed the co-operation of the laity in the form of voluntary

contributions to enable him to improve the financial standing of the poorest parish priests, and this he singularly failed to get. His far-sighted plan to relieve the lowest paid clergy had scarcely been launched before he and Mary died, and Elizabeth resumed the State's taxation of the Church which killed the scheme entirely by removing its financial backing.

Mary and Pole together had more permanent success in re-habilitating representatives of the higher clergy. The Queen's dealings with the episcopate still await detailed investigation on a national level: it may well be found that the economic independence, albeit a limited one, which the Elizabethan bishops enjoyed came in considerable measure from Mary's restitutions. The see of York provides an example which almost certainly had parallels elsewhere. Through the exchanges of archiepiscopal lands which Archbishops Lee and Holgate had been forced to make with the Crown in the reign of Henry VIII the income of the archbishop had fallen to approximately half of what it had been on the eve of the Reformation. Very soon after Heath's translation to York in 1555 Mary began to make recompense for her father's gains. First she released the see in perpetuity from the payment of annual rent charges of almost £260 and granted the archbishop a London residence in return for one previously confiscated. Two years later, acknowledging that the revenues of the archbishop were much diminished by the surrender of estates formerly belonging to the see, the Queen restored the lordships of Ripon, Scrooby and Southwell and other ancient archiepiscopal manors still in royal possession. These lands increased the archbishop's income by something like £575 a year. With justification a local antiquary could later claim that the see of York owed to Mary and Heath more than a third part of its post-Reformation revenues.

It is hardly surprising that the laity in general paid small atten-tion to Mary's restitution of land to the regular and secular clergy, apart from grumbling in Parliament that these actions would inevitably increase the Crown's need for further taxes, for lordly bishops and fat monks had long been targets of anti-clericalism. In addition the possessors of Church lands could argue that they, in most cases, had acquired their lands from the Crown at full market rates and consequently could not contemplate making restitution without compensation. Nevertheless it would be wrong to depict the Marian laity as altogether out of sympathy with the Queen's policy of restoring Catholicism. There is evidence to suggest that some of Mary's actions attracted support from her more conservative subjects. They did not want to pay more for their religion and tried to avoid a too detailed scrutiny of their beliefs but many wholeheartedly welcomed a somewhat undemanding return to the old religious ways.

Robert Parkyn, priest of Aldwick le Street in Yorkshire, probably spoke for many of the laity as well as for a majority of his fellow clergy in the more conservative parts of England. He made Pole's entry into England bringing papal absolution and the country's reconciliation with the Papacy the climax of his account of the acts of 'gracious Queen Mary'. He clearly understood that there could be no Catholic orthodoxy without the recognition of the papal supremacy but he cherished most the return of the old ceremonies with all they symbolized and above all the restoration of the Mass. Even before Mary had taken any action, he recalled, Catholic lords and knights commanded priests to say Mass in Latin with consecration and elevation. Then in August 1553 came the royal proclamation licensing the Mass and by the following month few Yorkshire churches had not returned to the Mass in Latin : priests laid aside the English service, re-erected altars and brought back holy bread and holy water. This revival of Catholic ceremonies, he asserted, happened particularly quickly north of the Trent. It is true that an element of revenge entered into his report, but here too he seems to have mirrored the reactions of some of the laity :

> Then began holy church to rejoice in God, singing both with heart and tongue, *Te Deum laudamus,* but heretical persons, (as there was many) rejoiced nothing thereat. Ho, it was joy to hear and see how these carnal priests (which had led their lives in fornication with their whores and harlots) did lour and look down, when they were commanded to leave and foresake the concubines and harlots and to do open penance according to the canon law, which then took effect.[4]

At the other end of England, in Dorset, the writings of a cleric of a very different persuasion tend to confirm initial popular enthusiasm for the restoration of Catholicism. Despite all Thomas Hancock's efforts to preach the Protestant gospel in Poole in the previous reign, the Catholic faction had persisted in the town. The moment Mary proclaimed herself a loyal Catholic the Poole conservatives attempted to bring back the Mass, and the wealthy merchant, White, with others built an altar in the parish church and employed a French priest to celebrate. In Poole, however, the Protestants, doubtless with Hancock's support, had enough strength to retaliate and they pulled the altar down. This merely resulted in White's setting up an altar in his own house, and having Mass there, while Hancock went on preaching in the parish church. Under Mary, however, Hancock could not hope for favourable government intervention to put down local rivalries and, when the Catholic party began collecting information against him, he did not need to be told that the Queen would not pardon his Protestant teaching. Like many of his fellow Protestant ministers he fled with his wife and children, going first to Normandy, but finally making his way to Geneva 'in the which city . . . I did see my Lord God most purely and truly honoured, and sin most straitly punished'.[5]

For most lay Catholics their main object seems to have been the restoration of the Mass, and once this had been achieved they lapsed into inactivity. The pious remembered the church in their wills, as at York where Alderman George Gale bequeathed a purple, red and blue frontal cloth with the resurrection embroidered upon it to the high altar of the Minster in return for prayers for his soul. Another alderman gave the Minster a canopy of red and green sarsnet under which the holy sacrament used to be borne. These, though, were unspectacular gifts and may even have been a restitution of vestments and furnishings which had formerly belonged to the church. The request for prayers for the dead shows that the years of Protestant preaching had not caused all laymen to abandon their belief in purgatory, but instances of fervent lay support for Catholic revival are hard to find. Many, perhaps a majority, of Mary's subjects somewhat passively welcomed a return to the ancient Catholic liturgy but, much like the Queen herself, seem to have been unaware of any present need to strengthen or recover Catholic doctrines which had not been taught in their entirety for almost a generation.

Despite its success in gaining the formal restoration of Catholic orthodoxy by the beginning of 1555 and its apparent widespread acceptance in very many areas of England, the Marian government still seems to have paid far more attention to casting down than to building up. Perhaps in her obsession with extirpating heresy Mary made her most costly mistake, for as a result of the persecutions she gave a prominence to Protestant zealots which they would not otherwise have attained. In addition, by her very severity, and that of some of the leading members of the hierarchy, she created something in the nature of a Protestant opposition, organized and directed by religious exiles who, in their turn, made the Protestant confessors in England the object of a highly effective campaign of religious propaganda. At first, in the early days after her accession, Mary did not stress her abhorrence of heresy, and many Protestant ministers, like Hancock, were able quietly to leave their livings and retire to the Continent with little more government harassment than had been experienced after Edward VI's death by those continental Protestant leaders whom Cranmer had brought into England. As is shown by Parliament's continued unwillingness to re-introduce the heresy laws influential laymen seem to have wanted this state of affairs to continue, but with the reconciliation of England to the Papacy and the eventual passing of laws against heresy at the beginning of 1555 the Queen no longer had any reason to conceal her intentions and embarked upon the campaign to stamp out heresy.

In the four years between the revival of the heresy laws and Mary's death in November 1558 almost three hundred people are known to have been burnt for heresy in England in addition to a considerable number more who died in prison awaiting trial or before their sentences could be carried out. The number of those who were burnt fluctuated between seventy and ninety-five in the years 1555, 1556 and 1557, falling to around forty in 1558. These figures did not amount to the holocaust that occurred in certain parts of Europe, but the numbers of Protestants who died made an immense impression in England. Even after the passing of the Act of Six Articles in 1539 the total of Protestants put to death in the closing years of Henry VIII's reign probably had not exceeded twelve: Mary annually permitted the burning of six or seven times that figure. The persecution, moreover, had a peculiar intensity in that the burnings were not equally distributed throughout the country. Fifty-eight Protestants died for their faith in London and Middlesex, over fifty in both Kent and Essex, more than forty in Sussex, over twenty in Suffolk, ten in Norfolk, nine in Bristol and Gloucestershire, six in Warwickshire, while Chester, Hertfordshire, Cambridgeshire and the Isle of Ely, Oxfordshire, Leicestershire, Northamptonshire, Berkshire, Wiltshire, Derbyshire, Surrey, Hampshire, Devon, Yorkshire, Wales and the Channel Isles could each claim between one and five martyrs. This pattern of burnings can only give a distorted picture of the distribution of Protestantism in England, since the government did not always keep to its policy of sending a Protestant to die in his own locality, allowing him instead to be put to death in or near London where he had been tried. To some extent also the number of burnings varied according to the diligence and zeal of the particular diocesan bishop, the attitude of local laymen, and especially according to the proximity of a county to London. Yet when these qualifications have been made it still remains substantially true that Protestantism had taken deepest root in London and its neighbourhood, in East Anglia and in South-East England.

The social composition of the Marian martyrs also proved significant for the future development of Protestantism in England. Not more than twenty-two were ministers, and of these five were bishops. Foxe records the names of nine gentlemen who suffered, and of one gentlewoman: he also lists an occasional schoolmaster and some merchants but describes the vast majority as tradesmen, weavers, husbandmen; over fifty were women. Catholic apologists used the lowly origins of those who died to demonstrate the unimportance of the burnings.

Contemporary Catholic propagandists, and some later historians, have gone to considerable lengths to emphasize the heterogeneous beliefs for which these martyrs died. Certainly all did not hold orthodox Protestant doctrine and some of those who spoke most vehemently against the idol of the Mass may have drawn their inspiration as much from a surviving Lollard tradition as from Protestantism. Nevertheless, if some of them, like a mason, tailor and husbandman burnt at Salisbury in 1556, could be denigrated as little more than illiterate Lollards, they were Lollards with a difference: in the persecutions of Henry VII and Henry VIII the Lollards were conspicuous for the frequency of their recantations; these Marian Lollards had the strength to face death for their convictions. Protestant leaders of the stature of Ridley and Latimer and their successors never questioned the ultimate rightfulness of the cause for which these so-called Lollards died and clearly considered that most had a grounding in true religion, but they did show great concern over the beliefs of those Freewillers who shared their imprisonment. The clash between the academic Protestants and the Freewillers provided Catholic writers with ammunition in abundance to reinforce their thesis that the Roman Church alone could maintain unity of doctrine. As early as 1554 Henry Harte, with Trew and Abingdon and a small band of followers, had been thrown into the King's Bench prison and it was there that John Bradford encountered them. 'In free will they are plain papists, yea Pelagians . . . They utterly condemn all learning,' he informed Cranmer, Latimer and Ridley in some distress. He strove unceasingly to win them over to the Calvinist doctrine of the total depravity of man, and Ferrar, Rowland Taylor and John Philpot joined him in his endeavours, while the controversy prompted Ridley to compose a treatise on election and predestination. Through the efforts of these Protestant theologians one or two Freewillers may have come over to the main body of Protestantism, but the academics failed to convert them all. When Careless in 1556 wrote a confession of faith in Newgate, Henry Harte promptly replied with a restatement of the beliefs of the Freewillers and the Papists continued to make the most of their dissentions.[6]

Yet the Catholic controversialists could not prove that more than a handful of the martyrs came from this small group of sectaries. In fact, the very existence of the Freewillers spurred on the academic Protestants to emphasize still further those Protestant doctrines for which they were prepared to die. Orthodox ministers and teachers made increasing efforts to publicize their beliefs from prison, and the weight of the evidence suggests that by far the greater number of the Protestants who died adhered to the religion of Latimer, Cranmer and Ridley. That the first martyrs were ministers gave their theological teaching a new authority in the eyes of humbler Protestants: John Rogers, Laurence Saunders, John Hooper and Rowland Taylor were all burnt at the stake in February 1555. In the succeeding months John Laurence, Robert Ferrar, George Marsh, John Cardmaker and John Bradford died, and in October 1555 Latimer and Ridley. The government itself added to the line of godly intellectual confessors when it chanced its arm too far in the expectation of a public recantation of Protestantism and allowed the apparently discredited Cranmer to make a last statement. Instead of an acknowledgement of the truths of Catholicism he found fresh courage at the last to confirm his full acceptance of the Protestant formularies he had devised under Edward vi. The examples set by men such as these at the beginning of the persecution gave magisterial Protestantism a reputation among the sympathetic laity such as the Freewillers never achieved and already by the end of 1555 there was emerging a Protestant hagiography. Children in London made rhymes about 'bloody Bonner', the Bishop of London, and an unnamed lady, according to Foxe, wrote to Bonner to tell him that every man had at his finger tips 'how many you for your part have burned with fire, and famished in prison; they say the whole surmounteth to forty persons within these three-quarters of a year . . . The blood of the martyrs is the seed of the gospel; when one is put to death a thousand doth rise for him.'[7]

Instead of obliterating Protestantism by burning its leading protagonists, the Marian government provided Protestant laymen with a clear demonstration of a faith for which to die. It miscalculated further early in the campaign by sending some of these Protestant pastors back to the scenes of their former ministry to die, since rather than giving a fearful warning of the end of all heretics as was intended the bearing of men like John Hooper at Gloucester or of Rowland Taylor at Hadleigh awakened compassion and a new respect for the beliefs for which they suffered. Their deaths stirred in some a desire to imitate their martyrdom and aroused a general revulsion against the practices of their persecutors. By early 1556 it was apparent that the government's attempt to break Protestantism by discrediting its leaders, and, when this proved impossible, by burning them, had failed. From this time the guidance of underground Protestantism in England passed increasingly to the laity and with surprisingly little deviation they chose to follow the example given by the Protestant academics.

These lay leaders came from very varied backgrounds. Thomas Hawkes, gentleman, who died at Coggeshall in Essex in 1555 had had a totally different experience of life from John Alcock, the woad setter, who tried as a layman to continue Rowland Taylor's ministry at Hadleigh. Hawkes had lived in the household of the Earl of Oxford until the death of Edward VI. When brought before Bonner on suspicion of being a 'scripture man', the combined attention of Harpsfield and Feckenham could not win him back to Catholicism. In prison he asked for the writings of Latimer, Cranmer and Ridley, and for Bradford's sermons, and before he died made a point of sending letters from prison to 'the congregation' in Essex. The Glover family of Mancetter had similar social origins. Foxe names John, William and Robert Glover as all being 'zealous professors of the gospel': Robert Glover had taken his MA at Cambridge and, besides, married Latimer's niece. From prison he wrote of the martyrs he would most wish to follow, Anne

Askew, Laurence Saunders, John Bradford. He was burnt at
Coventry in 1555 and both his brothers, though they died natural
deaths, were refused Catholic burial. Mrs Joyce Lewes, a Mancetter
gentlewoman, confessed that she had gone to Mr John Glover's
house where he had instructed her in the ways of the Lord and
had exhorted her against the Mass: she also died for her faith at
Lichfield in 1557. Geoffrey Hurst of Shakerley in Lancashire
resembled Robert Glover in that he, too, was related by marriage
to one of the academic martyrs. He had married the sister of
George Marsh, and had clearly learnt much from his brother-in-
law. In Mary's reign he refused to attend church and his neighbours
called him a heretic and a Lollard. To escape persecution he fled
into Yorkshire, but sometimes returned secretly to his family,
bringing preachers with him; on occasions they gathered together a
congregation of over twenty and held a communion service. Hurst
kept hidden at home a translation of the New Testament by Tyndale and a Prayer Book of Edward VI.

The lay leaders in Sussex and East Anglia lacked these close
links with university Protestants and by no means all were members
of the gentry. Richard Woodman, an iron-maker of Warbleton in
Sussex, claimed to have lands which brought him over £50 a year
but he seems to have been unusually prosperous. He was imprisoned
for a year and a half in the King's Bench, fled into exile, returned
to England, was recaptured and finally burnt with nine others at
Lewes in 1557. He left a detailed account of his many examina-
tions, revealing a thorough knowledge of the Bible and some
acquaintance with Latin. He denied that he had preached in public,
but admitted teaching in his own household. He sent a letter from
prison to Mrs Roberts, a gentlewoman of Hawkshurst and one of
his protectors; she in her turn asserted she had never gone to the
church service in Mary's reign. John Careless, though only a weaver
by occupation, equalled Woodman in his command of scriptural
knowledge. He took part in the controversy with the Freewillers
in the King's Bench prison and made explicit his belief that he had
been predestined to eternal life. From prison he wrote letters to
comfort others about to suffer martyrdom, reciting the names of
the godly ministers who had gone before, Cranmer, Latimer, Ridley,
Rogers, Hooper, Saunders, Ferrar, Taylor, Bradford and Philpot.
His own letters sounded very clerical in tone; he wrote one letter
of reassurance to a lady troubled by having attended Mass, and
another to a minister and his wife to confirm them in the holy

state of matrimony. Careless himself did not have to face the fire since he died in prison before he could be condemned.

In Sussex a Swede, but one who had lived in England for at least a decade, had charge of a Protestant congregation. Dirick Carver of Brighthamstead, a brewer, had been born near Stockholm. He specially admired the martyrs Hooper, Cardmaker and Rogers, and in his house in 1554 he and eleven others used to assemble and say the service in English according to the Edwardian Prayer Book. Though very articulate and a leader of Protestants in Sussex he only learnt to read in prison. Robert Smith, who had held a clerkship at Windsor and was burnt at Uxbridge in 1555, knew about Carver's congregation. But it was the counties immediately north of London which had the worst reputation with the government for secret Protestant meetings. Lord Rich in 1555 accused Thomas Wats of Billericay, a linen draper, of holding 'your conventicles, a sort of you, in corners, contrary to the King's and Queen's proceedings'. At Bentley Ralph Allerton, much like Alcock at Hadleigh, would go to his parish church, and when he saw the people merely sitting there, gazing about or talking, he exhorted them to pray and meditate on God's word, and after prayers had ended read them a chapter out of the New Testament. When forbidden to do this, as he was not a priest, he kept to his house and did not attend church. The hostile Catholic incumbent of Much Bentley alleged that Allerton had said that the Catholics were 'the malignant Church of Antichrist, and not of the true Church of Christ'. Yet of his Protestant orthodoxy there can be no question: he used the Prayer Book of Edward VI daily and from prison wrote to congregations at Barford, Dedham and Colchester to commend to them the faith for which Latimer, Ridley and Cranmer had died. Other obstinate heretics in Much Bentley, who later died for their beliefs, included William Mount and his wife, Alice, and Rose Allen, Alice Mount's daughter by a previous marriage, who not only refused to go to church but encouraged their neighbours to do the same. Their priest complained to Bonner that 'they assemble together upon the Sabbath day in the time of divine service, sometimes in one house, sometimes in another, and there keep their privy conventicles and schools of heresy . . .' In Norfolk Thomas Hudson, a poor glover, who had only learnt to read in Edward's reign, held similar schools. Because of the persecution he went into hiding for a time in his own home at Aylsham and the people came to him to hear his readings, prayers and exhortations. His enemies reported that he had called the Mass 'a patched monster and a disguised puppet', and the authorities feared he had infected many in Aylsham with his opinions; they burnt him at Norwich in 1558.

Out of this practice of instruction by laymen there developed something of a theory of lay ministry. Edmund Allin, a miller of Frittenden in Kent, produced the most articulate surviving justification for what the Catholics regarded as an invasion of the clergy's prerogative. When Catholic officials accused him of preaching, not being in orders, he replied:

Why are we called Christians, if we do not follow Christ, if we do not read his law, if we do not interpret it to others that have not so much understanding? Is not Christ our father? Shall not the son follow the father's steps? Is not Christ our master, and shall the scholar be inhibited to learn and preach his precepts . . . ?

He cited the example of Christ, when he was only twelve years old, disputing with the doctors in the Temple, and went on to maintain that true Christians

are all kings to rule our affections, priests to preach out the virtues and word of God, as Peter writeth, and lively stones to give light to other. For as out of flint stones cometh forth that which is able to set all the world on fire, so out of Christians should spring the beams of the gospel, which should inflame all the world. If we must give a reckoning of our faith to every man, and now to you demanding it, then must we study the scriptures and practise them.[8]

If some fervent Protestants interpreted the concept of the priesthood of all believers in this way, it is scarcely surprising that they held their popish priests in correspondingly low repute. In 1556 certain inhabitants of Norfolk objected to the papal supremacy and the Latin service, and petitioned to be permitted to keep the English service and to retain communion in both kinds. 'The priests complain that we laymen love them not,' they continued

nor have them in honour, but it is their own fault, for how should we love them, that only seek to keep us in blindness and ignorance, to damn our souls, to destroy our bodies, to rob and spoil our goods and substance under colour of pretended holiness?[9]

The experience of persecution which in many cases automatically deprived congregations of Protestant ministers placed lay zealots in a position of judgement which they had never quite previously attained, and which some subsequently never relinquished. The intellectual freedom and initiative achieved by these lay Protestant leaders, however, did not necessarily imply an increase of anti-clericalism. Time and again, as has been seen, these laymen spoke with reverence of the examples set by the ministerial martyrs, and the Protestant ministers in prison and their few fugitive colleagues at liberty continued to be heard with respect. This was particularly true of the Protestant church in London which, despite the persecution, probably maintained an unbroken existence throughout the reign. Foxe thought that the London congregation had a membership of forty which rose on occasions as high as a hundred and even sometimes attracted two hundred hearers; towards the end of Mary's reign it greatly increased. Meeting in lofts, inns, church-yards, even in ships, the congregation had a succession of faithful ministers: Edmund Scambler, later Bishop of Norwich, then Thomas Fowle, who had been a fellow of St John's at Cambridge, John Rough, a companion of Knox, Augustine Bernher and lastly Thomas Bentham, the future Bishop of Coventry and Lichfield. Both Rough and Bentham returned from the safety of exile to serve the church and Rough in 1557 paid for his bravery with his life. Particularly earlier in the reign the zealots also received instruction from other Protestant ministers passing through London on their way to exile. Bartlet Green, a gentleman who had been educated at Oxford and the Temple, admitted in the autumn of 1555 that he had never gone to the Catholic Mass but for two years running he had participated in a Protestant communion in London at Easter, once at the house of John Pulleyne, one of King Edward's preachers, when Christopher Goodman, formerly divinity reader, had mini-stered the service, and once with Pulleyne and one Rimneger, an Oxford MA. On both occasions he had received the bread and the wine and Pulleyne had read the words of institution as given in the Book of Common Prayer.

Mention of the use of the Prayer Book, normally the Second Prayer Book of Edward VI, occurs with frequency in the confes-sions of those imprisoned for religion. The martyrdom of the leading Edwardian clergy had conferred on the book a new reputation: men who wished to follow Cranmer, Latimer and Ridley's religion would now also reverence their book. Perhaps this was why heterodox Protestant ideas proliferated far less than might have been expected considering the scarcity of Protestant ministers, and certainly far less than Catholic propagandists tried to pretend. Two-thirds of the 190 people charged with failure to attend church as a result of Bonner's visitation of London in 1555 can definitely be linked with magisterial Protestantism; they objected to the Mass, to Catholic ceremonies and to fasting. The authorities convicted a few for possessing heretical books, others for rejecting services in Latin, but they did not discover any evidence at all of Anabaptist doctrines. Even in East Anglia, apart from the unique example of the Freewillers at Bocking, Catholic officials found very little opinion outside the Protestant mainstream. An investigation at Ipswich in 1556 heard of many who had fled the town, some of whom had refused to attend Mass, other still resident who would not go to Mass or observe ceremonies, yet even those recorded as not allowing their children to be dipped in fonts seem to have objected because of the Catholic ceremony involved and not to the sacrament itself. The thirteen martyrs, mainly from Essex, burnt on 27 June 1556, set out a profession of faith to confirm their orthodoxy: they believed in one God, in the divinity and manhood of Christ, and held both the Apostles' and the Athanasian Creeds. They recognized justification by Christ alone, and denied that good works could in any way contribute to a man's deliverance. They regarded the Lord's Supper as a sacrament of redemption, rejecting any idea of a perpetual sacrifice, and approved of infant baptism. Above all they dwelt upon the 'sweet, pleasant and unspeakable comfort' to them of the knowledge of their predestination and election in Christ.

In the face of their persecutors' taunts these Protestants could generally establish their orthodoxy, but they had much less of a defence when challenged with their lowly social status. The majority of the three hundred and more who were burnt or who died in prison came from below the gentry class. This may partly be explained by the fact that, even in Mary's reign, a man's position in society still offered some protection against persecution. Bonner's secretary wrote to his master in 1556, 'I do see by experience that the sworn inquest for heresies do, most commonly, indict the simple, ignorant and wretched heretics, and do let the arch heretics go; which is one great cause that moveth the rude multitude to murmur, when they see the simple wretches (not knowing what heresy is) to burn.' At Ipswich the commissioners particularly wanted Ralph Carleton, the curate, to be examined to see 'whether by corruption of money he hath crossed his book of any that are there named, and hath not received [communion] indeed, as it is reported'. The nonagenarian Lady Knevet, of Wymondham in Norfolk, was but one of several gentlewomen named by Foxe who would not go to church or have any 'papistical trash' ministered to her. Despite the threats of the Bishop's messengers she contrived to have the service of the Second Prayer Book of Edward vi read to her either by Mr Tollin, whom she preserved in her household, or, in his absence, by one of her ladies or servants. She survived, as did many other female protectors of Protestants, to die peacefully in the reign of Elizabeth. Other gentlemen, while they did not enjoy the same immunity as some of these ladies, could yet keep relatively safe by moving from one part of the country to another. Edward Underhill, a gentleman pensioner and self-styled 'hot gospeller', notwithstanding his boast that 'there was no such place to shift in, in this realm, as London', retired with his family during the persecution to the outskirts of Coventry, having first got a fellow zealot, old Harrydaunce of Whitechapel, to brick up his heretical books for him in his London chamber.[10]

It may well be that a disproportionate number of Protestants in the upper ranks of society evaded the attentions of royal officials through their influence and wealth. Their financial resources gave them the further advantage that, in the worst extremity, they could afford to emigrate while the poor had little alternative but to remain in their own country. As might be expected, an analysis of the eight hundred or so English people who fled to the Continent in Mary's reign on account of their religion produces a pattern totally different from the analysis of those who suffered martyrdom in England. Whereas the largest proportion of the Marian martyrs came from the lower sections of society, by far the greatest number of the exiles consisted of gentlemen and university students with their dependents. Out of 453 male exiles who could be classified, 166 were gentlemen, 67 Protestant clerics and 119 theological students; a further 40 were merchants, 7 printers and 6 professional men. Of the remainder, not attached to the households of gentry or clergy, 32 only seem to have been artisans. The exiles settled principally in the Swiss and German cities of Basle, Frankfurt, Strassburg, Wesel, Zurich and Geneva.[11]

These exiles probably did not consciously plan their exodus as a means by which the Catholic restoration in England might be defeated, but seem rather to have turned for help in their adversity to some of their foreign colleagues, like Martyr, whom they themselves had so recently befriended. Nevertheless, very soon after the full persecution began in England some of the clerical exiles deliberately set to work to make known the sufferings of the Protestant confessors and to train up a new generation of Protestant clergy ready to labour in their native land if they should ever be given a fresh opportunity. John Foxe, probably influenced by Bale who had written the life of Anne Askew from contemporary sources when he was in exile in the 1540s, may have planned a history of the professors of the truth from the time of Wyclif until the ending of persecution under Edward VI before Mary came to the throne. He had finished his *Commentarii*, a first draft of the first half of the *Acts and Monuments*, before he left England for the Continent in 1554. However, with the renewal of burnings in 1555, he changed the whole emphasis of his work and, with the help of Grindal, attempted to gather all the information he could from England. Consequently the very first martyrs, and these, moreover, clerical intellectuals, appreciated that they were acting in a drama not on a national but on an international stage. They could well hope that the reports of their trials, their exhortations and letters to their congregations would, through the mediation of such men as Augustine Bernher and Thomas Hilles, be conveyed not only to their correspondents in England but ultimately to the clerical exiles on the Continent. Many laymen had the education and the zeal to copy the literary enterprise of the clerical martyrs, and Foxe and his helpers amassed a storehouse of hagiographical material, the substantial accuracy of which has never been successfully challenged. The death of a martyr in Marian England might seem to be of only local interest, but in the pages of Foxe it achieved a lasting significance. Foxe published his Latin account of the Marian persecution in 1559, following it with a revised edition in English in 1563: from that time onwards convinced Protestants needed little persuasion to see Mary's attempt to restore Catholicism in England as an anti-Christian, un-English campaign to divert the nation from the true Church. 'If any be so far beguiled in his opinion [as] to think the doctrine of the church of Rome, as it now standeth, to be of such antiquity, and that the same was never impugned before the time of Luther and Zwinglius now of late, let them read these histories . . . ,' Foxe wrote in his preface to 'the true and faithful congregation of Christ's universal Church'. '. . . We have sufficiently proved before, by the continual descent of the Church till this present time, [that] the said Church, after the doctrine which is now reformed, is no new begun matter but even the old continued Church by the providence and promise of Christ still standing.'[12]

Mary reigned long enough to pursue a campaign of Protestant persecution which, because of Foxe's endeavours, has never been forgotten, but she and her churchmen, though they tried hard to reintroduce Catholicism, did not have time to revive a vigorous Catholic tradition in the country at large. By 1558 the overwhelming majority of Englishmen had become conforming Catholics, a fact which Foxe's vivid narrative tends to obscure, but the allegiance of this majority to the Papacy proved to be only skin deep. Indeed, because of her passionate loyalty to the Pope, and to her Spanish husband, Mary unintentionally had made Catholicism appear to some of her subjects as a foreign form of religion, which it had never done before. The Queen and Pole died defeated by their labours within a few hours of each other in November 1558, and Elizabeth came to the throne. As the only surviving child of Henry VIII and, moreover, the sole issue of his marriage to Anne Boleyn, she was unlikely to feel her sister's devotion to Catholicism, and Protestant enthusiasts took her accession to portend the renunciation of the papal supremacy. The future of the English Church, as Foxe had foreseen, did indeed lie with the Protestant exiles and their sympathizers in England.

CHAPTER 6

THE ELIZABETHAN CHURCH:
SETTLEMENT AND SEPARATION

Both negatively and positively Mary's short reign did much to determine the subsequent development of the English Church. The persecution caused articulate Protestants to see the Roman Church as antiChristian and foreign, and no Church for Englishmen; while, more constructively, the five years of the reign marked a rapid growth of congregational independence in the underground churches in England as well as in the churches of the exiles. Experience gained then influenced the settlement of 1559 and lay behind many of the crises of the following thirty years. Because of the reversals of religious practice in the reigns of Henry VIII, Edward and Mary, it was only after 1558 that Church and State had time to undertake the long-term task of implementing the Protestant Reformation. Yet these very changes may have already made it impossible to impose a rigid Protestant uniformity upon the nation. The Queen never abandoned her goal of a totally comprehensive Church, but her churchmen's efforts to carry out her wishes led quickly to the appearance of dissent and even separation among conservatives and radicals alike. England did indeed become a Protestant country in the course of Elizabeth's reign but the religion many Englishmen chose to adopt probably diverged considerably from the supreme governor's intentions.

The disputes among the English exiles over the form of worship and the nature of Church government foreshadowed the problems which later rent the Elizabethan Church, and in particular the troubles which occurred at Frankfurt am Main became a precedent for future strife. The first Englishmen who fled to Germany soon after Mary's accession had not held high office in Edward's Church and had not personally shared responsibility for the decisions concerning religion taken then. Like Hooper they believed that the Church still contained many impurities and the relative freedom of exile gave them the opportunity there and then to set up the type of reformed religion they desired, without the constraints previously imposed by the civil magistrates. Even John Knox, their first minister, who had earlier shown little enthusiasm for the

Second Edwardian Prayer Book, felt that they might be moving too fast and hesitated to abandon the Prayer Book entirely in favour of an English translation of the Genevan service book as his congregation was pressing him to do. The more senior English clerics who, by the autumn of 1554, had settled in Zurich displayed much greater concern over the liturgical experiments at Frankfurt. They wrote to the church there counselling it to be less precipitate in altering a prayer book which in any case had been in use in England for under a year, 'lest by much altering of the same, we should seem to condemn the chief authors thereof (who, as they now suffer, so are they most ready to confirm that fact with the price of their blood); and should also both give occasion to our adversaries to accuse our doctrine of imperfection and us of mutability, and the godly to doubt in that truth wherein before they were persuaded'. Grindal came in person from Zurich to urge the Frankfurt church to keep 'the book of England: not that they meant, as he said, to have it so strictly observed but that such ceremonies and things which the country could not bear, might well be omitted; so that they might have the substance and effect thereof'. For a few weeks an uneasy compromise lasted but it seems that the English at Zurich still thought that the Frankfurt church did not fully appreciate the need for the exiles to maintain a common front. Then in the spring of 1555 Cox and a company of his friends arrived in Frankfurt. Cox had worked with Cranmer in devising the Edwardian Prayer Books and he insisted that in exile 'they would do as they had done in England; and that they would have the face of an English church'. Through a series of manœuvres which reflected little credit on the newcomers, Cox and his party succeeded in getting Knox and his supporters banished from the city, and the Knoxians retired to Geneva, the one city where they knew they could use the Genevan service book undisturbed. One group of English Protestants had already explicitly committed themselves to Calvinism.

The actions of the Knoxian radicals might well have been predicted; in some ways the English church which the victorious Coxians set up had more significance for the future, for, as Cox explained to Calvin, it was an English church with a difference. 'When the magistrates lately gave us permission to adopt the rites of our native country,' he wrote in April 1555, 'we freely relinquished all those ceremonies which were regarded by our brethren as offensive and inconvenient. For we gave up private baptisms, confirmation of children, saints days, kneeling at the holy communion, the linen surplices of the ministers, crosses and other things of the like character.' They had discontinued them, he went on to say, not because they considered them impure and papistical but because they were of their own nature indifferent, and so not worth retaining at the expense of offending some of the godly. Coxians and Knoxians could at least agree on some of the ceremonies to be abandoned, even though they disagreed on the precise form of a fully Protestant liturgy.

In the long run the disputes which divided the Frankfurt congregation in 1557 over the government of their church were perhaps even more important than the disputes over ceremonies. Cox did not stay long in Frankfurt after his triumph, and after an interval Horne succeeded him as pastor. Soon after his appointment some members of the church began questioning his allocation of money sent from England, and from this arose an issue of principle over where ultimate authority in the congregation lay. Taking offence at the criticism directed at them, Horne and his seniors temporarily withdrew from the church; forty or so members replied by asserting 'that the church was above the pastor, and not the pastor above the church . . .' They argued that 'the assembly which remained and tarried behind [was] a lawful assembly, and had authority to make effectual decrees, by which they might bind all and every member of the church without exception'.

As in the previous dispute, both sides had moved much further along the road to reform in exile than they had apparently considered necessary earlier in England, and there seems little doubt that the experience of congregational independence had clarified their thinking on matters of church polity. Horne and his little party had willingly accepted that the church should be governed by a pastor, preachers, elders and deacons; they had drawn up a simple body of rules about the reception of new members into the church and the ordering of the congregation which those who wished to progress further called the old discipline. In the future the church wanted to make clerical domination impossible. In their new discipline they proposed to have two ministers, elected by the congregation, 'and that the said two ministers and teachers of the word shall, in all things and points, be of like authority, and neither of them superior or inferior to the other'. This, they believed, conformed to the practice of the best reformed churches and had been recommended by Calvin in his *Institutes*. The two ministers administered discipline in co-operation with the six seniors, though the ultimate power to make decrees remained with the full congregation. Annually they elected the seniors, the four deacons who looked after the church's funds and the four wives or widows who cared for the sick, and they permitted every member of the congregation to speak his mind in the assemblies as long as he did not offend against God's truth. That a majority of a church which still proclaimed that it kept 'the form and order of the ministration of the sacraments and common prayer, as it is set forth by the authority of the blessed King Edward of famous memory in the last book of the English service' could in effect draft a wholly new scheme of worship and government suggested that they would not find it easy to revert to the Edwardian service book on their return to England. Yet however intense the quarrels between the exiles in Geneva and the other English exile churches, the different factions resembled each other more closely in their practice and aspirations than either party resembled the majority of Protestants in England who had conformed under Mary.

On Elizabeth's accession the church at Geneva tried for the last time to achieve supremacy over the other English churches in exile and wrote to the congregations at Aarau, Basle, Strassburg, Worms and Frankfurt in an attempt to agree upon a common policy concerning the ceremonies acceptable in a reformed national Church. The Frankfurt church replied early in 1559 that contention over ceremonies had now become a somewhat futile exercise since 'it shall lie neither in your hands or ours to appoint what they shall be, but in such men's wisdoms as shall be appointed to the devising of the same, and which shall be received by [the] common consent of the Parliament . . . But we trust that both true religion shall be restored; and that we shall not be burdened with unprofitable ceremonies.' In fact certain members of the exile churches did far more than express pious hopes; they ensured that they had spokesmen in Parliament when the time came for a decision to be made on the settlement of the Elizabethan Church.[1]

Elizabeth's first Parliament met late in January 1559 and sat until the beginning of May. Many of the leading laymen among the exiles had already returned home by the time it opened, but some of the ecclesiastics, particularly those in Geneva, remained on the Continent, deliberately holding their hand until they saw what the Queen and Parliament would decide about the Church. Knox had in any case gravely prejudiced his chance of coming back to England by the unfortunate publication at the end of Mary's reign of his *First Blast of the Trumpet against the Monstrous Regiment of Women*; Whittingham and Gilby stayed behind to oversee the publication of their revised English translation of the Bible, subsequently known as the Geneva Bible. However, despite the absence of these representatives from Geneva, the lay exiles from the other English churches in Switzerland and Germany took a decisive part in the parliamentary proceedings with outside support from their clerical colleagues. Early in the session Sir Francis Knollys, who had spent from 1556 to 1557 in Basle and then moved to Frankfurt, and Sir Anthony Cooke, who had lived most of the time since the spring of 1554 in Strassburg, assumed the leadership of the Protestant group in the House of Commons. In February 1559 Cooke urged the House to adopt the modified form of the Second Edwardian Prayer Book which the Frankfurt church had formerly used, quite ignoring the fact that the exiles' aims appeared to be totally at variance with the designs of the Queen.

Very soon after her accession Elizabeth had demonstrated her aversion to Roman Catholicism; her refusal to be present at Mass at the time of elevation and her brusqueness towards the abbot and monks of the newly restored monastery at Westminster contrasted strongly with her gracious acceptance of the English Bible from the citizens of London. Yet up to the time Parliament assembled she had revealed little of her plans for the settlement of religion. Probably Elizabeth would most have welcomed a policy of very gradual change, permitting Parliament to make a break with Rome in this first session but leaving the question of services and doctrine to be resolved at a later date. Such a policy would antagonize continental powers least at a time when England still remained in a state of war with France and so was dependent on the continuation of her alliance with Spain, and also give least offence to the conservative majority in England. The 1559 Act of Supremacy, which in addition to recognizing the Queen as supreme governor over the Church allowed communion henceforth to be celebrated in both kinds, seems to confirm the cautious nature of the government's thinking. At this stage the Queen may have considered proroguing Parliament and postponing any further decisions on religion until a future session. If so, she changed her mind for Parliament resumed its sitting after Easter. It then debated and passed the Act of Uniformity and, in consequence, authorized the legislation which constituted the Elizabethen settlement in one sitting. Undoubtedly the easing of the foreign situation in March, through the signing of a peace treaty between England and France, had given the government more freedom of action, but the apparent change in the Queen's attitude may well have been partly caused by the demands of the group of vociferous Protestants in the Commons.

Yet their notable success in extracting from the Queen a more Protestant settlement of religion than she seems to have wanted was by no means an unqualified victory. The Queen had said in public, admittedly to a Catholic auditor, that she wished religion in England to return to the state in which it had been during the last years of her father's reign, and it seems highly likely that she would have been content to have restored the relatively conservative First Prayer Book of Edward VI. The exiles, together with some of their more forward brethren who had joined the underground Protestant churches in Mary's reign, would certainly have preferred a purified version of the 1552 book such as they had themselves devised. In fact, the Act of Uniformity provided for the use of the Second Edwardian Prayer Book but with the important addition of sentences at the communion service which would allow of a more than commemorative interpretation of the sacrament, and with the equally important deletion of the 'black rubric'. Further, it prescribed that ministers should wear those vestments that had been worn in the second year of Edward VI.

The Elizabethan settlement of religion was in all senses an Erastian one, and a singular achievement of the laity. In the House of Lords the churchmen, still Catholic since the Marian bishops could not be legally displaced until Parliament had restored the royal supremacy, opposed the government's policy to a man, seconded by a few Catholic lay peers. Convocation, also overwhelmingly Catholic, had not been permitted to take any part in the decisions concerning religion. Thus the settlement reflected, more or less, a middle way between the preferences of the Queen, the Church's royal governor, and the aspirations of leading Protestant laymen. Nowhere can this be seen more clearly than in Parliament's appropriation to itself in perpetuity of the right to define heresy. Clause twenty of the Act of Supremacy laid down that the Queen's representatives could pronounce as heretical only such matters 'as heretofore have been . . . adjudged to be heresy

C.A.P.   E by the authority of the canonical scriptures, or by the first four general councils . . . or such as hereafter shall be . . . determined to be heresy by the high court of Parliament of this realm, with the assent of the clergy in their Convocation'.[2] To the limits of their capacity laymen were trying to ensure that never again would the clerical estate have the power to enquire into religious beliefs in the way it had done during the Marian persecutions.

At first Elizabeth's intention to resume the royal supremacy had posed some difficult theological problems, for convinced Protestants as well as religious conservatives expressed doubts about whether a woman could be head of the Church. To still these, Elizabeth styled herself in the Act of Supremacy Supreme Governor rather than Supreme Head, though this apparent concession in no way affected either her determination to rule her Church as her father had done, or her attitude towards her churchmen. Elizabeth quite clearly considered her bishops first and foremost as her servants and she left them in no doubt of their subordination to the Crown. In spite of the protests of Parker and Cox, the Queen, relying on an act of the 1559 Parliament, proceeded to arrange exchanges with the bishops elect of those dioceses which up to that time had managed to retain their ancient episcopal lands. As a result, combined with the earlier unfavourable exchanges, almost all Elizabeth's bishops came increasingly to depend upon impropriate livings and even, as at Ely after the death of Cox, on clerical taxation for a substantial part of their income. Through no fault of their own bishops found themselves living literally at the expense of their lower clergy. Yet while Elizabeth had little compunction at continuing to take considerable wealth from the Church, albeit to a more moderate degree than had her father or brother, from the first she tried to curb lay exploitation of the Church by prohibiting bishops and deans and chapters from leasing property to anyone except the Crown for more than twenty-one years. Thus after 1559 only the Crown, or privileged royal servants, were allowed to make large profits at its expense and the earlier indiscriminate spoliation of the Church came to an end.

Since the Queen meant to control her Church through the bishops she could not afford to undermine their local standing too drastically. Indeed, once episcopal subordination to the Crown had been established the royal governor's own interest lay in preserving the bishops' powers. Under Elizabeth, and clearly in accord with her wishes, the English Church kept its essentially medieval, and outdated, character. The division of the Church into the two provinces of Canterbury and York persisted, as did the great discrepancy between the size of the different sees: even though they had lost lands when Henry VIII had set up the new dioceses of Peterborough, Oxford and Chester, the dioceses of Lincoln and York remained enormous and beyond the supervision of one man, while those of Rochester and Bristol, discontinuous and poorly endowed, may well have been too small. In exile John Aylmer had devised a new scheme of dioceses in England with boundaries conterminous with county boundaries which would have made the pastoral superintendence of a reformed bishop a possibility, but in terms of the Crown's control, it was a case of the fewer bishops the better. In consequence no change took place in diocesan organization until the nineteenth century. The same sort of discrepancies as regards size and endowment were perpetuated between parishes. Some ancient cities such as London, Norwich, York and Bristol retained a large number of tiny parishes, poorly endowed and totally inadequate to maintain an educated preaching minister. York, for example, still had some thirty parishes while its rapidly growing neighbour, Leeds, had only one. In the country-side too the parishes differed greatly in extent and wealth. On the whole a diligent incumbent could manage most parishes in the South, the Midlands and in the Yorkshire plain, but farther north and particularly in the North-West, where the parochial structure had never fully evolved and where a titular parish like Halifax might include twelve dependent chapelries, a parochial minister stood no chance of knowing his parishioners in the way that reformed teaching demanded. Yet in this respect also the Crown, the bishops and the lay patrons combined to prevent any change. This failure of the Crown and Parliament to conceive of any fundamental reorganization of the Church's structure meant that the new bishops, charged with implementing the new religious settlement, had to work within the confines of a system at variance with the requirements of a fully reformed Protestant Church.

Just as the Queen, under pressure from the House of Commons, had to accept a more Protestant religious settlement than she seems to have intended, so she had to select as bishops to enforce the settlement men whose decidedly Protestant convictions ran counter to her more conservative tastes. To Elizabeth's disappointment, in spite of overtures from the government, with one possible exception, none of Mary's bishops would serve in her Church after the passing of the Acts of Supremacy and Uniformity. A considerable number of higher clergy followed their example, and royal commissions prominently staffed with former exiles, which toured England in the summer and autumn of 1559, discovered that, as at York and Durham, as many as half a cathedral chapter might refuse to take the oath acknowledging the royal supremacy. Consequently the Queen, faced with having to fill an unprecedented number of vacancies at the higher levels of the Church at one time, had little alternative but to turn to the committed Protestant clergy who had gone into exile in the previous reign and experienced life in reformed congregations on the Continent. Matthew Parker, the Queen's new Archbishop of Canterbury, who under Mary had lived privately and undertaken no clerical duties, proved an important exception, but virtually all the other major bishoprics went to exiles. Elizabeth appointed Barlow to Chichester, Pilkington to Durham, Cox to Ely, Bentham to Coventry and Lichfield, Bullingham to Lincoln, Grindal to London, Parkhurst to Norwich, Jewel to Salisbury, Horne to Winchester, Sandys to Worcester, Berkley to Bath and Wells, Scory to Hereford, and Young to York; all had taken refuge on the Continent in Mary's reign. Parker's consecration took place in December 1559, and thereafter a handful of new bishops received their sees in fairly quick succession, though some dioceses, and especially those in the North, had to wait until the spring of 1561 for their bishop; in several cases bargaining over exchanges of land with the Crown was responsible for the long delay.

The deprivations of the Marian bishops and the slow process of their replacement left all bishoprics without active episcopal leadership for over a year after Elizabeth's accession, and some for over two years. This opportunity was seized by godly laymen from all sectors of society in certain parts of England to advance the cause of reformation. At court the Earl of Leicester soon built up a reputation as a patron of Protestants and he and Cecil, married to the very Protestant and highly educated daughter of Sir Anthony Cooke, almost certainly had the greatest influence in the nomination of the first Elizabethan bishops. The Lord Keeper, Sir Nicholas Bacon, a convinced Protestant himself and the husband of another of Cooke's formidable daughters, handled much of the Queen's subsidiary patronage and appears when possible to have made Crown livings available to sound Protestants. Marriage also linked Leicester and his brother, Warwick, with the Earls of Bedford and

Huntingdon, and this group of noblemen, imitated at a lower level by countless like-minded gentlemen, in the early years of the reign consciously employed their own patronage and, when they could, that of the Crown to place leading Protestants in key positions in the Church. The promotion of William Whittingham after his return from Geneva illustrates the extent of their power. In 1561 Huntingdon actively encouraged Whittingham in his work as an itinerant Protestant preacher in Leicestershire and the surrounding counties and tried to install him in the valuable family living of Loughborough but failed through lack of co-operation from his Catholic uncle. Whittingham next joined Warwick as chaplain at the siege of Le Havre and from there Leicester secured his promotion to the important and rich deanery of Durham. Another Genevan exile, Anthony Gilby, who refused to accept office within a church insufficiently reformed, also benefited from Huntingdon's protection and until his death in 1585 lived at Ashby de la Zouch as a lecturer, greatly influencing the sort of Protestantism which developed in the surrounding area.

The establishment of lectureships, indeed, from very early after Elizabeth's accession became the chief channel through which the godly laity made their inclinations known within the Church. These voluntarily financed preaching posts attracted advanced Protestant clergy who, like Gilby, had scruples about conforming to the Prayer Book and enabled the laity to obtain frequent preaching which often their ill paid and poorly qualified parish incumbent could not provide. London, with its continuing tradition of underground Protestantism under Mary, saw the growth of parish lectureships very soon after the persecution ended. The lectureship at St Antholin's had been founded in Edward's reign and, after Elizabeth's accession, rapidly developed into a centre of preaching for a whole city, supplying a regular series of preachers and sermons on almost every day of the week. Some towns outside London displayed an equal enthusiasm, and Coventry, in particular, whose mayor had been in exile, acted with notable enterprise and independence. By the summer of 1559 some leading citizens had procured Thomas Lever as their preacher, as Lever himself recounted to Bullinger, his erstwhile protector in exile:

And there is a city in the middle of England, called Coventry, in which there have always been, since the revival of the gospel, great numbers zealous for evangelical truth: so that in that last persecution under Mary, some were burnt, others went into banishment together with myself: the remainder, long tossed about in great difficulty and distress, have at last, on the restoration of pure religion, invited other preachers, and myself in particular, to proclaim the gospel to them at Coventry. After I had discovered, by the experience of some weeks, that vast numbers in this place were in the habit of frequenting the public preaching of the gospel, I consented to their request, that I should settle my wife and family among them; and thus, now for nearly a whole year, I have preached to them without any hindrance, and they have liberally maintained me and my family in this city. For we are not bound to each other, neither I to the townsmen, nor they to me, by any law or engagement, but only by free kindness and love.[3]

Lever did not in fact remain long in this somewhat precarious situation as a preacher supported solely by voluntary alms-giving. Thomas Bentham, a fellow exile, consecrated Bishop of Coventry and Lichfield almost a year after his arrival in Coventry, regularized Lever's position by making him an archdeacon in the diocese.

Other provincial towns where Protestantism had persisted under Mary went ahead on their own initiative in encouraging Protestant preaching in the very early years of the reign. Ipswich corporation resolved in 1560 to have a lecturer and appointed Kelke, another exile, to the post, voting him a salary of £20 a year. Colchester possessed its common preacher by 1564. The corporation of Yarmouth had to deal with a more complex but not unusual situation: in 1563 it decided to supplement the income of the curate of St Nicholas, presented by the dean and chapter of Norwich but allowed a quite inadequate stipend, and seven years later the merchant guild took the logical step of purchasing the living for the town, at the same time raising a benevolence to pay for the town preacher. These towns appear to have acted merely in response to what they considered to be a local need; elsewhere some towns made similar arrangements but in collaboration with a local patron. At Leicester, where one martyr had died under Mary, the Earl of Huntingdon and the corporation jointly had set up a lectureship in St Martin's Church by 1562, and at Warwick under the aegis of the Earl of Leicester the corporation authorized a lectureship in the collegiate church at a similar early date. These laymen took it for granted that they should participate in the spreading of Protestantism in their own neighbourhood and never subsequently relinquished this freedom of action assumed in the first years of the reign.

In consequence, when some of Elizabeth's new bishops at last came into full possession of their sees, they found themselves having to deal with groups of determined laity unwilling to submit themselves unquestioningly to clerical guidance from above. In London Grindal, almost from the moment of his consecration, had to contend with members of Protestant congregations reluctant to give up the independence they had experienced under Mary, while he discovered in Essex radical Protestant congregations which their incumbents felt unable to control. Similar problems with partially conforming lay people beset Parker in Kent, while in Coventry and Lichfield, and in Norwich, Bentham and Parkhurst attempted to co-operate with the forward laity in their dioceses. Although some bishops, especially in East Anglia, parts of the Midlands, London and the South-East, had to contend with pockets of Protestant radicalism, for others the great difficulty remained the winning over of the majority of their flock from a conservative Catholicism. Jewel's impression of the religion of the West Country which he visited as a royal commissioner in 1559 had been of apathy and indifference. He reported back in dismay to his friends in Zurich on 'the wilderness of superstition' which 'had sprung up in the darkness of the Marian times. We found in all places votive relics of saints, nails with which the infatuated people dreamed that Christ had been pierced, and I know not what small fragments of the sacred cross. The number of witches and sorceresses had everywhere become enormous.' From the moment they assumed office Jewel and many of his episcopal colleagues, eager to start work as reformed Protestant superintendents, came up against this lay antagonism which threatened to impede or distort their policy of advancing Protestantism in the localities.[4]

Since in 1559 neither the Queen nor Parliament had contemplated altering the diocesan judicial machinery the bishops had to rely largely on the ancient ecclesiastical courts in enforcing conformity to the settlement. The Reformation changes under Henry VIII and Edward VI and the return to Rome under Mary had scarcely at all affected the operation of the diocesan courts and they continued to administer discipline until the outbreak of the Civil War, almost as they had done in the late Middle Ages. Rectors and vicars, and now increasingly lay impropriators, could still sue defaulting parishioners in these courts for tithes withheld, laymen bring cases against laymen for the inadequate or improper administration of wills or for cases of slander or defamation, while the bishop's own officers in response to information obtained at diocesan visitations could advance charges against doctrinally or morally delinquent clergy or laity. But the antiquated procedure of the Church courts, even more cumbersome than that of the secular courts, allowed determined defendants many loopholes and the penalties the courts could impose often seemed to be little more than slightly updated versions of medieval Catholic forms of public penance. Nevertheless, the courts functioned vigorously and indeed, in the diocese of York, court business actually increased between 1560 and 1640.

However, in implementing the Elizabethan settlement, the bishops did gain one virtually new judicial weapon. For the Queen could delegate her powers to commissioners and, very soon after Parliament recognized her as Supreme Governor, in 1559 two formally constituted ecclesiastical prerogative courts, the Courts of High Commission, were established for the provinces of Canterbury and York which could be supplemented, when the need arose, by local and often temporary High Commission courts for particular dioceses. These Courts, unlike the ancient diocesan and archiepiscopal courts, could both imprison and fine and through them the Queen's commissioners had at least some chance of compelling into conformity the more socially eminent recusants, whether clerical or lay, conservatives or radicals. Although by the end of the reign the churchmen seem to have gained a preponderant influence in the High Commission courts, laymen continued to be nominated to sit on the Commission and in the last analysis, since the Queen controlled all appointments to the commissions, ecclesiastics there had little freedom to act against the monarch's known wishes. Despite appearances, despite the emergence of the prerogative ecclesiastical courts, Elizabethan churchmen had far less jurisdictional independence than their medieval predecessors.

Elizabeth's bishops learnt very early in the reign the extent to which they depended upon the royal will, discovering that not only in matters of discipline but also of doctrine they had little power to act without at least implicit authorization from the Queen. One of the first collisions between the Supreme Governor and some of her bishops occurred over the Queen's conservative religious inclinations. Elizabeth, partly because of the exigencies of foreign policy, partly from a desire not to provoke reaction from the conservatives in England, but also, it would seem, because of her own personal tastes, wanted the English Church to continue looking like a Catholic Church. Not surprisingly her Protestant ecclesiastics found it exceedingly difficult to understand her motives. Men like Jewel and Sandys who, as royal commissioners in 1559 had cast out what they considered to be idolatrous and superstitious monuments from cathedrals and parish churches, seriously thought of resigning their bishoprics a few months later when Elizabeth seemed on the verge of ordering the restoration of crucifixes. On this occasion the Queen, untypically, bowed to their protests and only insisted on keeping these ornaments in her own Chapel Royal, but five years later she aroused Protestant susceptibilities anew in the related but much more serious vestiarian controversy. In 1559 Sandys had taken it for granted that Parliament had included the clause in the Act of Uniformity retaining vestments as they had been early in the reign of Edward VI merely for form's sake, but believed that the Queen would never force them upon Protestants who had scruples over their use. In the first years of the reign some latitude in fact does seem to have existed, especially outside London. Grindal certainly allowed one Essex minister not to wear the surplice until he could wean his congregation from their abhorrence of all that recalled the popish Church, and many forward clergy appear to have accorded themselves a similar licence. Elizabeth, however, had envisaged no such toleration in ceremonial matters; in January 1565 she remonstrated with Parker over the lack of outward conformity in the Church and ordered the vestments clause to be strictly observed in future. The Queen then withdrew, leaving the Archbishop and his fellow bishops with the unenviable task of attempting to dragoon the parochial clergy into obedience. All Parker required of his clergy, in fact, was for them to wear not the vestments but the linen surplice, yet even this garment had been rejected by the exiles on account of its association with Rome. The controversy began at the universities; at Oxford Humphrey and Sampson led the academic protest, while at Cambridge almost the entire membership of St John's college refused to wear surplices in the college chapel. To Parker's plea of matters indifferent the recusants replied that if indeed the wearing of surplices did constitute a matter indifferent then the bishop could have no justification in forcing them on those with tender consciences. Because of pressure from the Privy Council Parker had to try to bring the parish clergy to order, enlisting Grindal very much against his will. In Lent 1565 the clergy of London assembled upon an episcopal summons to observe a correctly attired minister whose dress in future Parker expected them all to adopt. The crisis came at Easter, when the Archbishop feared that some forty London clergy would decide not to officiate in order to avoid celebrating communion wearing a surplice. Sampson, indeed, suffered deprivation rather than conform over the issue, and other clerics chose at least temporary non-conformity, though their number proved not to be so high as Parker anticipated. In London feeling reached such a pitch over the incident that a number of citizens' wives took to the streets in a public demonstration on behalf of their deprived ministers, denouncing Grindal to his face for his severity.

Over England as a whole the vestiarian controversy provoked rather less tension than it did in the universities and in London, partly because in dioceses farther from the court bishops were more lenient and only sporadically attempted to enforce the surplice on unwilling clergy. Early in the seventeenth century members of one Leicestershire town parish asserted that their ministers had never worn it throughout the whole of Elizabeth's reign, and there must have been other similar exceptions. Yet in London the crisis immediately led to an even graver development : the campaign to enforce conformity there occasioned the first conscious Protestant separation from the national Church. In 1567 Grindal's officers discovered a congregation worshipping in secret at Plumbers' Hall in the city and brought some of its members before him and other High Commissioners. Their spokesman informed the Bishop that when he had displaced their ministers for not wearing the apparel with the result that they could no longer hear them preach 'we bethought us what were best to do; and we remembered that there was a congregation of us in this city in Queen Mary's days; and a congregation at Geneva, which used a book and order of preaching, ministering of the sacraments and discipline, most agreeable to the word of God; which book is allowed by that godly and well learned man, Master Calvin, and the preachers there : which book and order we now hold'. When Grindal tried to quote Bullinger and even Calvin on the duty of conforming in matters indifferent he received the crushing reply, 'We reverence the learned in Geneva or in other places wheresoever they be; yet we build not on them our faith and religion.' Members of the group knew Foxe's 'book of the monuments of the church' and they had read there about 'many which were burned in Queen Mary's time, [who] died for standing against Popery, as now we do'. They also cited the example of Scotland where the Church 'hath the word truly preached, the sacraments truly ministered and the discipline according to the word of God: and these be the notes by which the true Church is known'. About a hundred people had been surprised at Plumbers' Hall, and despite threats made then and subsequent imprisonments, searchers found seventy-seven men and women from all over London assembled for worship in a goldsmith's house in St Martin's in the Fields in 1568.[5]

One or two members of the Plumbers' Hall congregation had almost certainly been members of the English church in Geneva during Mary's reign. Similar continuity of membership connected the Plumbers' Hall group with the congregation of Richard Fitz which in 1571 put out a statement to justify its separation from the established Church. More clearly than the Plumbers' Hall group, Fitz's congregation objected not only to the surplice but to the lack of a reformed discipline in the English Church. On his entry into Fitz's church a new member, having condemned the Prayer Book ceremonies as the 'relics of Antichrist' and having disassociated himself from those who by conforming had received 'the marks of the Romish beast', made the following declaration:

> I have now joined myself to the Church of Christ wherein I have yielded myself subject to the discipline of God's word, as I promised at my baptism, which if I should now again foresake and join myself with their traditions, I should then foresake the union wherein I am knit to the body of Christ and join myself to the discipline of Antichrist. For in the Church of the traditioners there is no other discipline than that which hath been maintained by the antichristian Popes of Rome, whereby the Church of God hath always been afflicted, and is until this day, for which I refuse them.

After each member had individually sworn his agreement to this protestation the group had apparently gone on to take communion together to signify their communal assent.[6]

The exiles at Frankfurt and Geneva had made formal agreements when they had founded their congregations to which later members had had to subscribe: now some of the godly, driven beyond endurance by the government's failure to carry out a thorough reformation within the Elizabethan Church, deliberately continued the practice. It seems highly unlikely that they intended to create a permanently gathered church of the elect and much more probable that they thought in terms of a temporary separation until the national Church had been cleansed of all traces of popery and they could again worship in their parish churches. Their actions show the depth of the Protestant convictions of certain Londoners rather than any coherent lay thinking about the nature of the Church. Some men, with the experience of Mary's reign in mind, determined to continue to worship as they felt to be right, quite disregarding the fact that the English Church in the meanwhile had officially become Protestant. Nevertheless the impulsive actions of these *de facto* separatists in theory wrecked the unity of the national Church and for this reason evoked the bitter hostility of the churchmen, including such bishops as Grindal, who had sympathized with their original grievances: with the recent example of Mary's reign before them, the Queen and Privy Councillors, equating separatism with political subversion, readily supported the bishops' efforts to break up these congregations wherever they appeared. Yet failure to grant more reformation served only to generate further protests.

Clerical opponents of vestments believed as strongly as the bishops in the need for preserving the unity of the Church but the actions of the bishops in attempting to enforce conformity did much to drive some to construct a framework for an alternative national Church. At the time of the parliamentary settlement of religion in 1559 the form of Church government had not come into question; even Calvin had recognized the first Elizabethan bishops while the churchmen of Zurich had openly rejoiced that so many of the Marian exiles had received promotion in the English Church. However, in the light of episcopal activity during the vestiarian controversy and afterwards, both Beza, Calvin's successor at Geneva, and the admirers of the Genevan church in England began to dispute the necessity for episcopacy in a rightly reformed Church. In the late 1560s former members of the English church in Geneva including Thomas Wood, once an elder there, had meetings with young clerics like John Field who had prejudiced their livelihood in London because of their refusal to wear the surplice. They already had in the French church in London a working model of a fully reformed church, governed by ministers and elders such as some of them had known in Geneva. In their persecution of nonconformists the English bishops appeared increasingly to be revealing their true nature, and this led the radicals to ask whether the office of a bishop could any longer be countenanced. They became even more discontented with the existing scheme of government when they discovered that Beza had recommended the total abolition of episcopacy in Scotland.

When, therefore, Thomas Cartwright delivered his famous lectures in Cambridge in the early months of 1570 he was not the first to assail a system of Church government which had passed unscathed in England up to that time. His importance lies rather in his academic eminence for he emerged as the first university teacher to give his support to Presbyterianism. As Cartwright expounded the Acts of the Apostles he constructed out of the biblical text a system of congregations ruled by pastors and elders, above them district assemblies (or *classes*) composed of representatives of local congregations, and in turn above them provincial and national synods. He offered this as the only authentic pattern of Church government to replace the popish English hierarchy of bishops, priests and deacons. The sensation caused by Cartwright's lectures extended far beyond Cambridge, and the government took immediate alarm since in his ideal Church Cartwright had made no provision at all for the exercise of the royal supremacy. In place of bishops in charge of dioceses appointed directly by the Queen the Presbyterians would have substituted at a stroke congregationally chosen ministers and elders administering the Church through local, provincial and ultimately national councils. The system can more accurately be described as oligarchic (and clerical) rather than democratic, as some of its enemies claimed, but whatever its exact balance it would have consorted ill with monarchy, as the Queen herself at once understood.

Fortunately for Elizabeth, Cartwright had a greater talent for expounding Presbyterian theory than for directing a Presbyterian movement. As the controversy intensified in Cambridge and as he more and more experienced the hostility of Whitgift, the head of his College and a life-long antagonist, Cartwright decided to leave England to observe actual Presbyterian churches on the Continent. Despite his withdrawal, Cartwright's theoretical justification gave a new strength to the London radicals among whom Field gradually assumed the position of an organizing secretary, collecting stories of the bishops' oppressions, bringing together sympathizers across England and popularizing the Presbyterian system. Field's hand can be discerned behind the *Admonition to the Parliament*, which came out in 1572 just after Parliament had failed to approve a new reformed scheme of ecclesiastical law to replace the old popish canon law. Now that Parliament had neglected yet again to provide the Church with true discipline, Field and his collaborators called upon the nation at large to take up the cause. 'Instead of an archbishop or lord bishop, you must make equality of ministers.' Instead of the antiChristian hierarchy 'the whole regiment of the Church [is] to be committed' to 'ministers, seniors and deacons'. 'Is a reformation good for France,' they asked, 'and can it be evil for England? Is discipline meet for Scotland? And is it unprofitable for this realm? Surely God hath set these examples before your eyes to encourage you to go forward to a thorough and speedy reformation.' Mingling reproof with exhortation, they made a final appeal to godly laymen to act on their own initiative:

> You may not do as heretofore you have done, patch and piece, nay rather go backward, and never labour or contend to perfection. But altogether remove whole Antichrist, both head, body and branch, and perfectly plant that purity of the word, that simplicity of the sacraments, and severity of discipline, which Christ hath commanded and commended to his Church.[7]

As might be expected, this new Presbyterian platform at once alienated the bishops since it undermined their very existence. Sandys in letters to Zurich condemned the young radicals, and his fellow bishops, many of whom had felt some sympathy for the earlier nonconformists in the vestiarian disputes, adopted a similar attitude. Less predictably, some of the old nonconformists, such as Humphrey and Sampson, held back from the new movement. Although Field and his colleagues insisted that they were working for the reformation of the entire English Church, they found themselves acting as semi-separatists.

Outside London and the universities the Presbyterians only raised meagre support for their *Admonition*, very largely because of its political mistiming. Only the most blinkered Protestant could consider the reformation of the English Church in a vacuum, and in the 1570s the godly hesitated for many reasons to disturb a Church where, despite Field's censures, Protestant clergy and laity together had some reform in hand: perhaps the most weighty of these reasons lay in the threat from Rome. In the first decade of the reign both the government and the godly had some justification for assuming that the Catholic problem was in the process of solution. The surviving Catholic bishops had accepted their sequestration quietly and did not organize an opposition or, it seems, even give much succour to their fellow Catholics. Elizabeth's policy of not enquiring too closely into a man's beliefs, though much disliked by fervent Protestants, seemed to be paying dividends. In all except the most inaccessible parts of England lay Catholics attended church, and among the lower clergy old priests like Parkyn who had unreservedly welcomed Mary's restoration of the Church to Rome reluctantly stayed on to minister the new Protestant service. The odds were that, once the present generation of middle-aged conservatives and waverers had died, all the Queen's subjects would have grown together in one national Protestant Church. The dream was shattered by the flight of Mary, Queen of Scots, to England, the rebellion of the northern earls in the autumn of 1569, and the papal excommunication of Elizabeth early in 1570. From that date most zealous Protestants saw English Catholics as actual or, at the least, potential traitors willing to supplant their lawful queen. Under Mary hatred of Spain had extended to hatred of the Spaniards' religion; the excommunication of Elizabeth (ironically long prevented by Philip II) completed the progression, and for centuries the majority of Englishmen looked upon Catholicism as inherently unEnglish.

This new mood very soon manifested itself in the House of Commons. In 1571 Parliament passed an act making it treason to question the Queen's title to the throne or to call her a heretic, schismatic or usurper, and followed it with another act prohibiting the bringing of bulls from Rome into England. From 1571 anyone in England who reconciled one of the Queen's subjects to the see of Rome or who received such absolution became guilty of high treason. Passions ran so high that some of the bishops in the Lords and a considerable body of the Commons wanted all Englishmen to be compelled to receive the (Protestant) communion. To this Elizabeth would not agree; but the laws already in being still made it possible for the persecution of Catholics to begin. Between 1570 and 1603 the Government permitted nearly 200 Catholic priests and laymen to be put to death for their faith: not a single Catholic had been executed between 1558 and 1570. Inevitably, this persecution both drove erstwhile conforming

Catholics into separation and stimulated further Catholic resistance to the royal supremacy.

From 1559 the migration to the Continent of Catholic fellows from Oxford and Cambridge colleges led to a propaganda campaign which culminated in the literary battle between Harding and Jewel over the legitimacy of the English Protestant Church. Yet the first Catholic exiles only gradually realized that if Catholicism was to have any chance of surviving priests had to be trained and organized to return to England to minister to the largely leaderless Catholics there. William Allen deliberately designed the seminary at Douay to meet this need, and it was there that he introduced English students, attracted in growing numbers from 1568, to the fervour of Counter-Reformation Catholicism. Consequently when in 1570 the Pope called for the reconversion of England, Allen already had young and eager priests in training to answer the summons. At Douay, Allen prepared his students to face, even to aspire to the martyrdom which the acts of the 1571 Parliament had indicated might be their fate: in 1574 the first four seminary priests reached England and by 1580 about a hundred priests had been sent over; in 1577 the first suffered death by hanging, drawing and quartering. Slowly and haphazardly the priests made their way to the parts of England where they believed the populace might still be Catholic at heart. Almost inevitably, because of the nature of rural society, the new priests had to depend upon local gentry households for protection, often for their very survival, and the government's panic reaction to the Catholic mission more and more took the form of searches of suspect Catholic households. When in 1580 the arrival of the first two English Jesuits, Parsons and Campion, coincided with an increasing state of war with Spain, English Protestants' fear of Catholics mounted to hysteria. Parliament passed yet more laws: by the Act of 1581 the saying of Mass became an offence punishable by death and Catholic recusants who did not attend church laid themselves open to the unprecedentedly high fines of £20 for the first offence, £40 for the second and £100 for the third. Yet priests still continued to enter England, perhaps as many as 180 in the five years between 1580 and 1585. The government retaliated by introducing the 1584 Act against Jesuits, seminary priests and other disobedient persons which expelled from the country all Catholic priests who had been ordained since Elizabeth's accession: those who defied the law and stayed in England together with their lay protectors might be sentenced to death.

The ministrations of the seminary priests and their constancy under persecution ending frequently in martyrdom, brought about a revival of Catholicism in England. In the past many of the old Marian priests had connived at the laity's attendance at their parish church but now some seminary priests and Jesuits forbade it absolutely, and their teaching inspired some members of the laity to demonstrate their faith openly. Just as Marian Protestants had had to make a public confession of penitence for being present at Romish services, so now the Catholic priests insisted upon their converts renouncing all links with the established Church before they would reconcile them to Rome. In Lancashire, in the North Riding of Yorkshire, in Hampshire, Essex and in other parts of England, particularly where gentry families could offer some element of protection, there developed substantial Catholic communities. Some of the lay recusants, often converts, shared the new priests' spiritual intensity and kept themselves rigidly apart from Protestantism. In York Margaret Clitherow, a citizen's wife, achieved her longed-for martyrdom, and, if the government had not intervened, Mrs Wiseman in Essex might also have succeeded in following her example. The number of well-born young men offering themselves for ordination rose significantly and certain gentry households went to great lengths to obtain Jesuit chaplains so that they could enjoy what they considered to be the most fervent form of Roman practice.

Allen and Parsons forbade their priests on the English mission to discuss politics, yet it is now clear beyond reasonable doubt that, given a favourable opportunity, such as the invasion of England by forces loyal to the Papacy or the possible substitution of a Catholic for a Protestant monarch, they expected the priests to declare for the Catholic side. The Elizabethan government thus had good reason for labelling the priests as potential traitors, and their 'bloody question', though cruel, corresponded to a certain grim logic. Priests who had experienced the seminary training must have subconsciously realized that they could not be both good Catholics and loyal Englishmen. Many of the Catholic laity, on the other hand – though less frequently the converts – refused to face this issue. The appearance of Lord Montague and his Catholic troop at Tilbury in 1588 to defend Elizabeth against the expected Spanish invasion demonstrated the eagerness of some Catholic laity to solve what for many of their priests constituted the insoluble problem of allegiance. The continuing existence of church Papists, heads of households who attended church while their wives maintained the tradition of absolute recusancy, despite priestly prohibitions, shows that other Catholics still regarded this token conformity as a way out of the impasse. From this lay practice the theory developed that men might be loyal to the Pope in all spiritual matters and yet remain obedient subjects of the Queen in all matters secular. Since it involved distinguishing between religious and secular allegiance and would ultimately have destroyed the very idea of an all-inclusive State Church, the doctrine proved as yet unacceptable to both the Elizabethan State and the Papacy. Incited by a Government-directed propaganda campaign which produced books like *The Execution of Justice in England* to justify the persecution of Catholics, most Protestants after 1570 went on regarding Catholics, particularly all Catholic priests, as possible or actual traitors.

The mounting popular fear of Catholics after the excommunication of the Queen may well have held back convinced Protestants from casting their lot with the Presbyterians. The zealots in Parliament believed in the necessity of a common front against Rome and their constant remonstrance against the Queen's leniency appeared to be gaining success in the recent passage of severe anti-Catholic legislation. When on Parker's death in 1575 Grindal became Archbishop of Canterbury he made a particular effort to retain the more forward brethren within the national Church by diverting their attention away from the Church's inadequacies, which he himself sincerely hoped to remedy, to the need for strengthening and deepening a common Protestantism in response to the Catholic revival. By practical reform, the enforcement of clerical education, the supervision of the morals of the clergy and laity alike, the ending of flagrant abuses which the Church had power to control, Grindal attempted to resolve the divisions among England's Protestants. Even Thomas Cartwright, in exile, accepted Walsingham's invitation to join the common attack on Rome by composing a reply to the Catholic Rheims translation of the Bible. Perhaps, however, Grindal gained most respect for what he was than for what he did, for he had so short a time in which to implement his desired reforms. The fact that an archbishop of Canterbury chose to undergo sequestration rather than acquiesce in the Queen's assault on frequent preaching gave the godly an example of a truly reformed bishop and restored credibility to an institution which had so recently come under Presbyterian attack. Late in 1576 in his famous and much circulated letter Grindal dared to write to the Queen in favour of the preaching exercises, or prophesyings, which Elizabeth saw as a vehicle of Presbyterian subversion, and his defence brought him a reputation for godliness that many Puritan clergy and laity never forgot.

Nevertheless in the short term Grindal seemed to have failed: Elizabeth never allowed his sequestration, imposed in 1577, to be completely lifted before his death in 1583, and she had her way in getting the prophesyings banned in the southern province. Thus one means of bringing the educational level of the ordinary parish ministers to a sufficiency of biblical knowledge requisite for the instruction of the people which the exercises, usually under episcopal superintendence, had been supplying came to a premature end. The action taken by bishops in the southern province to stop prophesyings during Grindal's sequestration, and the attempt to limit Protestant preaching which this implied, sparked off a new outbreak of Separatism, more serious than before since Separatism was now endowed with a theoretical justification. At Cambridge, Robert Browne rebelled against a system of episcopal licensing of preachers, arguing that all inspired by God should have freedom to preach, but he did not enter into deliberate separation till 1581 when he had gone to live with Robert Harrison in Norwich. There some Protestants, distressed by what they saw as episcopal harassment, 'gave their consent to join themselves to the Lord in one covenant and fellowship together, and to keep and seek agreement under [God's] laws and government; and therefore did utterly flee and avoid suchlike disorders and wickedness . . .' Episcopal oversight in Norwich prevented the permanent establishment of a Separatist church in the city, so Browne and Harrison together with their congregation emigrated to the Netherlands. Perhaps Browne had some knowledge of Fitz's congregation in London, uncovered ten years previously; certainly his action in removing himself and his fellow believers from the contamination of the ungodly had several precedents; but the reasons he set down for his action in *A Treatise of Reformation without tarrying for Any* and *A book which showeth the life and manners of all true Christians*, both published in Middleburg in 1582, gave to Separatism a new intellectual vindication. Browne wrote of the gathered congregation of the elect and avoided almost entirely any discussion of the organization above the local level of these ideal, voluntary congregations, which had been the Presbyterians' major concern. He did not question the primacy of the congregation: the congregation called the minister from which he drew his authority, and without which he had no standing. Browne advocated a severance between the congregations and the State which would have proved just as destructive to the preservation of a national Church as the somewhat inarticulate aspirations of the lay Catholic loyalists.[8]

In *A Treatise of Reformation without tarrying for Any* Browne directed his most bitter criticisms not against the conforming members of the English Church, whom he seems to have considered beyond redemption, but against the Presbyterians who had seen the light but had not followed it. His attacks brought emphatic declarations from Cartwright that an English Church must be a church inclusive of the whole nation. The doctrinaire Presbyterians had a horror of being classed as Separatists and now admitted that despite its manifold imperfections the English Church did constitute a Church of Christ, redoubling their assertions that reform could only come through the intervention of the godly monarch. Yet in practice the problem remained that the monarch did not share their spiritual enthusiasm. Indeed, with the suspension of Grindal and the ascendancy of Whitgift, who succeeded Grindal at Canterbury in 1583, Elizabeth's ecclesiastics appeared not more but less sympathetic to reform than they had done in the previous decade. Whitgift marked his assumption of power by issuing three articles to be subscribed by all the clergy in his province. Most advanced Protestants would, as he required, recognize the Royal Supremacy and agree to the Thirty-Nine Articles approved by Convocation in 1562 and Parliament in 1571, but they could not conscientiously swear that the Book of Common Prayer contained nothing contrary to the word of God. Confronted with mass protests, Whitgift made a judicious retreat and only demanded full subscription from new ministers on ordination. Even so, the readiness of the bishops, in compliance with the Queen's wishes, to renew the attempt to achieve conformity sparked off, as Parker's attempt had done, a fresh outburst of nonconformity.

The revival of Presbyterianism in the 1580s coincides almost exactly with Whitgift's elevation to the see of Canterbury, and John Field, the movement's organizer, certainly believed that the new Archbishop's intolerance of Protestant nonconformity brought recruits into the fold. It may well be that hostile contemporaries and more recent historians have greatly over-estimated the extent and the efficiency of the Presbyterian movement, but a voluntary association of Presbyterian ministers did emerge at this time on something like a nation-wide scale, presenting at least a potential threat to the integrity of the established Church. Field tried to co-ordinate the movement from London while in certain parts of the country, most notably in East Anglia and the Midlands, groups of like-minded ministers met on a regional basis in what could be considered Presbyterian *classes*, though they had little or no representation of lay elders which a fully developed Presbyterian system would have presupposed. Representatives of these local assemblies came together in what might be seen as provincial meetings at the universities at degree-giving and even in national meetings in London at Parliament time. For a few years something approaching a Presbyterian alternative to the established Church existed in embryo.

The records of one *classis*, that of Dedham in Essex, have survived, and they reveal both the strengths and the weaknesses of the movement. For seven years certain ministers from the Dedham area held frequent meetings at which they discussed common ministerial problems and even the extent to which they might institute within the law the changes advocated in the Presbyterian *Book of Discipline*. They made a point of keeping in contact with neighbouring conferences. Cartwright himself, who returned to England in 1585, later confessed to having participated in a conference of this type at Warwick, though he maintained that he and his colleagues had never exceeded the bounds permitted by the law. The voluntary nature of the gatherings subsequently provided a valuable legal defence to Presbyterians on trial for their activities but in the 1580s it proved to be the movement's chief limitation. Ultimately there could be no compulsion if a member of a *classis* did not wish to obey a group's decision. Bartimaeus Andrewes, for example, a member of the Dedham assembly, received a call in 1584 from the church at Yarmouth and resolved to accept it without first fully consulting his brethren. When, however, his fellow ministers came to discuss the matter, they decided overwhelmingly that his duty lay in remaining with his present congregation at Wenham. Yet for Andrewes a richer living and a more welcoming flock outweighed the opinion of his colleagues and they could do no more than record that he had gone from Wenham without their consent.

Bancroft, in his highly tendentious account of the activities of the Presbyterian ministers, emphasized the support they received from the laity, instancing the eagerness of the burgesses of Bury St Edmund's to entertain favoured ministers after their sermon. This he interpreted as placing unjustifiable pressure upon the clergy to supply teaching in accord with the prejudices of influential groups among the laity. In many respects Bancroft did report on the situation fairly accurately : many gentlemen and leading towns-men would on occasions sit in judgement upon their local incumbent, demand better educated clergy and give them active encouragement; but he was exceeding his evidence in assuming that many laymen supported the Presbyterian system of Church government just because they supported Presbyterian ministers. Members of the House of Commons would always rise to condemn non-residence, pluralism, ill-educated ministers and criticize the action, or lack of action, of the bishops, but when in 1587 Hatton, Mildmay and Egerton expatiated to them on the degree of clericalism to which Cope's revolutionary Presbyterian bill and book would subject the country, the great majority recoiled. Most godly gentlemen continued to approve the proposal made, though not passed, in the Dedham *classis*, 'that a reconciliation should be offered to the bishops that since we profess one God and preach one doctrine we may join together with better consent to build up the church'.[9]

In 1588 John Field died and the tenuous organization of the movement fell apart. With the death of Leicester in the same year, the great patron of the godly and Whitgift's implacable opponent, Whitgift was at last able to prosecute Cartwright together with other eminent Presbyterians before the High Commission and the Court of Star Chamber on charges of seeking to overthrow the established Church. Though neither Court secured a conviction, the ministers were not formally acquitted. To their evident alarm they realized that, had they been found guilty of seditious activi-ties, they might, like their foes the Catholic priests, have paid with their lives. Ministers who all along had proclaimed that further reformation could only come through the Queen and Parliament, and who until 1588 had been remarkably persistent in lobbying members of the Commons to obtain these reforms, now had little choice but to accept the decision of the Supreme Governor in Parliament. Cartwright and his fellows recognized the danger of engaging further in any form of ministerial organization which could be labelled as Presbyterian, and the Presbyterian movement as such disappeared.

In part the virtual surrender of the surviving Presbyterians can be attributed to their concern at being thought to be Separatists, but also to the fact that, with the emergence of new Separatist leaders in London in the 1580s, they were the readier to admit a fundamental identity of aim with the national Church. Henry Barrow and John Greenwood, though they repudiated Robert Browne on account of his partial conformity after 1585, nevertheless shared a belief in the need for immediate reformation by congregations and for that separation of the godly from the ungodly about which Browne had written at length. They were both arrested in 1587 but not silenced, for from prison they contrived to compose and publish a whole stream of apologies for Separatism. Their congregation, left leaderless on their imprisonment, probably had at least one member whose separation went back to the group at Plumbers' Hall, and it continued to meet despite harassment, citing in justification the actions of London Protestants in Queen Mary's days. Early in 1593 the Bishop's officers surprised members of the depleted congregation in a wood in Islington, and under examination several confessed that 'he hath made a promise to the Lord in the presence of his congregation when he entered thereunto that he would walk with them as they would walk with the Lord'. From the detailed information which the ecclesiastical authorities uncovered then a whole spectrum of dissent emerges. Some members of Barrow's and Greenwood's church seem to have been temporary Separatists who refused to go to their parish churches until the word of God was preached according to their beliefs. Others denounced State interference in the Church, and Church involvement in the State, objecting specifically to Whitgift's membership of the Privy Council. To the consternation of some of the godly, who in no sense countenanced Separatism, Barrow and Greenwood together with Penry were executed in 1593 under the law which most members of Parliament had intended to be directed only against seminary priests. The congregation did not dissolve with the deaths of Barrow and Greenwood – indeed Francis Johnson came back from Middleburg to serve it – but its members soon concluded that it could only continue as a community in exile. In 1595 some of the London Separatists reached Holland and two years later the government freed their leaders who eventually joined them there. Separatism had not been entirely eliminated in England, but by 1593, like Presbyterianism, it had been discredited as a viable alternative to the established Church in the eyes of most of the influential laity who still worked actively to advance a further reformation.[10]

The evident failure of Presbyterianism and even more of Separatism by the last decade of Elizabeth's reign did not mean that uniformity had triumphed, at least not uniformity as understood by the Queen and Whitgift. In the final resort convinced Protestant laymen did not in any numbers support the alternative schemes for Church government because they had already discovered that the reforms they desired could to a considerable extent be achieved within the confines of the national Church. Whatever the Supreme Governor may have thought, a great many convinced Protestants considered the English Church to be still in the process of becoming a thoroughly Reformed Church. Looking back over a generation they could count their very real achievements in their own localities, and they had every reason to be confident that in the future they could continue to participate in Protestant evangelism.

CHAPTER 7

PROTESTANT CONSOLIDATION

Perhaps at the time and certainly later the Elizabethan disputes over ecclesiastical polity concentrated attention upon conflicting theories of Church government at national level at the expense of the less spectacular and less controversial process of winning the countryside to informed Protestantism. The success of Whitgift and Bancroft towards the end of the reign in imposing a degree of outward Protestant uniformity and the failure of Presbyterianism and Separatism to maintain their positions as organized movements did not in any sense bring to an end the quest for further Protestant reform in England. Admittedly, by the 1590s, in the face of the Queen's refusal to contemplate any decisive change, the bishops had mostly reconciled themselves to accepting the unreformed structure of the Church, and for them Hooker wrote his great justification of the status quo. Yet for generations *The Laws of Ecclesiastical Polity* held few attractions for committed Protestant laymen. Even in Parliament these men showed far more concern with practical reform than with rival systems of Church government, and their priorities in the long run help to explain the bishops' lack of success in imposing more than a token uniformity. The hierarchy of the late Elizabethan and Jacobean Church never became a unified or independent body and continued subject to clerical disagreement within and to constant and often contradictory pressure from the Crown and the laity without. Throughout Elizabeth's reign Protestantism made remarkable progress through active co-operation between zealous local clergy and local lay people. Bancroft, when he became Archbishop on Whitgift's death in 1604, tried to curb this local initiative as Whitgift had done, but his measures to obtain total conformity, again like Whitgift's, could never be fully carried through. In James I England had a godly monarch such as it had not seen since Edward VI, and while he remained as Supreme Governor of the Church, King and bishops in practice allowed considerable freedom to all but the most radical Protestants, a freedom which enabled godly laymen to proceed with the building of a fully reformed Protestant Church in their own particular areas.

By 1590 the seeds planted by certain advanced clergy and laymen in the earliest years of Elizabeth's reign had matured and
were bearing fruit abundantly. The enthusiasm that had been
awakened for frequent Protestant preaching, however, served only
to draw further attention to the glaring inadequacies of the existing Church structure. Some years earlier, with the aim of demon-
strating the urgent need for a wholesale reorganization, Field had
arranged for county surveys to be conducted; and these revealed
the limitations of the generality of parish clergy. To Presbyterians
the solution seemed obvious: if the State permitted the redistribution of the wealth of bishops and higher clergy and equality in
the Church, every parish would have the funds to finance a godly
preaching pastor. After the trial of Cartwright and his ministerial
colleagues Presbyterians must have realized that at least for the
remainder of the Queen's reign their system could at best be a
distant goal. Yet in the counties the problems to which they had
drawn fresh attention seemed the more obtrusive as the laity came
to expect increasingly high standards of their incumbents, and,
because no improvements had been made to those many livings
appropriated to ecclesiastical or lay landlords, well-qualified clerics
had some substance in their arguments that they needed to hold
two benefices with cure of souls in order to gain a reasonable
livelihood. In consequence zealous lay people increasingly looked
upon impropriations and pluralism as the source of all the Church's
evils. The churchwardens of Headon in Nottinghamshire represented these feelings exactly when, soon after James I's accession,
they remonstrated against the abuses in their parish:

> We have both a parson [i.e. a rector] and a vicar. Our parson
> being a preacher, but very unprofitable and non-resident with
> us, suffering both the parsonage house and chancel to be very
> ruinous: our vicar being a learned, painful and profitable and
> godly preacher, and by degree in the schools, a Master of Arts . . .
> Our parson hath two parsonages the value of one viz Headon
> where he is nonresident being fifteen pounds in the King's Books
> [the *Valor Ecclesiasticus*]. The value of the other where he is
> resident being ten pounds in the King's Book: our vicar hath
> but one poor vicarage where he is continually resident, which
> is but four pounds, three shillings and four pence in the King's
> Books, the smallness of whose living we lament, considering his
> learning, degree, pains, charge and piety.

Understandably laity and clergy saw the acknowledged abuse of impropriations in different terms: for the laity the scandal consisted chiefly in their minister being defrauded of his due by a more senior ecclesiastic in the Church hierarchy; for the clergy in lay ownership of impropriations by which tithes went to line the pockets of laymen. Robert More, the evangelical rector of Guiseley, considered this to be the great rock of offence. 'But most woeful and lamentable above all other abuses are those dangerous and sacrilegous robberies and spoils of our churches both in the south and in the north parts whereby our rectories and parsonages are impropriated and wrongfully turned into the possession of covetous worldlings and so into vicarages and miserable curateships of £5, £10 or 20 marks pensions per annum or the like.' The laity believed the problem would be solved by divesting the bishops and cathedral clergy of their unearned wealth; the clergy, on the other hand, thought relief could come only by lay landlords returning their tithes to the Church; neither achieved any widespread restitutions. When first Elizabeth and then James refused to countenance any radical restructuring of the Church, laymen came to realize that any improvement in the standards of the parish ministry depended on their own efforts. Despite clerical denunciations of covetous worldlings some godly laymen would pay, and pay handsomely, for the sort of clergy they wanted, but gave on their own terms, with the result that the control of the ecclesiastical hierarchy was weakened yet further. Laymen who wanted to attract more zealous ministers to their parishes had two alternatives open to them: they could either unofficially supplement the rector's or vicar's stipend, or they could create and finance new posts quite separate from the parish living.[1]

Combined with the Church's intrinsic weaknesses, the economic power of the godly laity may well have been a major cause of Whitgift's inability to impose a rigid Protestant uniformity across the country. He found himself powerless to halt the lay advance which had forged ahead under his predecessors Parker and Grindal: in the northern province, where the authorities considered Catholicism to be the major threat, no archbishop attempted to hamper the ambitions of reforming laymen. Like any others, the great lay patrons had to contend with livings inadequate to maintain a learned preacher. Occasionally they did what churchmen were continuously exhorting them to do and returned impropriations they owned to the Church or otherwise permanently increased the value of the livings to which they held the presentation. The pious Earl of Huntingdon, for example, when he chose Arthur Hildersham, a pupil of Cartwright's and a distant family connection, for the cure of Ashby de la Zouch in 1593 promised him that the 'pastoral charge at Ashby . . . by that time I have finished my long intended purpose shall be a sufficient place for any learned preacher'. Much more often, however, they, like lesser lay patrons, preferred to make their control over their livings doubly sure and supplemented the living only so long as it was occupied by an incumbent of whose opinions they approved. When patronage was exercised by a group of laymen, they seem to have been especially reluctant to restore revenues permanently without first ensuring their rights over the living in perpetuity.[2]

Throughout the latter years of Elizabeth's reign town corporations or influential groups of townspeople had been improving the finances of their town livings in order to obtain more zealous ministers, and this movement continued on an even greater scale in the reign of James. Particularly in towns which had a multiplicity of poorly endowed parishes local inhabitants seem to have been spurred on to take action. In the year of the Armada the more substantial inhabitants of Leeds bought the advowson of the parish church, ultimately vesting the patronage rights in twenty-five lay trustees. They chose a committed Protestant, Robert Cooke, for their new incumbent to replace their elderly, non-preaching vicar, and when Cooke died in 1615 they gave the vicarage to his only partially conforming brother, James, who had previously been their lecturer. By 1630, in London, very different from Leeds in the number of its churches, thirteen city parishes had acquired their advowsons and administered their patronage through the vestry. In the large parishes of the North-West, which often included half a dozen or more chapelries within the formal bounds of the parish, the inhabitants of the individual chapelries attained very considerable authority over their curates. It became customary in some chapelries in the West Riding to levy a rate on the wealthier parishioners; the rate payers then selected the curate, subject only to the approval of the parish incumbent and the archbishop which, since the rate payers raised the money, was usually given almost automatically. In this way Robert Booth, curate of Sowerby Bridge, a chapelry of Halifax, was 'elected by the general approbation and consent of all or the most part of the inhabitants . . . together with the approbation, consent and liking of Dr Favour, then vicar [of Halifax]'. The inhabitants of Sowerby Bridge rewarded Booth with the not inconsiderable sum of £26 14s 4d a year for his services. In this way, without challenging the law, some parishes had come near to the congregational choice of a minister advocated by Presbyterians and Separatists.[3]

Where they did not possess the advowson of the parish church, and perhaps only in a small minority of town parishes did the laity gain so much control, leading townspeople could still decisively influence a town's religious life by the skilful use of lectureships which normally entailed upon their holders the duties of preaching on Sundays and frequently also on weekdays. In the earlier part of Elizabeth's reign towns often financed their lectureships on a voluntary basis, entering into annual contracts with their preachers. Increasingly, however, the lectureships attracted a permanent endowment or, in the case of civic lectureships, became a regular charge on a corporation's finances. Often, if a parish had an incumbent whose ministry it appreciated, it also gave him the lectureship and thus temporarily raised the value of the living. A bishop could refuse a lecturer a licence to preach, or recall it after it had been issued, but the laity, since they managed the finance, retained the ultimate sanction. Should a bishop attempt to impose a lecturer upon a parish, or assume that a parish would grant a lectureship to an incumbent of whom the leading parishioners did not approve, they could and did retaliate by discontinuing the lectureship's funds.

Bancroft opposed the foundation of lectureships because he suspected that the lecturers would preach to please their auditors, but for this very reason lectureships continued to grow in the laity's esteem. After 1610 one out of every three London parishes had a regular lecturer; previously a lecturer may have been active in one parish out of four. In the diocese of London, excluding the archdeaconry of London, one parish in eight may have established a lectureship between 1583 and 1637. By the time of the Civil War almost all towns of any standing outside the London area had at least founded civic lecturing posts if they had not also set up parish lectureships. Yet not all towns were equally responsive to the attractions of civic sponsorship of Protestant preaching. The city of York told the Lord President of the Council in the North when he pressed them to create a lectureship in 1579 that since the Minster dignitaries supplied them with sermons at no cost to themselves they saw no need to raise funds to provide additional preaching. Upon further urging, however, they complied and in time came to value the lectureship so highly that in the early seventeenth century they petitioned to be allowed to set up Sunday preaching in each of the four wards of the city. Town governors relished preaching for its own sake, but it also did not escape their notice that preaching could effectively add to their powers of social control. York corporation in 1607 wanted more preaching partly to occupy and convert the irreligious. The corporation of Northampton had thought along the same lines earlier; in 1571 it had decided that the mayor and his brethren, together with the preacher, the minister and other gentlemen, should every week enquire into any 'notorious blasphemy, whoredom, drunkenness, railing against religion or the preachers thereof, scolds, ribalds and such like'. By these enquiries, which, if they had been fully implemented, would have entirely superseded the antiquated episcopal courts, they considered 'ill life is corrected, God's glory set forth and the people brought in good obedience'.[4]

As towns increasingly undertook to provide regular Protestant preaching, so the individual godly patrons were freed to concentrate on those areas of the countryside in which their particular interests lay. Where there had been one zealous lay promoter of Protestantism in 1560, forty years on there might well be four. The Earl of Huntingdon, active in furthering Protestantism from 1560, had taken special pains to pass on his religious convictions to succeeding generations and his good works mirror those of many other committed noblemen and gentlemen. One of the Earl's younger brothers, Francis Hastings, whom he had sent to Oxford to be educated under Laurence Humphrey, developed a special aptitude for Protestant theology which extended in later life to exchanging letters with Cartwright on biblical exegesis. In 1583 Sir Francis had the opportunity of moving from his native Leicestershire to Somerset to oversee the family estates for his brother and within a decade had established a centre of Protestant piety at his house at North Cadbury. There he and his equally godly wife entertained the local preachers, relieved those in want and, by example, taught their tenants to do the same.

In Somerset, Hastings joined a group of Justices of the Peace, which included Matthew Ewens of North Cadbury, Sir John Popham of Wellington, Edward St Barbe of Ashington and Sir Edward Phelips of Montacute, who shared similar religious interests. At the opposite end of England other young protégés of the Earl of Huntingdon found their path less smooth when they embarked upon the same mission. Margaret Dakins of Linton in Yorkshire had received her education in the Countess of Huntingdon's household in York: in 1596, when still under thirty, in obedience to Huntingdon's dying wish she married for the third time and took as her husband Sir Thomas Posthumous Hoby, son of Lady Elizabeth Russell and grandson of Sir Anthony Cooke. Of two young people of such irreproachable Protestant ancestry and upbringing much was expected and they did not fail in their trust. Setting up their household in the village of Hackness, some miles west of Scarborough, and in an area previously noted for its recusancy, they created a pattern of sober Protestant living. Lady Hoby together with her chaplain entered into a continuous round of sermons, repetitions, and Bible study in which she involved both her extended household and the villagers. In the family devotional exercises she had her servants read aloud from Foxe's *Acts and Monuments* while more privately she nourished her own piety on the devotional works of Perkins and Greenham. Lady Margaret lived in Hackness until she died in 1633 and after her death her widower built a chapel as a fitting memorial in an outlying part of the parish to succour the souls and bodies of the inhabitants of Harewood Dale, binding himself and his assigns for ever to support an educated preacher to lecture and catechise there every Sunday.

Members of families like the Hastings, the Russells, the Bacons and the Cookes felt an urgent sense of mission to what they believed to be the Church of God. As Sir Francis Hastings wrote in 1602, 'My duty to father a good people to a good minister, a longing people to hear to a labouring speaking minister to teach them, is a bond of duty that I may never forget, and a work of duty that I must ever be ready to perform.'[5] Such patrons did not hesitate to approach bishops in order to place their favoured ministers in positions of authority in the Church. If their nominees proved too radical for the established Church to contain, they could always as a last resort become chaplains in noble and gentry households. William Bradshaw, the author of *English Puritanism*, for whom Sir Francis interceded with Whitgift in vain to get confirmation of his lectureship at Chatham, ended his life under the protection of the Redlich family of Newhall. From their household in Derbyshire he kept in close contact with the only slightly more conformable Arthur Hildersham at Ashby de la Zouch. Lady

Bacon made Gorhambury in the 1590s a safe lodging for Presbyterian clergy at the time of the Star Chamber proceedings, and until their deaths in 1620 and 1616 respectively the dowager Countesses of Huntingdon and Cumberland went on protecting zealous young clerics, so continuing for over fifty years a tradition of piety.

Wise bishops co-operated as far as they could with this sort of Protestantism which, by late in Elizabeth's reign, had become entrenched among many sectors of the laity, and to oblige importunate patrons frequently admitted to office scrupulous clergy whom they knew at best would only partly conform. Resentment over the bishops' behaviour towards certain clerical leaders of the Presbyterian opposition has tended to obscure the fundamental identity of attitude of the majority of Church leaders and influential godly laity on both matters of Church government and Protestant doctrine which still persisted and may even have been reinforced during the last years of Elizabeth's reign. Members of the House of Commons had drawn back from the clericalism inherent in the Presbyterian system and many would have wholeheartedly concurred with Archbishop Sandys's acknowledgement that as 'our ecclesiastical policy in some points may be bettered, so do I utterly mislike even in my conscience all such rude and indigested platforms as have been more lately and boldly, than either learnedly or wisely preferred, tending not to the reformation, but to the destruction of the Church of England . . . The state of a small private church, and the form of a learned Christian kingdom neither would long like, nor can at all brook, one and the same ecclesiastical government.' Yet as late as 1587 Sandys could use this preamble to his will also to declare that 'concerning rites and ceremonies by political constitutions authorized amongst us, as I am and have been persuaded that [they] . . . are no way either ungodly or unlawful . . . so have I ever been and presently am persuaded that some of them be not so expedient in this Church now, but that in the Church reformed, and in all this time of the gospel (wherein the seed of the scripture hath so long been sown) that they may better be disused by little and little, than more and more urged'. When an archbishop at one of the most sombre moments of his life could thus publicly express his reservations concerning the state of the national Church, laymen might well continue to hope that in the future another Royal Governor would permit them and the churchmen together to go forward to further reformation.[6]

In many ways Sandys's death marked the end of an era: thereafter few bishops remained who had experienced life in reformed Protestant churches abroad, and the English bishops who followed were more reticent in admitting the Church's imperfections. Yet in matters of doctrine the godly laity continued to find little to offend them in the teachings of the leading churchmen. However much they might criticize Whitgift as an authoritarian prelate, with Whitgift the theologian they enjoyed much common ground. The Archbishop's involvement in the 1590s in the controversies at Cambridge, where some young Masters of Arts had had the audacity to question some of Calvin's leading tenets, won him the approbation of the heads of the houses even though it earned him the Queen's displeasure. Elizabeth, striving to the last to keep the Church as comprehensive as possible, would not permit divisive doctrines to be aired in public. Whitgift, nevertheless, had in a statement to the Cambridge theologians committed himself to the unequivocally Protestant belief that 'God from eternity predestined certain men to life and condemned others to death'. He had also gone on to affirm that 'the moving or efficient cause of predestination to life is not forseeing of faith, or of perseverence, or of good works, or of any other thing which is in the person predestined, but the will of the good pleasure of God alone'. The Lambeth Articles, of which these clauses form part, largely because of the Queen's intervention never became an officially accepted statement of doctrine in the established Church, but their very existence reinforced the belief of the godly among the laity that further outward Protestant reform might yet be attained.[7]

A change had also taken place in the nature of Protestant writings by the 1590s which fostered further Protestant harmony between clerics and zealous laymen. The bitter arguments over the precise form of a Christian church laid down in the New Testament, which twenty years previously had absorbed so much of the energy of Cartwright and Whitgift, had given way to a more pacific school of writers who put far more emphasis on practical Puritan piety. The pastoral works of the Cambridge preacher William Perkins achieved an immense and lasting popularity, and the sermons of Richard Greenham, the godly rector of Dry Drayton in Cambridgeshire, became the staple reading of devout lay people for generations to come. Ministers of their stature advocated the virtues of a limited conformity, teaching that it were better for a

Protestant to serve in the Church of God as far as he could than by over-scrupulosity withhold his labour from the harvest. Partial conformists and Elizabeth's chief ecclesiastics were at one in their support for establishing a learned ministry in the Church and (despite the Queen's own lack of enthusiasm) on the need for frequent preaching, the ordinary and chief means of salvation.

The increase of Protestant, Calvinist inspired preaching, which occurred during Elizabeth's reign, continued unchecked under James, often with the active encouragement of the bishops. About 1560 most bishops did not consider the majority of their diocesan ministers capable of preaching: in Devon in 1561, for example, only one out of twelve beneficed clergy held a preaching licence, in Worcester one out of four, and in Rochester one out of five could preach. By the 1590s, when standards had risen considerably, nearly a quarter of the ministers in Norfolk were licensed preachers, rather more than this in Gloucester, Chester and York, and in the diocese of Ely, favoured by its proximity to Cambridge, 79 out of 117 incumbents held preaching licences. This great alteration in the standard of qualifications of those entering the Church, maintained unchecked until 1660, came about through the rapid expansion of higher education. From the accession of Elizabeth the number of students attending Oxford and Cambridge grew decade by decade until between 1620 and 1640 there were more students in proportion to the total population of the country studying at the two universities than ever again before the twentieth century. Although the demand for education seems to have developed of its own momentum, godly laymen made it their purpose to ensure that this should be to the Church's advantage. Sir Walter Mildmay designed his new Cambridge college of Emmanuel in 1584 expressly to produce preaching ministers, and twelve years later Frances, Countess of Sussex founded Sidney Sussex College with the same intention. London, with its many opportunities for attracting notice and thus promotion, had 40 per cent of graduates among its clergy in 1560: in 1595 the figure had risen to over 70 per cent. The proportion of graduates in other dioceses remained much lower than this at the turn of the century, but it increased steadily throughout England as more and more graduates came out of the universities. By 1642 the English Church was within reach of acquiring an all-graduate clergy, and most bishops assumed that all conformable graduates could, indeed would, preach.

With the accession of James I the tension was relaxed between the Supreme Governor and the Protestant clergy and laity over the necessity for frequent preaching which had continued throughout Elizabeth's reign. Now as royal Governor the English Church had an unquestionably godly king. James had been educated in what all but the most extreme English Protestants acknowledged to be a fully reformed Church and he never abandoned the Calvinist convictions he had learned there. Yet to their cost some Protestants in 1603 failed to understand that their King did not hold the same reverence for the Presbyterian form of Church government as he did for Calvinist theology. On James's arrival in England those Presbyterians whom persecution had silenced in the last years of Elizabeth dared once again to seek further reformation. In the Millenary Petition, organized by Arthur Hildersham, they did not ask for the full substitution of a Presbyterian system of Church government, but for much more moderate concessions, a universal preaching ministry which they knew the King approved, limited toleration for ministers who could not conscientiously conform to all the requirements of the Book of Common Prayer and a purge of abuses still remaining in the Church's discipline. They stated quite emphatically that they did not intend an equality of ministers within the Church and hence the abolition of episcopacy, nor in any other way seek to undermine the Church's existing stability. James sympathized sufficiently with the petitioners to permit a conference to be arranged between their representatives and those of the bishops; and in the interim made a gesture which seemed to indicate his practical reforming intentions by stating that the leases of impropriate livings retained by the Crown should in future only be granted to learned, preaching ministers without increase of rent, urging the two universities to follow his example. Whitgift, anticipating further and more drastic change, ordered an enquiry into the abuses in the ecclesiastical courts.

The reforming party at Hampton Court may well have lost their case largely because of their moderation. If at the Conference they had attacked the bishops more strongly and asked more insistently for reform they might have obtained greater concessions. Their restraint misled James into thinking that most Englishmen had little desire for further reform in the Church and that the demands of a tiny minority had not sufficient support to justify his antagonizing the bishops. Yet Whitgift and his fellow bishops did not manage the Conference entirely to suit their own interest, as their official apologist tried to imply. With the Authorized Version the reformers eventually achieved the more scholarly translation of the Bible which they had long considered to be necessary. In addition the Canons of 1604, by at last providing a codification of ecclesiastical law appropriate for a Protestant church, did make the established Church a little more tolerable for tender consciences. The Canons imposed some restriction on autocratic bishops by recommending that at an ordination a bishop should be assisted by some members of his chapter or at least three senior clerics, and that at a deprivation he should similarly act in company with other grave preachers. The Prayer Book, reprinted after the Conference, also seemed to exclude the possibility of baptism by women in the future, a practice which even some Elizabethan bishops, including Sandys, had long wanted abolished.

Yet these proved to be sadly meagre concessions for those who had seen the Conference as a vehicle for the long-delayed reform of abuses. Any radical change in the government of the Church now seemed out of the question and this realization destroyed any hopes the surviving Presbyterian ministers still had: in accordance with Cartwright's teaching many became partial conformists rather than contemplate separation. The reaction of the clergy to the thirty-sixth of the Canons of 1604 illustrates their fundamental loyalty to the concept of a national Church which they felt that they should serve so far as their consciences would permit and to their own flocks whom they believed it would have been treachery to abandon to less committed Protestants. This Canon contained the three articles which Whitgift had attempted to enforce upon the clergy twenty years previously, with the extra refinement that the clergy's subscription had now to be given 'willingly and *ex animo*'. Unless he subscribed, no incumbent or lecturer might retain or enter upon any office. There were vociferous protests, and many laymen rushed to defend their threatened ministers; but the county petitions offered to the King on their behalf did little to help them since James considered the petitions dangerous and politically subversive. He retaliated by having some of the gentlemen who had presented them temporarily imprisoned and stripped of their local offices.

Bancroft, again like Whitgift, threatened more than he could perform. His canons appear to have gained more outward conformity. In spite of the fears of the godly, not more than a hundred ministers may have been deprived of their livings throughout the whole of England, although this may have partly been because many bishops moderated the terms of subscription. Apparently in most dioceses only those clergy who refused both to subscribe and to make some show of conformity lost their offices. Anthony Rudd, Bishop of St David's, reminded Bancroft that Whitgift, when he had dealt with the clergy already in livings, had allowed 'many learned preachers' to enjoy their liberty on condition 'that they did not by word or deed openly disgrace or disturb the state established'. When they asked their clergy to subscribe in 1604 many of Rudd's colleagues seem to have acted with this qualification in mind. At York during Matthew Hutton's archiepiscopate only four clergy in the whole diocese lost their livings for non-conformity, though limited nonconformity over the Prayer Book ceremonies continued unabated. The Bishop of Lincoln tolerated among others Simon Bradstreet, the vicar of Harbling, who would neither use the sign of the cross at baptism nor wear the surplice, and allowed him to remain in his living in the ultimately vain hope of his eventual conformity. Throughout James's reign the bishops received reports of ministers who refused to wear the surplice, would not use the ceremonies and gave communion to their parishioners sitting or standing. Most seemed to believe that men with scruples of this kind who yet agreed with them in doctrine should be offered some latitude rather than that they should be driven out of their ministry. Yet the bishops were not alone in making concessions: on their side even partial obedience to the regulations on ceremonies proved hard for many advanced Protestant ministers. As one confessed, 'the greatest part by far of resident and painful preachers amongst ourselves rather chose to yield than to leave their livings and ministry, yet is there hardly any one who had not rather they were removed than received'.[8]

Ineffectual as Bancroft's attempt to impose total conformity turned out to be, it nevertheless caused much bitterness among lay protectors of these nonconforming clergy, particularly because at the same time as the Archbishop appeared most insistent on demanding submission from Protestant ministers, the government was showing unprecedented leniency towards Catholics. In this matter public opinion as expressed in Parliament had almost no appreciation of the King's foreign policy: most gentlemen loathed the very idea of peaceful relations with Spain or of any conciliatory moves towards English Catholics, and the news of the Gunpowder

Plot brought all the hatred and fear of Rome to the surface in a plethora of frantic denunciations. Sir Francis Hastings, who six months earlier had been deprived of all his offices under the Crown for presenting a petition on behalf of the Northamptonshire ministers, on hearing of the Plot at once dashed off a letter to the Earl of Salisbury. 'What Christian prince,' he asked.

> can promise any safety to himself, so long as the teachers of such divinity, I mean the seminary priests and Jesuits, be endured and their scholars permitted, not only to live in ease and plenty . . . but also to bear office, carry countenance and credit in the countries [counties] where they live? . . . If Christian princes love themselves and their posterity, and tender the Church and people of God committed to their charge it is high time, and will prove the best policy in all divine and human reason to suppress and disable by wholesome laws duly executed such wasting caterpillers and cankerworms of all true Christian estates and commonweals.[9]

At the height of the panic Parliament passed laws more stringent than any previously, with the intention of compelling all Catholics to receive communion in the state Church. More importantly, for in practice the courts did not enforce the new laws systematically, the government made a distinction between Catholics, predominantly the Catholic laity, who would live peaceably and loyally under Protestant rule, and their ultra-montane priests who would not entertain any suggestion of curbing the Papacy's power to depose heretical monarchs. In the aftermath of the Plot a number of eminent Catholic laymen did agree to take an oath of allegiance to James explicitly rejecting the Pope's authority in the temporal sphere. Most Catholic priests could not make such a concession, but they still suffered less harshly under James than they had done under Elizabeth: in the first years of his reign twenty Catholics, three-quarters of them priests, died under the treason laws, but only seven between 1612 and 1625. By this latter date it was clear that the priestly counter-attack to reconvert England to Catholicism had failed, and for this failure the lay Catholics must bear some of the responsibility. In parts of England, especially the North, priests had gradually built up a separate clergy fund under their own management, but they never became sufficiently strong to sever their economic links with the gentry, and throughout the whole period of the operation of the penal laws priests continued to be largely dependent upon gentry households for their livelihood. Their financial reliance upon the laity may in no small measure have prevented the more radical seminary priests and Jesuits from creating a lasting revolutionary spirit in English Catholicism. Gentlemen who wished to practise their religion in their households but who had lost sight of any vision of regaining the entire nation for Rome deliberately chose not to patronize priests who might endanger their security or involve them in suspicion of treasonable plotting.

If the Catholic laity could thus in the long term exercise a determining influence upon the fate of English Catholicism, the importance of the laity within Separatism requires little demonstration: from the beginning Separatists had stressed the primacy of the congregation and taught that the minister derived his authority from the community of true believers. Jacobean Separatism, which first appeared somewhat unexpectedly in the northern province, could only have arisen through the active intervention of certain committed laymen. William Brewster, a Cambridge graduate and former servant of William Davison, Elizabeth's secretary, had left his employment in London to return to his family estates in Scrooby in Nottinghamshire in 1589. Ten years later he came before the episcopal courts on a charge of repeating sermons and of not attending his parish church when there was no sermon. The godly commonly repeated sermons among themselves; as Brewster explained, 'he with others do note the sermons delivered by the preacher and in the afternoon they that have noted do confer with one another what they have noted or lost unnoted'. At precisely this date Lady Hoby at Hackness regularly took her household through such practices, and Brewster merely received an admonition for his excess of zeal. Yet within a decade he had moved from comprehension within the Church to open Separation, and for him the Canons of 1604 seem to have been the last straw. In 1604 four Nottinghamshire clerics, Bernard, Clifton, Southworth and Gray, who had previously contrived to officiate without wearing the surplice, refused even a conditional subscription and lost their livings. John Smyth, who had been dismissed from his post as preacher at Lincoln, came to Gainsborough to join them, and John Robinson, who had also been ejected from his Norwich lectureship for his failure to subscribe, did the same. In 1606 these deprived ministers gathered at the house of Lady Bowes at Coventry to consider the state of the national Church. The seniors present, dominated by Arthur Hildersham from Ashby de la Zouch, would not even think of separation, but the radical minority decided that the English Church, because of its manifold abuses and the persecution inflicted by its bishops, could no longer be held to be a true Church. John Smyth went home and bound his congregation at Gainsborough with a covenant to form a separate church. Bernard similarly formed a covenanted congregation, though he later retracted his separation. Besides Brewster, Thomas Helwys, another local gentleman, became one of Smyth's most dedicated lay supporters, and Separatist ideas seemed to spread rapidly among the laity in Nottinghamshire in 1607. Several lay people refused to attend church where the incumbent had no licence to preach: Thomas Jessup of Mattersay told the ecclesiastical authorities he would not receive communion 'until he be resolved whether he may take it kneeling, sitting or standing lawfully'. Archbishop Matthew felt compelled to act and went to Bawtry to preach against the 'Brownists'. In November 1607 another gentleman, Gervase Nevile of Scrooby, appeared before the Archbishop in the High Commission Court suspected, with reason, of being a Separatist. He rejected the *ex officio* oath and in the tradition of Barrow bitterly attacked the 'Antichristian hierarchy'. He was imprisoned in York for four months: in the spring of 1608 three other leading lay Separatists, John Drewe, Thomas Jessup and Joan Helwys, joined him in prison, while Brewster and Richard Jackson of Scrooby were both cited to appear before the court. These lay people and their ministers soon realized that they could not both retain their principles and live unpersecuted in Nottinghamshire. So in the summer of 1608 Smyth, Robinson and the laymen Helwys, Brewster, Nevile and their households left England for the Netherlands where ten years earlier the chief remnant of Barrow and Greenwood's London church had taken refuge. Archbishop Matthew had made it clear yet again, just as Whitgift had done, that separation which denied any validity to the established Church would not be tolerated in England. Once the Separatist leaders had been driven out, the northern High Commission no longer enquired too minutely into nonconformist practices in North Nottinghamshire, even though it seems that Separatist sympathies remained. In 1610 churchwardens from North Collingham presented a parishioner for 'maintaining by public disputation, that whosoever cometh into the church in time of divine service and shall kneel down to pray, that he may hear with edification, offered the sacrifice of fools and his prayer is abominable'. Occasional Separatists, holding 'horrible erroneous opinions', came before the judges at both the Assizes and the High Commission Court until the end of the reign.[10]

Those Separatists who left England, however, found no ready solution to their troubles once they reached the Netherlands. John Smyth had previously been a pupil of Francis Johnson and he seems to have taken his group of Nottinghamshire Separatists to Amsterdam with the intention of uniting with Johnson's church of 'the old separation'. In fact, this never happened, perhaps partly because almost since Johnson's arrival in the Netherlands the congregation had been riven by disputes in much the same way as Browne's congregation had been a generation before. In Johnson's case his quarrels with his brother George, which he described at wearisome length in *A Discourse of some Troubles in the banished English Church at Amsterdam*, made matters worse. At bottom the contention seems to have been over the authority of the minister and elders in the church: Francis Johnson favoured ministerial power, while his brother supported the rights of the whole congregation. Though Francis Johnson seems to have kept control over the church, it was at the expense of almost continuous strife.

Smyth's congregation developed in a very different way. In exile his teaching on the nature of a true Church moved rapidly in an unprecedented direction: from considering the covenant as the distinguishing mark of a true Church he began more and more to emphasize the importance of baptism as a qualification of entry into a gathered community. He could discover no church in Amsterdam which, in his view, had kept the seal of baptism unsullied and in consequence late in 1608 or in the early months of 1609 he took the momentous step of re-baptizing himself, and then of re-baptizing his followers. Until this time, because of the association of adult baptism and re-baptism with the social anarchy of the Anabaptist communities of the 1530s, the English Separatists had shied away from giving baptism particular prominence, and indeed had stressed the legitimacy of infant baptism for the children of believers. But once Smyth and his congregation had dared to make this radical departure they progressed further and further from the main Calvinist tradition. In contrast with Johnson's congregation, they defended the autonomy of the community

of believers against the powers of the minister, and their services
became less structured, and more disordered and subject to
individual inspiration. According to a description of their meetings
which two members of the congregation sent to friends in England,
they began with prayer and a chapter or two from the Bible;
they then laid aside their books, and one speaker after another
prophesied out of the text for an hour or so. The morning exercise
started at eight and lasted till twelve, and a similar session lasted
for three or four hours in the afternoon. Smyth, concerned by his
spiritual isolation, eventually recognized a true Church among the
Dutch Mennonites and went over to them, taking part of his
congregation with him. Thomas Helwys, however, remained convinced of the rightness of Smyth's original inspiration and sought
to keep the identity of the surviving English Baptists. He made
the break with Calvinism absolute by writing a treatise expounding
the theory of the general redemption of all men and in so doing
became the first to revive in print this strand of popular Protestantism since Henry Harte had defended his stand against
Calvinist predestination in the reign of Edward vi. At first these
English General Baptists formed only a very tiny community, but
their actions had considerable importance for the future. Helwys
led his followers back to England in 1612 and, although he died
in 1616, his church maintained a tenuous existence in London until
the outbreak of the Civil War when it vastly extended its mission.
Even in the reign of James i, when most influential Protestants
strongly opposed any questioning of Calvinist orthodoxy, some
expansion was taking place, and in 1626 the Dutch and English
churches in Amsterdam received news of General Baptist churches
in Lincoln, Salisbury, Coventry and Tiverton as well as London.

Thus the Jacobean Church did not succeed entirely in eliminating
these pockets of Separatism, but as an institution it had the strength
to prevent a Separatist movement emerging in England, and English
Separatists could only practise their faith openly abroad. The
hostility which the generality of advanced Protestants continued
to feel for Separatism indicates both their reluctance on a
theoretical level to cut themselves off from the national Church
and also, perhaps more importantly, the fact that they could still
live and, to some degree, work within the established Church.
Bancroft's attempt in 1604 to impose conformity had not had lasting results and he did not repeat it : no other Jacobean archbishop
even tried. Rather than as an initiator of a new policy of re-

construction, Bancroft can more accurately be placed as the last of the late Elizabethan authoritarian prelates. He continued, as far as he could, the policy of Whitgift, but unlike Whitgift, apart from a short interval around 1604, he did not enjoy the unwavering support of the royal Governor.

James had disappointed the radicals at Hampton Court by his outburst against Presbyterian government, but his very opposition to clericalism meant that he would not countenance any increase in clerical pretensions among his own bishops. Bancroft himself had been attacked by Knollys after his famous sermon at Paul's Cross in 1589 for stressing the God-given authority of bishops and thus by implication lessening the powers of the Supreme Governor. So long as James ruled an effective check remained on the elaboration of prelatical ideas of this kind. In addition, James did not share that ambivalence towards Calvinism displayed by a small group of late Elizabethan clerics, of whom Bancroft was one, and the King's own opinions effectively curbed any public dissemination of theology not in accord with the generally accepted Calvinist orthodoxy. Whatever the controversies over ceremonies in the Church or the disputes over the ideal form of Church government, the great body of churchmen, partially conforming ministers and zealous Protestant laymen, shared a common allegiance to Calvinism. James's intervention in 1616 at the Synod of Dort on behalf of the ultra Calvinist party among the Dutch set the seal upon his orthodoxy in England and as long as he remained Supreme Governor allowed the godly to continue to consider the English Church a true Church in all essentials.

In approving Bancroft's elevation to Canterbury in 1604, James may have meant to demonstrate his acceptance of the existing form of Church government. Certainly his other episcopal appointments indicate that Bancroft's promotion had not been intended to mark a new trend in the development of the Church. George Abbott, who followed Bancroft in 1611 and held the see of Canterbury until his death in 1633, was a convinced Calvinist and a latitudinarian concerning the significance of episcopacy in a Church in the tradition of Sandys, if not of Grindal. He believed as firmly as any of the godly that the Bible contained all the essentials for salvation and placed little emphasis on tradition in the Church. At York a man of similar complexion, Toby Matthew, a preacher, scholar and renowned literary opponent of Catholics, succeeded Hutton in 1607 and held the see until his death in 1628.

Other bishoprics went to men of the same stamp, and the advancement in 1621 of John Williams to Lincoln illustrates the long
persistence of the tradition. James had indeed gone far towards
fulfilling both the threat and the promise he made to Parliament
at the beginning of his reign : 'In things that are against the word
of God I will with as great humility as any slave fall upon my
knees or face; but in things indifferent they are seditious which
obey not the magistrate. There is no man half so dangerous as
he that repugns against order, yet some which make scruple I
would use with clemency; but let them meet me with obedience.'
Jacobean Calvinist churchmen offered unquestioned obedience to
the royal Governor, and received in return a commensurate
reward.[11]

With a godly monarch ruling over the Church, with the advancement of a continuing succession of Calvinist bishops, a wide general
tolerance came to be extended to all but the most radical Protestants in most dioceses throughout James's reign. In the North
the winning of the populace to an informed Protestantism
dominated the episcopates of Grindal, Sandys, Hutton and Matthew
virtually without a break from 1570 until 1628. With this as their
first priority, archbishop after archbishop turned a blind eye to
quite major irregularities committed by convinced Protestant
clerics as long as these did not extend to Separatism. Godly
ministers and godly laymen, setting their sights lower than Elizabethan Presbyterians had done, could pursue reformation in their
own parishes. Just because the northern archbishops only rarely
sought out nonconformity its prevalence is difficult to gauge, for
sympathetic churchwardens would not voluntarily uncover diver-
gencies in their parish services at ecclesiastical visitations. It seems
likely, however, despite the Canons of 1604, that many clergy with
the support of their parishioners disregarded the prescribed ceremonies of the Church, only rarely, if ever, wearing the surplice,
not signing babies with the cross at baptism, ministering the
communion to congregations which stood or sat rather than
knelt, even omitting large portions of the Prayer Book service
to give greater prominence to sermons. William Carte, the vicar
of Worksop from 1615 to 1627, well represents these partial conformists. Accused by an antagonistic parishioner of wearing the
surplice only at holy communion, of neglecting set services on
holy days and week days, of not reading the litany and the
Athanasian creed, of not using the sign of the cross at baptism

and of giving communion to those who did not kneel, he frankly admitted most of the offences. Yet episcopal officials dismissed him with no more than an admonition. Preaching flourished with the active encouragement of the northern bishops, most towns enjoyed preaching exercises, and the appreciative laity supported their lectures with growing enthusiasm.

After Elizabeth's banning of prophesyings in the province of Canterbury in 1576, the Elizabethan government seems to have tolerated considerably more Protestant dissent in the northern province (because of the supposed greater danger from Catholicism there) than in the southern. This distinction does not appear to have continued under James; rather, a similar latitude seems to have been granted to the South as to the North. In London, a key diocese, the Jacobean bishops permitted considerable Protestant deviations. George Abbott and then John King believed firmly in frequent preaching and sabbatarianism. To this congenial oversight the citizens of London responded by massively increasing the permanent endowment of lectureships. At both universities emphasis continued to be given to the pastoral tradition in Calvinist theology. At Cambridge Chadderton among many others perpetuated the influence of Greenham and Perkins, and at Oxford Abbott placed his brother, Robert, in the Regius Chair of Divinity and gave the Lady Margaret professorship to another convinced Calvinist, Benfield. In the absence of harassment the unrelenting religious controversies of the previous reign died away.

The English Baptists and the English Catholics stood at opposite poles of English recusancy. The mainstream of English Protestantism, conforming and only partially conforming, kept loyal to Calvinism, and this remained true even of the majority of the Separatists, particularly after Henry Jacob had devised a form of partial separation which allowed some of the godly to experience congregational discipline and yet to stay in outward communion with the Church of England. Jacob instituted a non-separating Independent congregation of this kind in London in 1616 whose members made a joint confession of faith and agreed to walk in all the ways God had made known or should in future reveal to them. John Robinson, who led the surviving English Calvinist Separatists from Amsterdam to New England in 1618, seems by then to have been converted to Jacob's more moderate, and still Calvinist, form of Independency.

To all except the Separatists and the Catholics who had

deliberately moved outside the confines of the established Church, the death of James I brought a sudden change in the life of the conforming and only partly conforming members of the national Church. Only months after his accession Charles I reversed his father's Church policy and admitted the intolerant Laudian party to power. Thus, within the space of two or three years these newly-advanced Caroline bishops were in a position to present committed Protestant clergy and laity, who had hitherto counted themselves as indisputable members of the national Church, with an alternative concept of the Church, offensive to them now not only in matters of ceremony and government but also in theology.

CHAPTER 8

THE LAUDIAN ASCENDANCY

In 1633 a censor asked Nicholas Ferrar to exclude from his forthcoming edition of George Herbert's poems the couplet

> Religion stands on tiptoe in our land
> Ready to pass to the American strand

because of its apparent topicality.[1] Yet the most superficial reading
of 'The Church Militant' would have revealed that Herbert had
taken as his theme not the local strife between the theological
parties in the English Church but the cosmic battle against the
forces of evil in the Church universal. That Herbert and Ferrar,
who in retrospect appear as some of the most loyal members of
the established Church in the early seventeenth century, could ever
have been suspected of in any way fostering subversion within
its confines illustrates the fundamental insecurity of the Laudians
even when their control seemed most strong. By 1633 they had
for some years enjoyed the unqualified support of the Supreme
Governor and secured many of the highest offices in the Church,
but they had not gained, and never did gain, the active co-operation of any substantial groups among the laity. More than anything
else this failure to win over the laity accounts for the transitory
nature of their triumph and the dramatic abruptness of their
eclipse.

The English Arminians who came to power on the accession
of Charles I could trace their ancestry back for at least two
generations, but until 1625 they had never formed more than a
very small minority among the higher churchmen. Within the
Elizabethan Church, where Calvinism had had such a predominant
influence, there had been some clerical dissidents who had not
accepted predestinarian theology and it was their disputes in
Cambridge in the 1590s which had led Whitgift to draft the
Lambeth Articles. Elizabeth's prohibition of the public discussion
of controversial theology had applied as much to them as it did
to the Calvinists, but it did not extend to their liturgical practice;
increasingly towards the end of her reign some of the higher clergy

began to give a new emphasis to the sacraments as a counter-balance to sermons in the Church's worship. Also, very cautiously after the snub Bancroft had received for his Paul's Cross sermon in defence of episcopacy, a few erudite clergy in the 1590s continued to elaborate, in Latin, the theory that episcopacy had been ordained by God and constituted for all time a necessary requirement of a true Church. Bancroft may have been the first cleric holding such views to attain high office since the Elizabethan Settlement had been passed, but it was not until after his death in 1610 that sufficient Arminian clerics emerged to make up a party. With Richard Neile at its head the group included Andrews, Overall and Buckeridge. Significantly these men still did not consider the time ripe to air their opinions either in print or in sermons but by some of their actions they demonstrated their belief in the sacraments, rather than in preaching, as the primary instrument of saving grace. In 1618, when he went to be Bishop of Durham, Neile converted the holy table in the Cathedral into an altar, and his dependant, Laud, did the same as Dean of Gloucester. A little later Andrews and Overall indicated their approval of the Roman form of private confession to a priest. From 1618, after the Synod of Dort, these churchmen through Neile began making overtures to James in an attempt to win him over to their views. Yet before perhaps the very last year of his life the King showed little sympathy for a group which seemed to be reasserting the importance of the clerical estate within the Church and which, at least potentially, could endanger the authority of the Supreme Governor.

Charles 1 inherited neither his father's love of theological speculation nor his political acumen, and ultimately this was to prove disastrous both for him and his Church. The King's introduction to the Arminians in general and Laud in particular came through the Duke of Buckingham. In his first years as James's favourite Buckingham had had close links with Calvinist members of the Church, acting as the chief patron of John Preston whom he advanced to be a royal chaplain, but towards the end of his life he veered towards the group organized by Neile from Durham House in London. Buckingham gave the Arminians access to Charles when he was Prince of Wales and later King, and they for their part seemed to be in a position to offer the new ruler all that he most lacked. They promised unquestioning support to a king who would reign in accordance with their image of a divinely inspired guardian of the Church and encouraged Charles to think of bishops as the natural pillars of the monarchy. In addition, Charles's tastes in religion, as in art, inclined towards the magnificent ceremonial which formed another plank in the Arminians' platform. In this respect his personal propensity may not have been very different from that of Elizabeth, but whereas she had always been on her guard against the resurgence of clericalism Charles seems not to have conceived that the rights of monarch and Church could ever collide.

From the moment he came to the throne Charles made no attempt to disguise his religious preferences. Archbishop Abbott had counselled James I against furthering the ambition of Richard Montagu, a man who had outraged many of his clerical brethren in 1624 by proclaiming, in a written defence of the Church of England, that the doctrine of predestination was not part of the theology set out in the Thirty-Nine Articles. In 1625 Charles, oblivious of the political consequences, created Montagu a royal chaplain. At the York House Conference of February 1626 the Arminians went to fresh lengths to show that the Prayer Book could also be used to modify the Calvinism which for generations ecclesiastics and laymen alike had assumed to be contained in the Articles. The King indicated his approval for their interpretation. and John Cosin, who under Neile's protection had already been introducing more ceremonial innovations at Durham, felt confident enough to claim that they had captured the Supreme Governor for their cause.

Without the active support of the Crown, the Arminian party could never have won control over the Church in so short a time. The right of the King to appoint bishops, deans, university chancellors and certain heads of colleges in Oxford and Cambridge meant that as the senior posts in the Church became vacant by death Arminians had direct entry to the highest offices. An Arminian bishop in his turn could exercise his patronage in cathedrals and in the parochial livings in his gift to promote members of his own party. The movement of bishops from one see to another of more strategic importance in the early years of the reign left Calvinist Protestants in no doubt of the direction from which the wind was blowing, and the advancement of Laud in particular provided the clearest indication of the King's intentions. In 1625 Laud held the poor and remote see of St David's; in the autumn of 1626 he came a little nearer the seat of power when the see of Bath and Wells fell vacant, but this position in no way matched the expectations of one to whom Charles that year had promised the metropolitan dignity. Then in 1628 Toby Matthew died, the evangelical Archbishop of York who had gloried in his frequent preaching throughout his diocese. Charles at once authorized the appointment of the Bishop of London to York, so that Laud could be made Bishop of London. But the highest office still evaded his grasp as George Abbott lived on in increasing isolation: Abbott died at last in 1633, and two days after his death, in his sixtieth year, Laud attained the Archbishopric of Canterbury.

By this date other leading Arminians had acquired some of the key English dioceses. In 1628 Neile had gone from Durham to Winchester, only to move north again five years later to become Archbishop of York. Montagu in 1628 secured the bishopric of Chichester, while Francis White, an equally flamboyant Arminian, received Norwich from the Crown. Matthew Wren, who had scandalized Cambridge conservatives by his changes in Peterhouse chapel, succeeded White, at one remove, first at Norwich, in 1635, and then at Ely. By 1633 Curle had been advanced to Winchester and Augustine Lindsell to Peterborough. These promotions more than justified the opposition's complaint that the Arminians held some of the best livings in the English Church.

Yet even in the highest reaches of the Church the Laudians never achieved an absolute dominance over the episcopate, since some of the men given bishoprics by James, for reasons quite different from those which weighed with his son, lived on to cause Laud endless frustration. Probably the least amenable member of the episcopal bench was John Williams, Bishop of Lincoln. Laud succeeded in getting him excluded from secular office, while he and Neile in 1627 became members of the Privy Council, but he could never oust him from the diocese of Lincoln, still one of the most extensive of the English sees. At Chester Bridgeman, appointed in 1619, only co-operated half-heartedly with the religious party in power, and the Arminians suspected Thornborough, who had been at Worcester since 1617, like Bridgeman of showing too much kindness to the nonconformists. Even some of Laud's own nominees disappointed his hopes. Goodman at Gloucester proved the worst liability since he confirmed all the Calvinists' dire forebodings by his conversion to Catholicism, which may have happened as early as 1636: by 1640 even Laud felt he had no

alternative but to suspend him from office. At Coventry and Lichfield Wright evaded compiling returns on his diocese for years on
end and did not enforce ceremonial changes. Richard Corbet, who
held the see of Norwich from 1632 until his death in 1635, proved
similarly unsatisfactory, and Roger Manwaring did not live up to
Laud's expectations either as Dean of Worcester or as Bishop of
St David's: Manwaring's successor in the see, Theophilus Field,
displayed little more concern for the Arminian interest. Nevertheless, despite these personal shortcomings, by the early 1630s the
Laudians had still attained very considerable power in the upper
reaches of the Church.

In many respects the Laudians discovered that they could obtain
a commanding influence within the Caroline Church more easily
than they could implement their policies once this supremacy had
been acquired. The very audacity of their plans made for major
difficulties in enforcement since they were seeking to change not
only the theological emphasis, exalting the place of the sacraments,
lessening the emphasis on preaching, but also, as a necessary
accompaniment, to restore the authority of the clergy to something
like it had been in the pre-Reformation Church. The Laudians
could have tried to disseminate their views by teaching but they
seem to have preferred actions to words, and in particular to have
hoped to instil a new attitude among the lower clergy and the
laity by the strict imposition of uniformity. In thus attempting
to return to practices of the past, little new legislation was required
since the somewhat imprecise clauses in the Prayer Book and the
Elizabethan Acts of Supremacy and Uniformity generally provided
sufficient authorization. In any case, given the hostility of the
House of Commons to any religious change of this kind in all the
sessions of Charles's early Parliaments, the bishops had no alternative but to work directly through the royal Governor; indeed,
in the 1630s, when the Prayer Book could not fully serve to
justify his proceedings, Laud chose to act under the protection of
the King and the Privy Council.

Although the Prayer Book supplied the Laudians with a means
to transform the churches of the nation, they were conscious that
it might prove to be a blunt instrument. In earlier decades the
Prayer Book had only received lukewarm support and the High
Churchmen's attempts to enforce uniformity soon revealed the
very wide latitude countenanced by previous generations. Laud,
however, was not one to allow his predecessors' failures to stand

in his way. He ordered all incumbents to wear the surplice, and through the persistence of his officials he seems to have gained a measure of success denied to earlier bishops who had often accepted a token conformity. In addition, from shortly after Charles's accession, at least in dioceses where the bishop sympathized with Laud, incumbents seem no longer to have been able to disregard the ceremonies of the Church, to baptize, for example, without using the sign of the cross, or to preach without first reading the Prayer Book service in its entirety. Subsequently Laud went on to require that all lecturers, whether appointed by individuals or corporations, should also hold a curacy. Since beneficed clergy could be sequestered from their livings if they did not observe the Prayer Book rubrics, this measure brought all ministers completely under ecclesiastical discipline for the first time since the Reformation.

To a certain extent the Prayer Book also gave the Laudians some authorization in their attempt to control the attitudes of the laity both towards their clergy and towards the sacraments of the Church. Since 1559 lay people had formally been expected to receive communion kneeling; now the Laudians rigorously enforced the practice, threatening the clergy with suspension if they gave communion to parishioners who stood or sat. The Prayer Book, however, did not give them the precise directions they needed on the placing of the holy table. In most dioceses it had been customary, since early in Elizabeth's reign, for the table to be brought down into the nave for the administration of communion and frequently the churchwardens had left it there. To change this state of affairs Laud in 1633 had to have recourse to the royal Governor to obtain a letter from the Privy Council instructing parish churches to follow the example of cathedrals and keep the holy table permanently as an altar, railed and at the east end of the church. The laity had now not only to show a new respect towards their clergy, once again set apart as a priestly caste, but also to observe a new outward reverence in ceremonial, kneeling at the reception of communion and at prayer, and bowing at the name of Jesus.

The essentially autocratic nature of Laudianism emerges with particular force from the manner in which the Laudians set about imposing these changes. They seem to have given the laity little guidance about the significance of the observances; they merely ordered them to obey. Laud appears to have thought that outward

obedience would in time effect a change of heart, but in this both
he and his supporters showed themselves singularly blind to
popular prejudices. They expected congregations who for almost
a century had been subjected to diatribes against the Papacy and
the Roman Church to reassume without much preparation ceremonies often disused for decades and long associated with
Catholicism. In place of explanations the Laudians imposed discipline to enforce compliance, as the metropolitan visitation carried
out for Laud in 1635 illustrates. At Bury St Edmunds Sir Nathaniel
Brent, Laud's official, deprived Mr Peartree of his licence to preach
for having indirectly glanced at the ceremonies of the Church in
his sermons. In Northamptonshire Brent suspended Mr Lewis, the
vicar of Rothwell, for not wearing a surplice when he read prayers
on Ascension Day. Mr Cave, a 'precise' minister of St Helens at
Ipswich – an 'exceeding factious' town according to Brent – suffered
the same punishment, as did a considerable number of other clergy
prevented from exercising their ministry about 1635 because they
had given communion to members of their congregation who would
not kneel.

There can be little doubt that these strong measures did achieve
some results and the metropolitan visitation suggests that by 1635
a preponderance of clergy and congregations would conform out-
wardly, at least in the presence of the Archbishop's representative.
Brent told Laud that the ministers and lay people in Stamford
remained uncovered all service time, and bowed at the name of
Jesus, though at Northampton many men wore their hats at
morning prayer and only took them off when he set them an
example; they stuck, however, at bowing at the name of Jesus,
even when threatened with a case in the High Commission Court.
Most of the lay people Brent encountered seem to have contented
themselves with this somewhat reluctant compliance and few spoke
out as brazenly as one Goodwin of Fairfield. He was rash enough
to assert that kneeling at communion was idolatrous, and promptly
found himself cited in the High Commission Court for contempt.
Most of the laity preferred to meet the Laudians' attempt to
enforce conformity by clandestine acts of disobedience. On his
visitation Brent repeatedly had to record, as in Gloucestershire,
that the people were 'much given to straggle from their own
parishes to hear strangers'. To circumvent this practice he arranged
in Coventry to have the two ministers preach simultaneously, so
that the people could not go from one sermon to another, while

he gave orders that the gallery built to receive strangers who had come to hear the preaching of the incumbent of St Pancras in Chichester should be pulled down; he seems also to have hoped that the great gallery in Kingston church would get the same treatment. Brent's report to Laud may have been unduly optimistic; the 'absolute obedience' to the laws of the Church promised by the chief men of Yarmouth did not last five years and the conformity of the better sort of Ipswich continued little longer; but at least in the southern province some sort of acquiescence seems to have been obtained by Laudian rule. Rarely did Brent come across a church like that of All Hallows at Worcester where the parish appears to have given its active co-operation to the new changes: the church had organs, singing men and a second service at the communion table and Brent commented to Laud that he considered it all very beautiful. Far more often the laity provided the bare minimum for church repairs and structural alterations necessary for the ceremonial changes, but all initiative for Laudian innovations seems to have been derived from the clergy alone.

When Brent had gone to Yarmouth he had discovered that the local magistrates wanted to appoint a lecturer, and he reported somewhat naïvely to his metropolitan 'but I find no inclination in them to give the choice of him to your grace'.[2] This problem of lay patronage, indeed of the economic power of the laity within the Church, in fact proved much more difficult for the Laudians than the achievement of some semblance of outward conformity. Undeterred by the failures of his clerical predecessors, Laud made a determined effort to regain lay impropriations for the Church. In a case of conscience referred to him by his former pupil, Sir John Scudamore, he took the opportunity of formulating the policy of the High Church party with respect to lay impropriations. With a submissiveness quite untypical of most of the laity, Scudamore had consulted Laud about the propriety of selling the impropriations his ancestors had bought in the reign of Henry VIII in order to improve his present financial position. He enquired of the Archbishop whether the holding of impropriations by laymen could be considered a sin, and whether the sale of them would also be sinful if the landowner did not return the proceeds of the sale to the Church. In reply Laud outlined the principles involved: tithes made up the bulk of all impropriations; if Scudamore believed that tithes were owed to the priest alone by divine right, then indeed for a layman to retain them virtually amounted to sacrilege. Laud realized, however, that Scudamore, in his straitened circumstances, could scarcely be expected to forfeit immediately the benefit from impropriations, so he advised him to sell them and aim by gradual steps at restoring the money to the Church as his financial state improved. In that way he and his posterity could make amends to the Church for what his ancestors had withheld from it. Laud's arguments confirmed Scudamore's own reservations and he gained fame in Herefordshire, and indeed outside the bounds of his county, for the number of impropriations he restored. The theory which Laud had enunciated in this particular case acquired a wider hearing in Sir Henry Spelman's writings, published posthumously as *The History of Sacrilege*, where he elaborated the unhappy fate of gentlemen who had tried to pile up riches on earth from property wrongfully detained from the Church. Laud's arguments and Spelman's book, however, could do little to overcome the practical weakness of the Laudians, who had no case at law, since it remained as legal for a layman to retain or sell impropriations as any other form of property. Only moral persuasion, exhortations and warnings of the fate destined for the sacrilegious could be employed to try to bring laymen to make voluntary restitution.

Scudamore's action received much comment for its singularity: very few landowners felt moved to follow his example, though, as Laud well knew, cupidity was not the sole reason for their failure to respond to his admonitions. By returning impropriations to a living a layman would have deprived himself not only of a profitable income but also of much cherished influence over a parochial living. By supplementing, or withholding, a pension to an individual incumbent an impropriator concerned about the state of his local church could relieve a godly vicar and yet still exercise considerable control over the living both then and in the future. One of Scudamore's near neighbours, Sir Robert Harley of Brampton Brian, opted for this second course. According to Thomas Froysell who preached Sir Robert's funeral sermon in 1658, he brought knowledge of the truth of the gospel to his whole area of Herefordshire by paying pensions directly to deserving clergy. 'And as God removed godly ministers by death, he continued still a succession of them to you. Not only Brampton Brian, but ye also of Wigmore, and ye of Leintwardine, owe your very souls to Sir Robert Harley, who maintained your ministers upon his own cost, that they might feed you with the gospel of Jesus Christ.'

Once a landowner gave back his impropriations to the Church he
would lose this close supervision over the living.[3]

Behind all the Laudian theorizing on the moral illegality of lay
impropriations remained the fear of the economic power of the
laity within the Church. Apparently an increasing number of laymen did develop scruples about the poverty of the incumbents of
impropriate livings about this time and at some cost to themselves
attempted to make amends, but in ways which would not deprive
them and their heirs of influence over the local incumbent. The
example of Mary Lady Weld who, in 1623, left £2000 for the
buying of impropriate rectories seems to have been more representative of lay action than Sir John Scudamore's unconditional
surrender. Lady Weld gave her money in trust to a London livery
company which she then made responsible for buying impropriate
rectories and for paying to the incumbents in the meantime two-
thirds of the value of the living until the impropriation should
have been bought out. By this arrangement the income of particular
incumbents could be substantially increased, but not at the expense
of lay oversight, a course which ran directly contrary to the
Laudian party's aims.

Laud was rather more successful in killing plans to extend still
further the laity's economic control in the Church than in
persuading laymen voluntarily to restore their impropriate tithes.
In 1625 a group of twelve Londoners formed themselves into an
unincorporated trust to acquire ecclesiastical revenues in lay hands
which they intended to use for the maintenance of a godly ministry
within the Church, reserving to themselves the right to determine
the criterion of godliness. In the six or so years of their active
operation they raised a great deal of money, often in quite small
donations, and also attracted bequests of impropriations and
advowsons. In 1628 alone nearly two hundred Londoners subscribed £1554 to buy impropriations to increase the endowment
of the St Antholin's lectureships and turned over the administration of this fund to the feoffees. With this and other substantial
funds that they collected the feoffees bought impropriations,
advowsons and leases of tithes in many different parts of England,
some in the Home Counties but others as far afield as Shropshire,
Hereford and Staffordshire, in fact wherever their London contacts
had a particular interest. However, they aspired to do much more
than merely supplement the impropriate livings they happened to
hold. They planned to maintain at St Antholin's a seminary for the

training of young preachers who, after some initial experience in
the city of London, could be sent out to livings owned by the trust,
thereby assisting the Church in the provinces. They dispatched
at least one St Antholin's lecturer, John Archer, to the parish of
All Saints, Hertford, and on some of their other impropriations
they contrived, by withholding the pension, to induce unworthy
incumbents to leave so that they could install godly candidates of
their choosing. But the Laudians soon realized the dangers to
themselves of this audacious undertaking. In 1630 Peter Heylyn
attacked the feoffees in a sermon at Oxford while Laud considered
their activities 'a cunning way, under a glorious pretence, to overthrow the Church government, by getting into their power more
dependency of the clergy, than the King, and all the peers, and all
the bishops in all the kingdom had'.

Early in June 1632 the Attorney General, Noy, summoned the
feoffees in the Exchequer court to answer a charge of forming
themselves into a corporation which made ordinances without
royal authorization. The feoffees had no adequate reply to this
accusation since they had considered applying for letters patent
but had put the suggestion aside until a more opportune occasion.
At the trial the basic objections of the Laudians came out: they
alleged that the feoffees had attempted to contruct 'a church
within a Church', acting as if they were a vestry of the whole
nation. In classical vein Weston blamed them for 'taking possession of Apollo's temple to make the oracle speak as they listed'.
By a decree of 1633 the court forbade the feoffees to meet again
and ordered them to restore their impropriations unconditionally
to the incumbents in the respective cures, and to make over all
the advowsons in their possession to the Crown. The feoffees'
defeat was complete. So long as Laud retained power it would
no longer be possible for lay trustees to acquire impropriations
corporately and use them to reward ecclesiastics whose theology
and life they found acceptable. In the final resort, the Laudians
preferred the unreformed state of the Church, despite the great
discrepancies in clerical incomes and the continuing drain of
clerical tithes into lay pockets, to any organized plan of restitution
which would have left the initiative with the laity.[4]

Despite the Laudians' concern to improve the condition of the
English Church in such innocuous ways as restoring church fabric,
bringing back more reverence into the services, recreating the
atmosphere of the beauty of holiness, their actions time and again

returned to the problem of the conflict between rival systems of power, ecclesiastical and lay. Laud was trying to implement a policy which ran counter to weighty lay interests in both theology and in pastoral care, a policy designed to substitute a priestly supremacy over the laity for the practical co-operation between ministers and leading members of parochial congregations to which laymen had been long accustomed. From the beginning Laud almost seemed to be deliberately planting the seeds of his own destruction. Perhaps only in frequent teaching and example had he and his colleagues any real hope of winning over the laity. Laud certainly was aware of the state of mind of leading laymen at the beginning of Charles I's reign, for from the outset Parliament resisted his designs to impose Arminianism upon the established Church. In the Commons Pym and St John, joined by Bedford in the Lords, led the attack upon a policy which they thought would have the effect of unchurching men who, until Laud's rise to power, had considered themselves orthodox Protestants. These men and their fellow members had not gone over to Presbyterianism, though they spoke as committed Calvinists, upholders of predestination who accepted episcopacy as a convenient form of Church government but did not think it to be of divine institution. At a time when the forces of Catholicism appeared resurgent on the Continent, when the Calvinist Elector Palatine had lost Bohemia, Huguenot La Rochelle had fallen to the Catholic troops of the French King, Poland, once a haven of refuge for Protestants, had been regained by the Counter-Reformation, members of Parliament felt especially sensitive to any weakening of the Protestant cause. Even in England they had good reason for alarm. At court a foreign Queen was openly proselytizing for her faith while it seemed that the party which had obtained supremacy in the Church might soon go over to Rome. Against this backcloth of Catholic advance and Protestant retreat, members of the Commons in 1629 remonstrated with Charles for allowing certain prelates to seize control of the administration of the Church, and so to prevent the advancement of 'orthodox', that is, Calvinist, clergy and to favour only those who shared their contrary opinions. This Commons' committee for religion, after deploring the increased activity of Papists in England and giving an acute summary of the theological differences between the Arminian sect and the 'orthodox' Protestants, demanded that the orthodox doctrine of our Church . . . may be established and freely taught, according as it hath been hitherto generally received, without any alteration or innovation; and severe punishment, by the same laws, to be provided against such as shall, either by word or writing, publish anything contrary thereunto . . . that his majesty would be graciously pleased to confer bishoprics, and other ecclesiastical preferments, with the advice of his Privy Council, upon learned, pious and orthodox men.[5]

The early Parliaments of Charles I proved singularly ineffective in curbing the King and his chosen advisers, but they at least provided a forum in which convinced Protestant laymen could voice their misgivings and try to defend the doctrinal integrity of the state Church. From 1629, when Charles chose to rule without a Parliament, the laity had not even this opportunity for concerted national protest. This disabling of the laity, who now could only come together in their own localities, presented the Laudians with a new chance to try to win over some by instruction, but they do not seem to have made much use of the opportunity. Little Gidding remained the chief and highly exceptional example of lay commitment to Arminianism. The family community which Nicholas Ferrar and his mother had established in a remote part of Huntingdonshire in 1625 very soon roused the suspicions of the Church's Calvinist wing. Although he never became a priest, Nicholas Ferrar entered deacon's orders with the intention of directing his sisters and brother, their wives, husbands and children in the religious life. They exhibited a devotion to the Prayer Book of a kind that few other lay people at this time seem to have shared, and in the intervals between the regular observance of set services gave themselves over to intellectual discussion, to compiling harmonies of the Gospels, and to good works to those living in their immediate neighbourhood. The King took a benign interest in their activities and visited Little Gidding on several occasions. Yet in spite of the recoil of the majority of Protestants from these apparently Romish practices and from what they saw fit to call an Arminian monastery, the Ferrar community in fact still had much in common with many godly Calvinist households. Nicholas Ferrar, disappointed by the failure of the Virginia Company in 1623, after helping extricate his elder brother from his financial ventures, had retired from the world to live a religious life free from mundane distractions. At Groton Winthrop experienced precisely the same sense of disappointment at the failure of his worldly hopes and of the corruption of the present time but in his case it led to the decision to conduct his family not to the fastnesses of the English countryside, but to the New World. Both families entered to the full into the pessimism, the general disillusion of the age, but one found a lasting source of spiritual refreshment in the Book of Common Prayer which the other would not have understood, for it was the Bible, and the Bible alone, which continued to be the inspiration of most Protestant laymen.

There is some evidence to suggest that perhaps other gentle people besides the Ferrars were beginning to adopt the belief of the Arminian clergy that the English Church had remained more faithful to the tradition of the Early Church and so was now more scriptural than other Churches, including other Protestant Churches. When Laud's disciple, Scudamore, went as ambassador to France in 1636 he somewhat ostentatiously refrained from attending Huguenot services in Paris and instead had his chaplains read the Book of Common Prayer in his embassy, a gesture his predecessors would never have thought of making. Yet again his action provoked attention because of its novelty: continental Protestantism had not lost its attractions for most of his lay contemporaries. The increased ceremonial promoted by the Arminians may have impressed rather more laymen than Arminian theology which still failed to awake any real lay appreciation: even the Ferrar family did not accord the sacraments that primacy in relation to the word which their clergy might have wished. Certainly outward show seems to have meant more to lay people than the inward symbolism of Arminian ceremonies. When certain gentlemen from Norwich viewed the sights of York in 1634 and attended a service in the Minster they admired enthusiastically the 'fair, large, high organ, newly built, richly gilt, carved and painted; a deep and sweet snowy robe of choristers', but then proceeded to marvel no less at the worldly splendour of the congregation, the lord mayor with his brethren, sword bearer and attendants, the vice-president of the Council in the North and his retinue, only comparable to a 'Paul's Cross auditory', 'a second London'. Gentlemen, it seems, might have been prepared to countenance greater ceremonialism in the Church, so long as this did not imply any reduction in respect for local secular authority. In this matter, however, the High Churchmen went on showing a dangerous insensitivity to lay susceptibilities, a point which is nicely illustrated by an incident which occurred at Uttoxeter when Brent was conducting the metropolitan visitation for Laud. When he went into the parish church he found that 'the walls of the chancel were almost quite covered with verses made by one Mr Archbold now living (who, as the common opinion is there, was 14 years of age when King Henry the VIII died) in commendation of divers learned divines whom he hath heard preach in that church, which I ordered to be wiped out and divine sentences of scripture to be put in their place'. Not surprisingly, 'the old gentleman was much offended' by this action, but Brent seemed quite unable to grasp that by this behaviour he had done much to shatter a sympathetic alliance between the clergy and the leading laity which clearly had existed for many years in the town. No inhabitant of Uttoxeter had cause to celebrate Brent's visit in rhyme.[6]

Elsewhere the Laudian clergy often offended other important laymen in similar ways, but they did not go on to justify their actions by instruction, at least not by instruction that the laity could make their own, and this constituted the greatest difference between the achievement of the Arminians and the Calvinist clergy of that and previous generations. Sir Henry Slingsby, who later suffered much on the King's behalf, in 1638 recorded in his diary misgivings about Laudian ceremonialism which persisted despite the explanations he had been given. In York he had become acquainted with Timothy Thurscross, a canon of the Minster who had recently undergone a conversion to Arminianism. He could approve of the canon's personal austerities but maintained his reservations about Thurscross's beliefs and practices. 'He is a man of most holy life, only he is conformable to the Church discipline that now is used, and to those late imposed ceremonies of bowing and adoring towards the altar . . . I thought it came too near idolatry to adore a place with rich cloths and other furniture and to command to use towards it bodily worship.' Sir Henry's wife felt even less attraction for these new ways; she retained her 'very great esteem' for Mr Ayscough, a safe Calvinist preacher in York, and continued to send to him for religious counsel, 'he being a man very eloquent both for his ordinary preaching and private discourse'.[7]

At the time of the calling of the Long Parliament Sir Henry Slingsby defended moderate episcopacy with the Erastian argument that the undermining of degree in the Church would by a logical progression extend to a demand for equality in secular government. This understanding, however, developed among conservatives only late in the reign. During the period of Charles's rule without a Parliament the actions of Laudian bishops seemed to many members of the governing classes in both towns and counties rather to circumvent their task of providing good order than to accord them the unquestioning support they expected from the Church. Laud never realized just how disruptive his attempts to impose a uniform religious observance could be upon the ruling classes in their endeavours to maintain the public peace. By the early seventeenth century sabbath observance and many other Puritan practices appealed to the local governors throughout England at least partly as a way of controlling the populace. Occupied in church or in religious exercises in the family on a Sunday, the poor could be kept from licentious excess. Sir Robert Harley, in his little corner of the world, honoured the godly ministers and vindicated the sabbath from contempt. 'By this means the congregations were frequented on the Lord's Day, and many thousand souls, prevented from their sinful sports, sat under the droppings of the word.' Justices of Sir Robert's persuasion looked upon Charles's reissue of the Book of Sports in 1633 as a cruel blow to their godly undertakings since it permitted lawful recreation on a Sunday after the Prayer Book services had ended. In fact it did not stop this trend towards increasingly severe religious discipline, especially in towns, but it brought home to local rulers their isolation both from the central Government and from the ruling party in the Church.[8]

In the 1630s in Salisbury a small but dominant clique within the town council had devised an ambitious plan intended simultaneously to relieve the poor and overcome licence. In place of the many local ale houses councillors decided to set up one municipal brewery and apply the profits to help the destitute. Laud's prosecution in the Star Chamber of Henry Sherfield, the recorder and former member of Parliament for the town, who had unwisely broken an 'idolatrous' window in his parish church on the authority only of the select vestry and without the permission of his bishop, did much to undermine the entire scheme. Indeed, the godly in Salisbury saw Laud's intervention as an attack by the central government on the local forces of order. Charles's government seemed to be favouring the unruly and superstitious rabble, and the local patricians considered that they had been abandoned by both Church and State. In York, though they had no comparable *cause célèbre*, the ruling group remained steadfast in their support of their godly ministers and in their bye laws continued to try to prevent popular disorder by implementing sabbath observance despite the fairly constant harrying of Archbishop Neile and his officials. Mayors, sheriffs and other members of the inner council appeared in the ecclesiastical courts for not receiving communion, for not kneeling and for wearing hats in church, but the Archbishop still could not break their adherence to their leading civic clergy, Shaw, Ayscough, White, Birchall, whom they continued to maintain at their own expense. In Newcastle also there was a similar group of civic governors who stood behind Dr Robert Jenison and other Calvinist lecturers against Alvey, the Arminian vicar, and who likewise suffered harassment in the ecclesiastical courts for their pains. On his perambulations Brent expected as a matter of course to find resistance to Laud's policies in towns, though he paid little heed to the effect his correction of local governors might have upon the governed.

The Laudians equally disregarded the susceptibilities of the county gentry. In Somerset they found no support from the central government for their attempt to put down unnecessary inns and licentious church ales; in Durham the gentry resented, largely on social grounds, the Arminians' meddling which would have had the effect of overturning the customary hierarchical seating in their parish churches. This failure to treat local Justices and others with the respect they regarded as their due in many areas, both in the North and the South, alienated the natural allies of the central government and tended to solidify the opposition. Godly gentlemen, merchants, and committed Protestants considerably below them in society discovered a common cause in their stand against autocratic bishops. In parts of North-West England the fossilization of the parochial system gave the laity a particular advantage. Despite the new outlook of senior churchmen the laity in many of the Lancashire and West Riding chapelries went on raising funds to provide for a preaching ministry. Sometimes aid came from an individual gentleman such as Richard Holland who in 1618 had endowed Denton chapel with £100 annually for the stipend of a godly minister. More often merchants took the lead: in 1635 the Manchester clothier, Humphrey Booth, built Salford chapel and endowed it with sufficient maintenance for the appointment of a preaching minister. Increasingly as Charles's reign progressed northerners seemed to have acted communally rather than as

individuals. The Bishop of Chester heard in 1636 that Darwen
chapelry in Cheshire had become accustomed to hiring a minister
who preached at the pleasure of the inhabitants. In the Wirral
at Shotwich Samuel Clarke derived his maintenance from the
voluntary contributions of 'Christians' purses'. In these places
Neile had good reason for suspecting the laity of usurping the
ministerial function, as he saw it, and of appointing ministers to
office in particular congregations only so long as they continued
to perform their duties to the satisfaction of the chief members
of the congregation.

Because of the peculiar status of these northern chapelries Neile
discovered that certain parts of his province lay virtually outside
his control. In 1638 Dame Dorothy Leigh of Worsley could determine when she gave £400 to help support a minister at Ellenbrook
chapel, 'that the bishop should have no hand in the putting in,
placing or displacing the minister there'.[9] Yet even in the South,
in a county like Essex where the parishes were of manageable size
and the bishop's oversight more close, this same congregational
enterprise appears. When he conducted a visitation of Essex for
Laud in 1632, Robert Aylett listed a considerable number of
parishes where either the incumbent, or the lecturer, or both, were
partly dependent on the parishioners' generosity for their livelihood.
At Castle Hedingham the churchwardens reported that 'the parish
is great and the living small, and that they allow £20 a year to
their minister'. The parish of Wethersfield had secured Mr Atwood
as their lecturer under cover of his being a curate to evade Laud's
ban on lecturers who would not associate themselves fully in
performing all the Prayer Book services: Atwood had already made
a name for himself for 'conventicles and unconformity'. A 'grave'
man from Oxford had been appointed as vicar of Great Waltham,
but the parish had brought Fuller in as lecturer, 'a young hot
fellow', 'who I fear will pull down faster than the builder can
build up in conformity'. In near despair, Aylett compared the
people of Colchester with 'those of Ephesus, their Diana is their
liberty, and none but the town clerk can appease their tumult'.
A year earlier Samuel Collins, the conformist vicar of Braintree,
had set out the practical problems of bringing parishes like these
to that reverential dependence upon the incumbent which the
Laudians demanded:

It is no easy matter to reduce a numerous congregation into

order that hath been disorderly these fifty years, and that, for the seven years last past, hath been encouraged in that way by the refractory ministers in the county, with whom they have had acquaintance in their private meetings and conferences, who have left divers schismatical books among them, and during their continuance here laboured to make my person and ministry contemptible and odious, because I would not hold conversation with them. If I had suddenly and hastily fallen upon the whole part of uniformity, I had undone myself . . . For, upon the first notice of alteration, many were resolving to go to New England, and others to remove elsewhere, by whose departure the burden of the poor, and charges of the town, had grown insupportable to those that stayed behind. By my moderate and slow proceedings I have made the stay of some, and do hope to settle their abode with us . . .

Laud, however, wanted quicker results: he could not wait for Collins's policy of winning over the laity little by little. When the lecturer of Earls Colne appeared before him he demanded to know what 'company of seditious, factious bedlams' had given him support. Yet, as Collins realized, the people would not be easily parted from their cherished ministers like Shepard or Thomas Hooker, of whom a wit had said, 'our people's palates grow so out of taste that no food contents them but of Mr Hooker's dressing'. As early as 1630 a company from Sudbury, led by their silenced lecturer, John Wilson, went out to New England. With the intensification of the attack on unbeneficed lecturers, the trickle of emigration from East Anglia to New England became a stream. John Eliot, who had been one of Hooker's assistants, sailed with governor Winthrop's wife and children. Hooker himself first took refuge in the Netherlands but in 1633 reached Cambridge in Massachusetts, followed by some of his faithful Essex admirers. A similar pattern of emigration can be discerned in the diocese of Norwich, especially between 1636 and 1638 when the strict Laudian disciplinarian, Matthew Wren, held the see. Nathaniel Rogers, a member of the godly ministerial family of Dedham, 'forseeing the approach of the storm towards himself . . . chose rather to prevent than to receive the censures of the ecclesiastical court' and, resigning his living of Assingham in Suffolk, crossed the Atlantic to settle at Ipswich in New England in 1636. The map of New England abounds in East Anglian place names and a great many of these townships owe their origin to ministers and laity who came to America between 1630 and 1640 at least partly to escape from the imposition of Laudian conformity. Perhaps the most renowned clerical emigrant was John Cotton who arrived in Massachusetts in 1633 with a considerable number of his Lincolnshire congregation : the settlers already there renamed the Indian township Boston in his honour. A considerable number of other New England immigrants, during the period of Laud's supremacy, came from the clothing areas of the South-West. Certainly economic depression did much to persuade lay people to abandon their homes for an uninhabited wilderness across the seas, but the pattern of emigration to New England differs significantly from contemporary emigration to Virginia. That those setting out for New England travelled in parties with their pastor, leaving areas in England where Calvinist Protestantism had long flourished and where Laudian bishops had been particularly active, goes far to indicate the overriding importance of religion in the great exodus.[10]

Emigration, whether to the Netherlands or New England, constituted only one, though the most radical, reaction of English Protestant zealots to the Laudian regime. Particularly among the laity, since necessarily the clergy had less freedom, resistance continued throughout the country on a wide scale in a variety of forms. Some committed Protestants saw complete outward conformity as preferable to exclusion from the ministrations of the Church. These acted like Mrs Ratcliffe, a gentlewoman of Chester, who, according to her biographer, after her spiritual conversion believed at first 'they could not be good and sound Protestants unless they showed themselves zealous detestants of whatsoever had been abused by popish superstitions'. The fear, however, that this nonconformity might bring about her excommunication and so deprive her of the sacraments subsequently caused her to alter her attitude. After conference with divines and others of the godly 'she received good resolution that she might safely receive the sacrament upon her knees, and so she did, and so continued without change of mind or scruple of conscience . . .' A Cheshire wheelwright adopted the opposite stance on the same matter. In 1625 Thomas Constable of Acton had appeared in the ecclesiastical court charged with not receiving communion, and he admitted that he had not taken communion because he would not kneel. Sixteen years later he came to prominence again as a confirmed recusant asserting 'that he did not value or care for any present-

ment that could be made against him by any of the churchwardens
or sworn men, for that for space of twenty years past he had
stood in the chancellor's teeth in defiance of his authority, and
for all the bishops they are as they have proved themselves –
the very scum of our country'.

Respect for the spiritual function of the Church brought some
to conform, while the Laudian attempt to enforce conformity
drove others into open defiance. Most opposition to Laud's policy,
however, tended to be clandestine and increasingly took the form
of Separatism or semi-Separatism. In the past the meetings of the
godly for repetitions of sermons, Bible reading, fasts had been a
tolerated, in places even a meritorious, activity within the Church.
Now the Laudians denounced such meetings as conventicles,
potentially if not actually subversive. This change of attitude
resulted in such unprecedented reversals of the normal order as
the wife of the Dean of York being accused, together with her
daughters, of attending conventicles in her own house conducted
by Mr Ayscough, one of the city's chief Calvinist preachers.
Ecclesiastical officers charged certain inhabitants of Burton-in-
Kendal in 1633 with 'separating themselves from the congregation
and running after a schismatical minister at Barwick called Richard
Fletcher'. Five years later they attacked Alexander Powell of Holt
for leaving his own church to go to others to hear ministers who
were 'suspended for their excess and nonconformity and did not
wear the surplice nor read public prayers according to the Book
of Common Prayer at such time as you so heard them pray, preach
or expound. And, therefore, you the rather did desire to follow . . .
them'.[11]

In the southern province a similar type of Separatism persisted,
and indeed increased. Henry Jacob's church in London, which in
the reign of James had come together to escape the corruptions
of the established Church, and yet sought to remain in communion
with the godly within the Church, continued despite Jacob's
emigration to America. In 1632 the ecclesiastical authorities
captured John Lathrop, Jacob's successor, and a large number of
members of his church at a meeting in Islington and brought them
before the High Commission accused of dishonouring God and
disobeying the King by running into the woods as if they had lived
in a time of persecution. In the English Church, the churchmen
maintained, preaching was freely available, and the sacraments
truly administered, yet this congregation had set up its own

reading, preaching, singing, and teaching, and most heinous of all, appointed its own ministers, the blind leading the blind. But the High Commissioners failed to extirpate this sort of Separatism in London. Even though Lathrop and thirty members of his congregation in their turn emigrated to America, a remnant of the congregation went on meeting under the guidance of Henry Jessey. In addition the 'ancient', strictly Separatist church which traced its origins back at least to Barrow and Greenwood contrived to keep some sort of corporate existence. The theology of these churches remained Calvinist, though already in the 1630s some members were expressing doubts concerning the validity of infant baptism and showing a preference for the baptism of adult believers.

Laudian persecution had the effect of driving reluctant conformists into semi-Separatism and semi-Separatists into outright separation. With some justification the authorities could emphasize the lowly social status and the poverty of the 'Brownist' church uncovered in Yarmouth in 1630, though even here one member was a brewer, and another, a grocer, had an estate valued at a hundred pounds. In general, however, their charge that Separatism had a particular attraction for social malcontents cannot be substantiated. Rather, the godly came from among the respectable citizens who felt themselves being compelled by the Romanizing activities of the prelates to move into partial, and sometimes into complete, separation. This progression from comprehension to separation happens to have been recorded with particular vividness in the city of Bristol. About 1670 Edward Terrill wrote the history of the congregation which had by then become the Broadmead Church, and traced its beginning back to the early years of the reign of Charles 1, when 'a people were raised up . . . to cast off the scraps of Church government [left] by the papal hierarchy, namely of lordly bishops'. Despite the oppression of their 'Egyptian taskmasters', who cited to their ecclesiastical courts any 'they knew did refrain out of conscience from their ceremonies . . . as cringing at the altar, bowing at the name of Jesus, imposing the cross, and divers other innovations', still 'those whose hearts God had touched would get together and pray, repeat their sermon-notes, and upon the Lord's day would carefully sanctify the Christian sabbath, and [perform] other such acts of living piety'. 'When they could hear of any minister that did savour of God, or of the power of godliness, they would flock to him as doves to windows . . .' In addition to their many other religious exercises, the Bristol godly were in a position to perform a unique service to their fellow sufferers throughout England by extending hospitality to families who came to the city to take ship to the New World. By 1640 the consciences of a handful of these semi-Separatists had been pressed too far. They had reached the point when they could no longer attend their parish churches which they now saw as fatally compromised, and under the leadership of Mrs Hazzard, widow of a Bristol grocer, and now wife of the zealous minister of St Ewins, five 'came to a holy resolution to separate from the worship of the world and times they lived in . . . And with godly purpose of heart joined themselves together in the Lord; only thus covenanting, that they would, in the strength and assistance of the Lord, come forth of the world, and worship the Lord more purely, persevering therein to their end.'[12]

The date of the final separation of the Church of Christ at Bristol has obvious significance. By 1640 the control of the Laudians over the laity, never absolute, could clearly be seen to be crumbling. The English government had tried to impose Divine Right episcopacy and a high version of the English Prayer Book on the Scots, and they had responded with an armed uprising. In 1640 at last Charles had no alternative but to call Parliament to raise money to meet the Scottish challenge. The Short Parliament failed to supply the King's necessities, and at this eleventh hour the Laudian party committed its final act of provocation. In Convocation the clergy took the unprecedented step of deciding to sit on after Parliament had been dissolved in order to grant the King clerical taxation and to formulate new Canons. These Canons, as well as professing that 'the most high and sacred order of kings is of divine right', and justifying all ceremonial 'innovations', now required from all clergy in England an oath approving the doctrine and discipline of the Church of England and undertaking never to 'consent to alter the government of this Church by archbishops, bishops, deans and archdeacons, etc., as it stands now established'.[13]

The Canons of 1640 illustrate yet again the blindness of the Laudian clergy to the claims of the laity within the Church. Ironically, their temporary triumph had brought about what the Elizabethan Presbyterians had never been able to achieve, a coming together of very wide sectors of the laity in opposition to the Church's ruling hierarchy. The Laudians had demonstrated themselves to be unsound in crucial matters of Calvinist theology, persecutors of godly ministers and godly lay people, the supporters of both Divine Right monarchy and Divine Right episcopacy. It is not surprising, therefore, that when the Long Parliament assembled in the autumn of 1640 the policy of the Laudian bishops was fiercely attacked and petitions began to be submitted for the abolition of episcopacy 'root and branch'. From the quiet of Herefordshire in January 1641 Lady Brilliana Harley, a gentlewoman far removed from any sympathy for 'popularity' within the Church, could write to her son: 'We at Brampton keep the day to sue to our God for his direction of the Parliament. I believe that hierarchy must down, and I hope now.' Three weeks later she added in a further letter, 'I have always believed that the Lord would purge his Church from all these things and persons, that have been such a hindrance to the free passage of his glorious gospel; and I trust, now is the time.'[14]

CHAPTER 9

IMPLEMENTING LAY SUPREMACY, 1640–1660

By 1640 Englishmen had become accustomed to having a lay governor in command of the Church for rather more than a century, but the previous fifteen years had given them a new experience of the royal supremacy. Many leading laymen had recently learnt to their cost that if the King allied himself with the clergy, then the laity's freedom of action in Church affairs could be severely limited. Their treatment at the hands of the Laudian clergy led many to demand restraints upon the King's power to act independently in religious matters and to claim supremacy over the Church for Parliament. Between 1640 and 1660 the laity in fact succeeded in attaining this dominance within the Church and resolved that from henceforth they should retain the right of ultimate decision in the definition of both faith and Church order. They regarded the Protestant clergy as their collaborators, but not as their mentors, as in 1650 Cromwell indicated in a remark to the governor of Edinburgh: 'We look at ministers as helpers of, not lords over, the faith of God's people.'[1] Laymen, however, agreed on little more than that they should have the supremacy: very soon after the Long Parliament assembled it became clear that members did not agree on how the faith of God's people should be expressed. The majority of those who continued to attend Parliament after the outbreak of the Civil War seems to have preferred an Erastian version of Presbyterianism and a uniform state Church, but even in Parliament some supported a far more loosely organized system of independent congregations. With the collapse of episcopal administration, the ruling classes in Parliament found they could no longer confine authority within the Church to themselves. The strength of sectarianism in the army in the end made the establishment of a form of Presbyterian Church which comprehended all English people an impossibility, and eventually a far less precisely defined Church emerged which allowed a wide range of Protestant opinions to coexist within its boundaries. The breadth of the English Church which developed in the 1650s and the extent of toleration both within it and without was due in no small measure to the influence of Cromwell.

Religion may not have been uppermost in the minds of those gentlemen who came together in Parliament in 1640; their own rights and privileges in both national and local government seem to have been their main concern; but few dissented from the prevailing opinion that prelacy, as it had been exercised by the Laudian bishops and their clerical supporters, must be curbed. In November 1640 Parliament set up a committee on religion which lost no time in deploring Laudian novelties, and the following month the Commons voted that Concovation had no right 'to make any constitutions, canons, or act whatsoever in matter of doctrine, discipline or otherwise, to bind clergy or laity of the land, without common consent in Parliament'. While many members contrasted primitive episcopacy favourably with Laudian prelacy, even before the end of 1640 Parliament had received the first petition calling for the extirpation of episcopacy root and branch. In the eighteen months between the summoning of the Long Parliament and the beginning of the Civil War most gentlemen in Parliament seem to have believed in the necessity for some moderate reform in the Church, a removal of Arminian innovations at the very least, and for a return to that form of Church government which they thought had existed under Elizabeth, when bishops and gentlemen had worked in harmonious co-operation to further Protestantism and punish the ungodly. The Grand Remonstrance which the Commons addressed to the King in November 1641 demonstrates this eagerness to return to a recent, though idealized, past. The Commons warned Charles against 'the bishops, and the corrupt part of the clergy, who cherish formality and superstition as the natural effects and more probable supports of their own ecclesiastical tyranny and usurpation'. These clergy, they continued, had tried 'to suppress the purity and power of religion, and such persons as were best affected to it, as being contrary to their own ends, and the greatest impediment to that change which they thought to introduce': Parliament now called upon the King to disown them.[2]

These demands by the Commons had some effect, and a month after their publication Charles sanctioned the translation of John Williams, a consistent opponent of Arminianism and Laud's chief enemy on the episcopal bench, to the archbishopric of York. Yet these royal concessions in Church affairs seemed half-hearted, and in any case came too late. In February 1642 the Commons passed the Bishops Exclusion bill, and later that spring Parliament decided to appoint an assembly of divines, nominated by the burgesses and knights of the shire, to deliberate upon Church reform. Schemes for moderating episcopacy went on being discussed in this assembly and found their apologist in the ecumenical Archbishop Ussher, but the onset of the Civil War sealed the fate of episcopacy in England for the next two decades.

It was not so much that those gentlemen who left Parliament to support the King on Charles's raising of his standard at Nottingham in August 1642 dropped their demands for reform in the Church out of loyalty, though the war understandably brought about a polarization of opinions on either side, as that those who remained with Parliament discovered constrictions upon their power to act independently in religion as in other spheres. Parliamentarians soon realized that they could not stand against the Royalist military forces without the aid of the Scots, and the Scots who had revolted against Charles's Church policy for Scotland had no sympathy at all for any plan for modified episcopacy. As the price of military aid which the English Parliamentarians needed so desperately, the Scots insisted upon the establishing of a Presbyterian Church in England. In January 1643, therefore, Parliament passed a bill abolishing episcopacy, and in September in the same year both Houses agreed to enter into the Solemn League and Covenant with the Scots and to impose this covenant upon England. The beheading of Laud in January 1645 belatedly marked the formal end of a system of Church government which had ceased to operate years earlier.

Although Parliament accepted the Solemn League and Covenant in the autumn of 1643, two and a half years were to elapse before, in the spring of 1646, it authorized the implementing of a Presbyterian system of government to replace the now hollow shell of episcopacy. The delay in establishing an English version of Presbyterianism largely resulted from the suspicions of leading laymen of any clerically dominated form of Church government, for many besides Milton came to think that 'new presbyter is but old priest writ large'. Especially during the years when they were at war with Charles, members of the Commons seem to have been quite content to assign to the Assembly of Divines the task of devising a new form of government for the Church and a liturgy to succeed that in the Book of Common Prayer, but without any intention of surrendering their final authority. The Assembly worked slowly, too

slowly for the Commons' liking, but at last in 1644 it produced
the Directory of Worship, a sober Calvinist form of service which
its compilers saw as the logical culmination of the long-drawn-out
Reformation in England. In January 1645 Parliament passed an
ordinance for the Book of Common Prayer to be replaced by the
Directory for Public Worship in every parish in England and Wales.
The laity in Parliament do not seem to have had serious reservations about the newly prescribed forms of worship, but they
exhibited the gravest concern over any attempt at reviving
clericalism. When ministers in the Assembly of Divines proposed
to give individual ministers with their elders the unrestricted right,
as in Scotland, to exclude scandalous parishioners from the sacraments, a majority in the Commons refused to grant them this
unfettered freedom. Presbyterian ministers in the Assembly bitterly
resented what they considered to be Erastian interference, but they
had to give way. Only when the Assembly reluctantly conceded a
right of appeal for those excluded from the sacraments first to
the local *classis* and then to a parliamentary committee would
Parliament agree to the setting up of Presbyterianism in England.
The Scottish observer, Robert Balie, perfectly understood the magni-
tude of the clergy's concession and referred in disgust to the 'lame,
Erastian presbytery'. This was the form of Church government,
with the laity in ultimate control, which Parliament allowed to be
put into practice in March 1646.

In all the controversy over the exact form of Presbyterianism
suitable for England, few members of Parliament had questioned
the need for one uniform state Church; their anxiety was largely
over the balance of power between clergy and laity within the
system. They intended that one exclusive form of Church should
follow another, and certainly by 1646 little remained of that
ecclesiastical organization against which the presenters of the
Grand Remonstrance had protested. The prerogative ecclesiastical
courts, through which Laud and his supporters on the episcopal
bench had been able to exert most pressure on lay and clerical
antagonists, had been the first to go; Parliament did away with the
courts of High Commission for both provinces early in 1641. The
bill abolishing episcopacy which they passed almost two years
later brought to an end any form of diocesan administration
throughout England and Wales and swept away the old type of
ecclesiastical oversight above the parochial level. Once the fighting
had ceased, Parliament dissolved cathedral corporations in the

wake of the abolition of episcopacy, setting in process a new
secularization of Church lands second in importance only to the
Dissolution of the Monasteries of the previous century. Yet in the
face of the all but irresistible demands of war and administration
Parliament nevertheless provided some augmentation for parish
livings out of the revenues of the former episcopal and capitular
lands. In the cathedral city of York, as in other similar cities, the
government created four preaching posts to take the place of the
cathedral clergy, and from late in 1645 each minister received the
handsome stipend of £150 annually out of the former revenues of
the dean and chapter; in addition the State allowed those of the
parish clergy who had stayed with their flocks a supplement which
for the first time gave to many of them a living wage. At last
those in authority were doing something to remedy the economic
disparity between the lower and higher clergy which had existed
for so long in the old Church and against which the Puritans had
complained in vain.

The years of the Civil War and those immediately following
inevitably saw much enforced mobility among the beneficed clergy.
The higher clergy lost absolutely, as Parliament deprived bishops
of their sees, deans of their deaneries, cathedral canons of their
prebends and all pluralists of the livings they held in plurality.
It did, however, permit both prebendaries and other pluralists to
keep one of their parish livings if they agreed to conform. Through
their membership of committees to examine politically or morally
scandalous ministers, leading laymen frequently could exert real
influence over the clerical personnel in their particular areas.
Anglican writers have tended to exaggerate the extent of this
clerical purge. Some beneficed parish clergy positively welcomed
the victory of Parliament and the ecclesiastical changes Parliament
introduced, while a majority of the clergy appears at least to have
acquiesced in them. It has been estimated that national or local
committees sequestered some 2425 parochial livings between 1643
and 1660 on account of the incumbent's loyalty to the King, his
'popish' innovations or devotion to the Prayer Book, his non-
residence or pluralism, or his moral inadequacy. As there were
about 9000 parishes in England at this time a change of incumbent
took place in approximately one living in three. Thus, despite the
conflicting demands of political and ecclesiastical obligations and
the pressures exerted by local committees, it seems reasonably clear
that considerably more clergy stayed in possession of their benefices

than were expelled.[3]

By the spring of 1646, when Parliament at last authorized the establishment of Presbyterianism in England, there was not only an absence of ecclesiastical organization above the parish structure, but often vacancies in those parishes where the incumbent had left out of loyalty to the King or been ejected for political or moral offences. At least in theory, many gentlemen believed that the English variant of Presbyterianism could best fill this ecclesiastical vacuum. Legally nothing now prevented the English Church from being transformed into a Presbyterian institution: for this to happen, however, individual parishes had to elect elders to exercise discipline in co-operation with the minister, these newly constituted presbyteries to form themselves into *classes* to which each parish presbytery sent representatives, while the *classes* in their turn needed to send representatives to provincial and finally to national assemblies. Although committed Presbyterians never realized their goal in its entirety and the English Church between 1646 and 1660 never became a fully functioning Presbyterian Church, in different parts of England during this period some clergy and laymen did work together to set up a form of Presbyterianism. The counties are few where local officials made no attempt to impose some formal organization above the parish level. On the one hand, records survive of active *classes* which met more or less continuously throughout the Commonwealth and Protectorate for parts of London, areas in Nottinghamshire and Derbyshire, and for Manchester and Bury and their neighbourhoods in Lancashire. Cheshire certainly had some type of classical organization, though no detailed records remain, and the same probably applies to Cornwall and Devon, and to Dorset, definitely to parts of Durham and Hampshire, perhaps to Kent and parts of Norfolk around Norwich, and perhaps also to parts of Northamptonshire, to the area of Northumberland near Newcastle, to part of Shropshire, to parts of Somerset, perhaps to parts of Surrey, and certainly to areas of Warwickshire, Wiltshire and the West Riding of Yorkshire.

When in obedience to Parliament's ruling county committees tried to activate Presbyterianism in the localities they encountered different but very real difficulties. In some parishes the incumbent showed the greatest reluctance to share his authority with lay elders; in others no lay elders would come forward to work with the minister. The Fourth London *Classis* soon had both these tendencies brought to its notice. It began keeping records in

November 1646, and by the following January received confirmation that eleven out of its fourteen constituent parishes had chosen
elders. From the first, however, the inhabitants of St Michael
Crooked Lane, proved delinquent: they had quarrelled with their
incumbent, Mr Browne, and refused to appoint elders to work with
him. The parishioners of St Margaret Fish Street presented a quite
contrary problem. They had no minister: Mr Brookes had offered
his services, but would only come to them on condition that their
lay elders gave up office, and the godly in the parish formed themselves into a gathered church. Similar conflicts arose in the North.
The Manchester *Classis* felt it necessary to confer with a minister,
Mr Clayton of Didsbury, over his objection to the 'unwarrantable-
ness of ruling elders' while at the same time finding it increasingly
hard to persuade laymen in the various parishes to agree to act as
elders. Doubtless the trouble caused by the activities of over-zealous
lay elders at Bolton made men there even less eager to seek the
eldership. The Bolton elders had been trying to compel all who
wished to receive holy communion on a Sunday to come to them
on the previous Friday to obtain a communion token. Oliver Heywood's godly father protested against the practice in the strongest
of terms, alleging before the eldership that it 'was not a divine
institution, but an human invention'. As seemed to be happening
at Bolton, objection to a particular activity of the elders could
easily develop into an objection to the very existence of the office.[4]

During the Interregnum neither the *classes* which remained
active nor the provincial assembly in London gained the necessary
civil backing to enforce obedience to their orders. They might call
upon congregations to obey their recommendations, but individual
parishes could ignore their exhortations with impunity. Though
they never ceased to encourage the voluntary operation of a Presbyterian system, more and more their chief function became the
examination of candidates for the ministry and the subsequent
ordination of those men who passed the comparatively stringent
academic and moral tests. Yet although only a shadowy form of
Presbyterianism ever operated above the parishes, and that only in
certain parts of the country and on a voluntary basis, in many
parishes throughout England the minister, sometimes together with
his elders, did exercise an attenuated form of discipline which the
incumbent and the local godly might well consider to be an
improvement upon anything which had gone before. This Angli-
cized Presbyterianism seems to have been particularly strong in

cities and towns. In York Edmund Bowles, brought to the area by
Lord Fairfax as his chaplain, sat with fellow ministers to approve
the worthiness of others to preach in the city. Bowles went on to
hold one of the four lectureships attached to the Minster and
worked in the closest collaboration with members of the corporation who enthusiastically supported him in all he did. His vigorous
oversight prevented any attempts to form independent congregations which might have disturbed the even tenor of the city's
religious life, and the corporation co-operated with the clergy to
impose compulsory church attendance upon all. In the city churches
the services took the form of those set out in the Directory : solemn
prayer conducted by the minister, readings from the Old and New
Testaments, communal psalm singing and a long and, where
possible, scholarly sermon. In fact the civic leaders maintained a
considerable continuity between the type of Calvinist worship they
had favoured in the 1630s and what they now secured. Even
gentlemen whose sympathies lay with the Royalists and Episcopalians, like Evelyn, considered it their duty to attend Sunday by
Sunday at parochial worship of this sort. Independency and the
yet more socially disruptive forms of sectarianism made into
'Presbyterians' gentlemen who subsequently vehemently denied that
they had had any such connection.

The evolution in the 1640s of this English variant of Presbyterianism, with a Calvinist type of worship but a discipline that
was little more than voluntary, came about partly because of the
political divisions among the supporters of Parliament but equally
because Presbyterianism, though the choice of many influential
Protestant clergy in the Westminster Assembly and of some important laymen in Parliament, had never been accepted as the only
alternative form of Protestantism to succeed the discredited
Episcopalian establishment. Small groups of advanced Christians
had worshipped apart from their fellows ever since the first reception of Protestantism in England, although most of these groups
failed to keep a corporate existence for very long; at least since
the publication of Browne's writings they had also been able to
claim a theoretical justification for their total or partial separation
from the national Church. Laudian innovations and the intolerance
of the Laudian bishops had induced a new growth of clandestine
religious meetings which had occasionally resulted in the emigration of congregations of the godly to the Netherlands or to the
New World. This development had greatly distressed Scottish

churchmen who from the first grasped the obstacle it would present to the setting up of the Scottish form of Presbyterianism in England. As early as the late autumn of 1640 Robert Ballie had resolved to go south to London with other Scottish ministers with the objective not only of attacking the episcopal Church system and advocating Presbyterian organization but also expressly 'to satisfy the minds of many in England who love the way of New England better than that of presbyteries used in our church'.[5]

The progressive breakdown of the bishops' control from the first calling of the Long Parliament enabled gathered churches to emerge rapidly in certain parts of England: some it seems were the conscious creation of ministers and lay people returning from exile in the Netherlands or New England, though others appear to have arisen spontaneously with the lessening of persecution. The Bristol Broadmead Church, which grew out of the reaction against Laudian innovations in the city and had few direct contacts with English churches overseas, had already entered into deliberate separation in 1640. Starting with only five covenanted members who included Mr Bacon, a young minister, as well as a countryman and a Bristol butcher and farrier, and who met at Mrs Hazzard's house at the upper end of Broad Street, the church soon increased to a hundred and sixty members from the city and surrounding countryside by June 1643. For most of this time the church had no constant minister, for Mr Bacon left them for a parish outside Bristol, yet 'not withstanding the loss of him, the church here kept together; having sometimes only the brethren of the church, that were not ministers, vulgarly so called, but only gifted, [who] did use to speak and carry on the meetings; and they multiplied and grew in the fear of the Lord'. The congregation, however, clearly felt the need of clerical direction: occasionally Mr Wroth from the church of Llanvaches in Monmouth would come over to preach to them and sometimes the 'professors' of Bristol went over to Wales to hear him and other good ministers there. 'Then there joined unto them one Mr Pennill, who had before been a minister at Leonard's [in Bristol], but being inclined to reformation was several times set on by Mrs Hazzard, like a Priscilla; so he left off his conformity and closed in with them.' The acquisition of Mr Pennill did not prove to be of much benefit to the congregation, but when the members of the church of Llanvaches with their new minister, Mr Craddock, fled to Bristol after the outbreak of the Civil War the two separated congregations united 'and after that they had the use of a small public place to themselves called [S]t Ewins, by the Tolzey, where they used to preach and celebrate the ordinance of the Lord as it was delivered. And so they continued and kept together in church fellowship, breaking bread, and prayers, until Bristol was delivered up to the king's forces.'[6]

During the two-year occupation of Bristol by the Royalists many of this Bristol church migrated to London where they worshipped in All Hallows the Great. London, indeed, very soon became a centre of Independency after the defeat of the Laudians, when the survivors of the hidden church of Henry Jessey and other less well known congregations were able to come out into the open. The former followers of Jessey finally settled with their minister in Southwark, though, despite the hostility of the civic authorities, other covenanted churches sprang up within the city. London also offered a haven to ministers who had spent much of the previous decade in exile on the Continent or in America. Dr Thomas Goodwin returned from Holland in 1640 and gathered a congregation in the parish of St Dunstan's in the East to which he ministered from 1640 to 1650. As early as 1641 Henry Burton, the rector of St Matthew Friday Street, declared in *The Protestation Protested*, 'Surely God's people must be separatists from the world and from false churches, to become a poor and holy people unto the Lord.' Three years later he saw his ideas being implemented when in his presence a Congregational church covenanted in Stepney 'to walk in all the ways of Christ held out unto them in the gospel'. In this way in London, which because of its size tended to draw the leaders of dissent, it is possible to trace both the spontaneous movement of little groups of laymen into separation and the considered advocacy of Independency by clerical leaders who had experienced congregational discipline in the New World or in Holland.[7]

One of these advocates of Congregationalism devoted himself, however, not to London but to East Anglia, and he had a decisive influence upon that part of England where Presbyterianism seems never to have gained a strong hold. In 1642 William Bridge came back from Rotterdam together with some thirty members of his English congregation, resolving to set up a gathered church immediately, though not yet clear where they should go. In November 1642 they came to Yarmouth and early in the next year secured the consent of the Rotterdam church for the appointment of Bridge as their minister. This church from the first included members who lived in Norwich, and in 1644 they obtained from the Yarmouth church the permission they had long sought to found a sister congregation in that city. From these two centres a network of gathered churches spread across Norfolk.

These churches are only a selection of the Independent congregations which had been established, or were in process of establishment, when the Assembly of Divines met in Westminster to decide upon a Church system for the nation. Both William Bridge and Thomas Goodwin participated in the Assembly and they, together with Philip Nye, Sidrach Simpson and Jeremiah Burroughes, published in 1643 *An Apologetical Narration* to defend their actions and remonstrate against any plan to impose a rigid form of Presbyterian government upon the nation. They emphasized that in their worship they confined themselves to the religious practices used in all other reformed churches: 'as public and solemn prayers for kings and all in authority etc.; the reading the scriptures of the Old and New Testament; exposition of them as occasion was; and constant preaching of the word; singing of psalms; collections for the poor etc. every Lord's day'. Indeed, there seems to be every reason to suppose that the form of service these Independents used and the form of service subsequently prescribed in the Directory and observed in the parish churches differed very little. The fundamental disagreement was over the matter of Church membership, whether the Church should be composed only of active Christians or should include the entire parish, and over the formal relationship of one church to another. Grieved with some reason at being labelled Sectaries or Brownists, the writers of the *Apologetical Narration* asserted, 'We believe the truth to lie and consist in a middle way betwixt that which is falsely charged on us, Brownism; and that which is the contention of these times, the authoritative presbyterial government in all the subordinations and proceedings of it.' Whatever the polity devised by the Assembly of Divines for the nation at large, they asked for latitude for their churches to remain free from external intervention. From this request for a special toleration, the denial of the possibility of one uniform national Church appeared a logical progression, and one that Burroughes himself made in *A Vindication* which came out in 1646. 'Where are any particular men standing church officers to the whole nation by divine institution?' he asked. 'What national worship hath Christ instituted? Doth our birth in the nation make us members of the Church? These things are so palpably plain to any that will understand, that 'tis tedious to spend time about them.'[8]

When Parliament, therefore, belatedly sanctioned the establishment of Presbyterianism in England in 1646 there already existed not only a growing number of separated churches but a developed theory which undermined the professedly biblical institution of the Presbyterian system. The foundation of one Independent church encouraged another: in 1646 Mrs Chidley set out from London to help form a local church at Bury St Edmunds, and others elsewhere followed in her footsteps. By the end of the Commonwealth period there may well have been over one hundred Congregational churches of the type described in the *Apologetical Narration* in more than twenty different English counties. Yet while men of the stature of Bridge may only have sought liberty for their own kind of Independent church, the break-up of unity made possible the appearance of churches of a far more radical and, many feared, more socially subversive type.

In *Gangraena*, published in 1646, Thomas Edwards dwelt upon the horrors of religious and social anarchy caused by the absence of any national ecclesiastical discipline. He claimed to have been sent a report from an eye witness the previous year of a love feast attended by eighty Anabaptists in a great house in Bishopsgate Street in London. At the feast five new members were baptized; afterwards the community fell to prayer, each one kneeling by himself apart. Edward Barber, their minister, went to every member in turn, men and women, and laid his hands upon their heads, praying that they might receive the Holy Ghost. (By this action, Edwards later explained, Barber gave authority to such persons as had gifts to preach publicly.) These ceremonies finished, they had eaten a meal together and after that participated in the Lord's Supper. The evening ended with a disputation over whether Christ died for all men or only for the elect. Edwards knew of other General Baptist churches in London, one conducted by Lamb, a soapboiler, in Bell Alley off Coleman Street, another to which Kiffin acted as minister. Young men and wenches flocked in particular to Lamb's meetings where such confusion reigned that a spectator might have thought he was at a play. Lamb himself had been preaching universal grace since 1644 in any church in London where he could get freedom of the pulpit and had also taught his doctrines in Guildford and Godalming and as far away as Portsmouth and performed adult baptisms there and elsewhere in Surrey and Essex. Kiffin's church also had sent out evangelists, Kiffin going in person to Kent where Edwards considered he had done much harm. These Baptist sectaries had not only penetrated counties near London, like Essex, Kent, Suffolk, Hertfordshire and Cambridgeshire, but even gone to the more remote parts of the country including Yorkshire, Bristol and Wales.

To a man like Edwards who considered a totally comprehensive, uniform, national Church absolutely necessary, the manner in which these Baptist evangelists visibly attracted the lower orders seemed likely to subvert the very basis of society. He probably did not unduly exaggerate the immediate appeal of Baptist teachings. By 1660 there may have been around three hundred Baptist congregations, although these were sharply divided in doctrinal matters between the Particular Baptists who adhered to a basically Calvinist theology and the General Baptists who preached universal salvation. Their strongholds lay in the midland and southern counties, near London and in Wales, and the two branches of Baptists taken together established three times as many churches between 1640 and 1660 as the Independents did. A prime reason for their success seems to have been that in the Baptist churches all sectors of the laity could take an active part in both the services and the ministry.

The unrestrained lay preaching associated with the sects appeared early in the army. Despite the godliness of herself and her husband, and their Parliamentarian sympathies, Mrs Hutchinson at first looked askance at the cannoniers who met privately in the Nottingham garrison, refusing to join in the public worship in the town churches but instead keeping conventicles in their own chambers. Upon Colonel Hutchinson's prompting, she began to realize that apart from their separation they were otherwise inoffensive and very zealous in their religious profession, and in the end she outstripped her husband by accepting the soldiers' arguments against infant baptism. Baptist churches flourished wherever the army established itself for long. At Hull, as at Nottingham, the ministers of the town churches opposed the preachers in the garrison for their sectarianism, and John Shaw recollected with bitterness his Separatist adversary and the darling of the soldiers, John Can. Whether they eventually adopted adult baptism or not, the soldiers seem to have especially cherished the fellowship of the gathered churches. Samuel Eaton, the apostle of Congregationalism in Lancashire and Cheshire, provides a further example of the army's influence: Colonel Robert Dukinfield brought him to the North, installed him as minister in the church which met separately in the chapel of Dukinfield Hall, and also made him pastor to the church gathered in Chester Castle. Eton went on to introduce Separatist ideas in an area otherwise strongly inclined to Presbyterianism.

Seen in this army context, Cromwell's broad religious tolerance becomes more readily understandable. He shocked gentlemen not connected with the army, and Scottish army officers, by suggesting in 1644 that a soldier who had refused the Solemn League and Covenant and was suspected of being an Anabaptist might yet prove a loyal officer: 'Sir, the State in choosing men to serve them takes no notice of their opinions; if they be willing faithfully to serve them, that satisfies.' In fact, the State as embodied in Parliament had by no means reached this advanced position of disinterestedness, but in many respects the army had, and Parliament dared not ignore the army. It may well have been through the intervention of Cromwell and his fellow officers that the Commons in the autumn of 1644 resolved that the committee appointed to treat with the Scottish commissioners and the Assembly of Divines over a form of Church government should 'endeavour the finding out some ways how far tender consciences, who cannot in all things submit to the common rule which shall be established, may be borne with, according to the word, and as may stand with the public peace'.[9]

In consequence, when the attenuated form of Presbyterianism came to be implemented, it was hampered not only by the ruling classes as represented in Parliament, who feared a new manifestation of clericalism, but also by the army which saw in Presbyterianism a possible weapon which might be used to curb the extended freedom of religious belief and practice which the soldiers had already achieved. Between 1646, when Presbyterianism seemed formally to have been accepted as the national Church, and 1653, when Cromwell assumed power, Parliament and the army collided time and again over the degree of toleration which could be allowed to Protestants outside the national Church. Late in 1646 Parliament passed a bill for the punishment of blasphemy and an ordinance against preaching by unordained men, the 'mechanic preachers' of the sects; the next year the army pressed Parliament for greater liberty. In his Heads of Proposals of June 1647, Ireton suggested some sort of toleration for all Christians except Catholics;

he got nowhere as the King rejected his proposals. Again in the Agreement of the People which came out of the Putney Debates of the autumn of the same year, the soldiers conceded the concept of a national Church but only in conjunction with the principle that there should be no compulsion of religion; all Christians might be tolerated except Catholics and Episcopalians. Parliament reacted early in 1648 by reiterating the necessity for the establishment of the modified form of Presbyterianism and by passing a savage new Blasphemy Act which prescribed the death penalty for atheists and those who questioned the doctrine of the Trinity, and imprisonment for those who taught a belief in universal grace or denied the validity of the sacraments. The army turned the tide decisively in its favour in December 1648 when, with Pride's Purge, it excluded the most committed political Presbyterians from Parliament. Nevertheless, even with the removal of some of the army's most intransigent opponents, the Rump still remained more conservative in religious matters than the army. In August 1650 it passed yet another Blasphemy Act directed particularly against Ranters, Familists, Adamites, Seekers and Levellers, all sectaries, in fact, suspected of aiming to overturn the accepted social morality. Parliament, however, did grant relief for 'religious and peaceable people' with the repeal of the Elizabethan Acts to enforce uniformity, to compel attendance at the established Church and to retain the Queen's subjects in their allegiance. All men and women had still to go to some form of religious worship on a Sunday, but they could now choose for themselves what form this worship should take. With the setting up in 1652 of the Committee for the Propagation of the Gospel, Parliament recognized the need for supervision over the churches and provided for local combined lay and clerical committees to oversee the parish churches and scrutinize the credentials of ministers. It intended that the Church thus loosely organized, adhering to certain fundamental Protestant tenets, should become the legally recognized Church of the nation. This in practice constituted the Church which Cromwell both enlarged and sustained.

In one sense Cromwell realized the ideal for which laymen had been striving for generations: liberty for every individual to determine his own religious destiny without external coercion. In another sense, he stood far in advance of most members of the ruling classes for he not only worked for freedom of religious observance for himself and other gentlemen but wished this freedom to apply to all men however humble. The fear of social anarchy, which so many Parliamentarians believed would come from permitting a plurality of religious opinions, seems to have had little weight with him. In his speech at the opening of the Barebones Parliament in 1653, the very language of which reflects his intense feeling, Cromwell besought the members to have a regard to the sincere religious beliefs of all men. 'We should be pitiful. Truly, this calls us to be very much touched with the infirmities of the saints; that we may have a respect unto all, and be pitiful and tender towards all, though of different judgements.' This passionate concern, which he never lost, that all men who faithfully tried to follow Christ should have the liberty so to do led him to widen very considerably the formal toleration permitted by the Instrument of Government. This laid down, in itself a substantial concession;

> That such as profess faith in God by Jesus Christ (though differing in judgement from the doctrine, worship, or discipline publicly held forth) shall not be restrained from, but shall be protected in, the profession of the faith, and exercise of their religion; so as they abuse not this liberty to the civil injury of others, and to the actual disturbance of the public peace on their parts : provided this liberty be not extended to Popery, nor Prelacy, nor to such as, under the profession of Christ, hold forth and practise licentiousness.

During the five years that Cromwell governed England there can have been few Christians of any kind, Catholics and Episcopalians included, who did not benefit from his broad tolerance.[10]

Cromwell's sympathy for the religious aspirations of all men in whatever form they might manifest themselves did not prejudice him against the national Church so long as its ministers did not attempt to compel the consciences of those who did not belong to it; indeed, he proved to be the defender of that establishment. The zealots in the Barebones Parliament, who considered that the remuneration of the clergy should be an obligation voluntarily undertaken by individual congregations, gained only limited support from him. Antiquated and inequitable as many recognized the tithing system to be, he would not allow its abolition until a new form of payment of the clergy could be devised, and Parliament never formulated an alternative scheme. By keeping the old system of tithing Cromwell did much to conciliate gentry opinion, since from the Reformation onwards many recipients of tithes had been lay landlords. Yet although society escaped the upheaval which any new scheme for clerical payment would have involved, the Cromwellian government continued to advance proposals initiated a decade earlier to ensure that all parish clergy had a more adequate and fair income. A committee of the Barebones Parliament made the suggestion that a committee of godly persons should carry out visitations and have powers, among others, to unite small and poorly endowed parishes, and this long-needed rationalization of the parochial structure in England did begin to take effect. In York, for example, the Commonwealth commissioners had already drawn up a plan in 1650 for amalgamating the twenty-five surviving city parishes to form eight parishes, each of which would then have sufficient resources to maintain a godly, learned minister: now central and local authority together made some serious efforts to implement the proposals.

Despite his very real reluctance to force consciences, Cromwell understood the necessity for some form of organization in the very loosely structured state Church and carried out, in a slightly altered guise, the Rump's scheme for county committees to look into the credentials of those about to be admitted to livings and to expel scandalous ministers already in possession. An Ordinance of March 1654 created a national commission of Tryers to approve candidates put forward by patrons and another commission of Ejectors who could remove unworthy clergy from benefices. The Board of Tryers in typically Cromwellian fashion included laymen as well as clerics and maintained a balance between Presbyterians, Independents and Baptists. Yet this diversity of doctrine did not inhibit action, and even Baxter, who would have preferred a far more strict, ministerially controlled form of discipline, admitted that

> they did abundance of good to the Church. They saved many a congregation from ignorant, ungodly, drunken teachers . . . so that, though they were many of them somewhat partial for the Independents, Separatists, Fifth Monarchy men and Anabaptists, and against the Prelatists and Arminians, yet so great was the benefit above the hurt which they brought to the Church, that many thousands of souls blessed God for the faithful ministers whom they let in, and grieved when the Prelatists afterward cast them out again . . .[11]

The clergy whom the Tryers permitted to take up or retain livings in the Church of the Protectorate held views on theology and Church government which stretched from moderate Episcopacy to forms of Anabaptism. Many ministers, episcopally ordained, found it possible to serve in this Church. Some actually preferred a non-episcopal system, others, like Thomas Fuller, who thought that episcopal government most nearly approached the form prescribed by God and observed in the primitive Church, acknowledged that it had not been kept in otherwise blameless reformed churches abroad. Men of his temper resolved that if they might not have that form of ecclesiastical government they most cherished they would conform to Presbyterian government and live quietly and contentedly under it. At the other end of the spectrum the Calvinist John Tombes, minister of Leominster, made no effort to move outside the established Church when about 1646 he changed his views radically on the admissibility of infant baptism. Although he sought re-baptism for himself, he went on to hold the living of Bewdley, his birthplace, and from there conducted preaching missions to spread his Particular Baptist tenets.

Belief in adult baptism did not always involve belief in the necessity of a gathered church, though clergy and laity alike often held the two doctrines in conjunction. The breadth of the Commonwealth Church is even more strikingly illustrated by those Independent clergy who accepted office within it. Over 170 Independent clergy may have received preferment at some time during the Commonwealth; and while about half of these held town lectureships, chaplaincies or academic posts which did not carry with them a cure of souls, at least 130 Independents went into parochial livings. Perhaps under the guidance of William Bridge, thirty clergy in Norfolk and Suffolk combined a pastorate of a gathered church with a living in the state Church. The arrangement indeed had precedents, for throughout the previous century zealous ministers had tried to serve their whole parish while reserving their particular exercises of prayer and exhortation for those of the godly who turned especially to them. It could, nevertheless, create practical difficulties. In 1649 the vestry of St Stephen's Coleman Street, London, apparently amicably agreed not only to permit the re-instatement of John Goodwin as their minister but also to share their church with his gathered congregation whom they allowed to use the church building once the parochial sermon had ended. Matters proceeded less harmoniously in St Bartholomew's parish when Cromwell appointed Philip Nye to the living: in 1657 the parishioners would not pay tithes to their minister because he had refused to give them the sacrament and to baptize their children unless they would first join his separated church; they also protested strongly against their church being filled with strangers. William Greenhill, who became vicar of Stepney considerably after he had set up a church of Christ there, acted more tactfully towards his parish, taking his part in the administration of poor relief and concerning himself over the repair of the church building, and the two congregations seem to have shared his ministry in peace.

These Independent churches may have been rather exceptional in that their ministers patently did not live solely upon the voluntary gifts of the brethren. Beyond these churches on the periphery of the Commonwealth Church, definably linked to it if only through the person of their minister, there were the exclusive churches totally separate, on the one hand some Independent churches, Arminian and Calvinist Baptist churches, and the congregations of the more radical sects, on the other the 'Prelatists' and the Catholics. Henry Denne, although for a time he derived some of his maintenance from the Disbrowe living of Eltisley in Cambridgeshire, still, according to Edwards, preached much against tithes and in consequence attracted many to join his Arminian Baptist church based upon Fenstanton. He drew his congregation from a wide area of Huntingdonshire and Cambridgeshire, and between 1645, the year of the church's foundation, and 1656 the records list the baptism of 178 adult believers. Fairly often the elders of this church had cause to rebuke their members for joining in public worship with the 'Church of England', as they called the established Church of the Commonwealth. Dr Chamberlen's Baptist church, the annals of which have been preserved for two tumultuous years between 1652 and 1654, practised a similar type of exclusiveness. Here Chamberlen, who had acted as Court Physician to James I, Charles I and their wives, completely dominated the group. A highly educated man and a convinced upholder of lay preaching, Chamberlen indulged in bitter doctrinal wrangling with his fellow elders, and the congregation suffered frequent secessions. Some members of this congregation also strayed by taking their children to be 'sprinkled' by the Presbyterians.

Some of the Independent churches with a popular following, and particularly the Baptist churches, in the Commonwealth period endured what the church at Cockermouth described as a great onslaught from the upsurge of Quakerism which they feared would sweep away all the churches in the nation. The Fenstanton elders constantly came across lapsed Baptists who had forsaken the saints and were asserting in 1651 that they had grown to perfection and become gods and denied the ordinances of prayer, preaching, baptism and the breaking of bread. These illumined ones, who put personal inspiration above the scriptures, provided a rich harvest for Quaker evangelists. With the early Quakers, who on principle disrupted the services of other Protestant churches, refused to observe the social conventions and themselves had no formal worship and no outward sacraments, the dissidence of dissent seemed to have reached its logical extreme. George Fox in the end succeeded in imposing order upon the apparent anarchy but not before the popularity of radical Quakerism brought about a movement towards unity among the far less socially disruptive religious denominations.

Only the Prelatists and the Catholics seem to have been untouched by the ecumenism of the 1650s. The Protestant clergy who remained in England between 1642 and 1660, and yet would not contemplate any sort of association with the Commonwealth Church, constituted a very small minority of those who had been episcopally ordained before the Civil War, and the number of laymen who joined them in total separation seems to have been even smaller, and notably socially exclusive. At least among these laymen Royalism appears to have brought about a newly awakened attachment to the Book of Common Prayer. In the private chapels of some Royalist gentlemen such as Sir Robert Shirley of Staunton Harold in Leicestershire, and in hidden congregations in London, the Prayer Book service continued to be used, on occasions with the connivance of the Cromwellian government; when he visited London, Evelyn could nearly always find an Episcopalian service and preaching. In their form of semi-secret organization these Episcopalians very much resembled the Catholics who, despite their fears, did not fall victim to a fresh and more severe persecution with the triumph of the Puritans: they, just as the Prelatists, benefited from the *de facto* Cromwellian toleration. Cromwell personally withstood the attempts of his later Parliaments to introduce new laws against Catholic recusancy and could with some justice claim to the French ambassador that he had plucked many of his co-religionists from the fires of persecution which in former times had tyrannized over their consciences.

The government, significantly, considered Catholics to be less politically unreliable than Prelatists, though it never fully trusted either group: neither, it now seems, attracted many members below the gentry. The intolerance shown by gentlemen towards the much less hierarchical and less clerically dominated separated churches may have been motivated as much by a desire for social control as by a desire for theological uniformity. Those accustomed to rule the nation both in Parliament and in their local areas evidently were very suspicious of what the populace might do away from the open assemblies of the parish churches, and they used economic pressure to prevent their dependents from going over to dissent. In Cambridgeshire one man sympathetic to the Fenstanton church dared not commit himself since, if he did, he feared his landlord would have him turned out of his farm; other widows and poor members of this congregation frequently fell away to their parish churches partly because in some villages attendance at public worship was a necessary qualification for poor relief. Cromwell, striving to maintain toleration, had to fight against gentlemen who had become increasingly convinced, after episodes of Quaker radicalism, that religious tolerance led inevitably to the dissolution of society as they knew it.

In the face of extreme radical sects, more moderate Protestant clerics also sought a greater ecclesiastical unity, and Baxter, and others working independently, took to sponsoring the Voluntary Associations to fill this need. In Worcestershire a company of 'honest, godly, serious, humble ministers' began to meet under Baxter's direction to discuss cases of discipline. A similar gathering came together in Cumberland and there were associations in Wiltshire, Dorset, Somerset, Hampshire, Essex and elsewhere: 'a great desire of concord began to possess all good people in the land, and our breaches seemed ready to heal'.[12]

Yet neither the eagerness of the more traditional Protestant clergy to regain a greater control over the religious activities of the laity, nor the wish of the influential laymen to restrain what they thought to be the religious licence of the lower orders had much chance of success so long as Cromwell lived to perform the office of a constable keeping the peace among the godly of different judgements and preventing them from coming to blows like braggards quarrelling in the street. Despite social and ecclesiastical pressure all sorts of men and women became accustomed to freedom of choice in religion. The vestry of St Lawrence Jewry in London in 1649 required their new vicar, as a condition of appointment to the living to which they held the presentation, 'to preach twice every Lord's day, besides once on the fast days, to administer the sacraments duly, and that of the Lord's supper (as heretofore) once every month. To admit all of his parish to that table that desire it, and are not known to be either grossly ignorant, or notoriously known to be of ill and scandalous life.' In this case the local laity, acting corporately, could impose real restrictions upon their minister. In a no less fundamental way lay people individually questioned clerical authority. The elders of the Fenstanton church reproved as very erroneous two village women of Over who had told them that those who believed the ways of the Baptist church to be true should walk in them, but also asserted that those who did not so regard them might yet walk in the way of God. Here some of the laity seem to have reconciled themselves to a wide diversity of doctrine and resented clerical attempts to enforce any type of uniformity. In Cambridgeshire, again, Widow Wiggs rejected Henry Denne's teaching that Christ died for all men : in London Mistress Browne of Limehouse left Greenhill's church in Stepney precisely because the pastor had declared that 'man hath not power of himself to do anything', and 'that God had made everything for himself, even the wicked for the day of evil'. She migrated to John Goodwin's church where she could hear in abundance the Arminian theology she favoured. Evidently many of the laity had chosen not uniformity but religious pluralism. Many others no longer felt the need of a minister to instruct them. All these individualists could enter fully into the thinking of Francis Rous who wrote in 1657 :

When Christ speaks to thee to follow him one way, thou mayest not with Peter make quarrels and questions concerning John's other way : for so mayest thou receive Peter's answer from the Master : 'What is that to thee? Follow thou me.' It is the Master's part to allot the way and work of his disciples, and therefore let both Peter and John walk that different way, to which their Master hath differently directed them.[13]

Attempts to limit religious liberty came quickly after Cromwell's death. The Parliament of Richard Cromwell, which sat in the early months of 1659, tried to re-establish a national Calvinist Church and repress dissent, and the Commons seized the chance to elaborate on the errors which had arisen through the laxity of the civil authorities who had had the duty of maintaining the purity of public worship and doctrine. After Richard Cromwell's resignation the revived Rump also voiced similar sentiments, but it clashed with the army, as it had in the previous decade, and again because of pressure from the army found it politic to profess freedom of conscience. When, however, early in 1660 Monck restored the Long Parliament religious reaction could appear in the open. Parliament once more declared the Westminster Confession to be the faith of the nation and re-affirmed the Covenant: in March 1660, only weeks before Charles II returned, members even took in hand the division of the country afresh into Presbyterian *classes*. Parliament clearly still upheld its right to decide the religious fate of the country, but now a majority of its members preferred to ally with the moderate Protestant clergy to ensure social stability rather than allow freedom of religion for all with its dreaded consequence of social upheaval. Feeling in Parliament against both Papists and Prelatists remained strong, and the resurrection of the old Episcopal Church seemed highly unlikely; yet between May 1660 and St Bartholomew's day 1662 a remarkable revolution took place. That an apparently resurgent Laudian Church could be brought back in 1662 might suggest that the years 1640 to 1660 had been entirely without lasting influence, but this would be to confuse the image with reality. The Anglican Church of 1662 was an Anglican Church with a difference. The Cavalier Parliament decided for an episcopal establishment but, as events soon demonstrated, in this restored Anglican Church the governing classes had now acquired an overriding control.

CHAPTER 10

EPILOGUE: THE ACHIEVEMENT OF
LAY POWER IN THE CHURCH

In 1662 Parliament actively participated in the re-establishment of a Church in which former Laudian clerics seemed to have achieved complete command, and historians of dissent have with some justice described the years 1660 to 1688 as the great period of the Puritan persecution. Yet in 1689 Parliament granted limited toleration to Protestant dissenters. These apparently contradictory trends within a single generation can only be explained in relation to the apprehensions and prejudices of the ruling classes which, soon after the Restoration, resulted in the passing of a series of harsh laws against dissenters by the Cavalier Parliament. An Anglican Church, seemingly more exclusive than ever before, came back in 1662, but on terms under which Parliament kept the ultimate control, as its subsequent actions clearly demonstrated. In its attempt to re-impose a Protestant uniformity upon the nation as a whole, Parliament succeeded much less well. Despite the severe penalties prescribed by Acts collectively known as the Clarendon Code, and despite fairly savage, though intermittent, persecution in various part of England, lay people in general refused to give up that diversity in religious practice which they had been in process of gaining, to some extent by default, ever since the Henrician Reformation, and had enjoyed freely since 1640. As the passive resistance of the Dissenters between 1660 and 1685 showed, the passage of time had made the ideal of uniformity in religion an anachronism, and in 1689 Parliament, in granting a degree of religious toleration, grudgingly conceded what had already become a reality.

The apparent revival of Laudian clericalism in 1662 came about largely because of the failure of the great majority of the clergy of the Caroline Church to maintain a separate existence between 1640 and 1660. Most parish ministers ordained by bishops before 1642 conformed either willingly or reluctantly to the various parliamentary settlements of the period of the Civil War and Interregnum. Perhaps in as many as three-quarters of the parishes in England the incumbent survived the Civil War in possession of his living: the Laudians bore the brunt of Parliament's hostility, and they had occupied the higher posts of the Church, the bishoprics and cathedral dignities, far more than the parishes. When, therefore, Parliament abolished episcopacy and cathedral corporations the holders of episcopal and capitular offices had been expelled, if they had not fled earlier because of their loyalty to the King. Many of these ecclesiastics could not in conscience conform to the Parliamentarian religious changes and, especially after the death of Charles I, lived in retirement in England or joined Charles II in exile. Although some of the bishops who stayed behind in England throughout the Commonwealth continued to exercise some of their episcopal functions, such as ordaining to the ministry those candidates who sought them out, they recognized that the *de facto* toleration they received depended upon their good behaviour; even hitherto committed Laudians among them held back from organizing a Church in opposition to the national Church. What theological direction existed among the Episcopalians in England came not from the bishops but from a group of High Churchmen associated with Hammond, Sheldon and Morley and other scholars and apologists who had not previously obtained high office. In spite of the promptings of this party, and of the pressure of vociferous churchmen at the court of Charles II led by Cosin and Bramhall and supported by Clarendon, the episcopal succession almost died out in England through inanition. Three times in the 1650s Clarendon tried to get the bishops still in England to meet to perpetuate their order, but made no progress at all. Since they benefited personally from the toleration established by Cromwell, they hesitated to offend his government and bring attention to themselves by such provocative action. Consequently by the beginning of 1660 considerably more than half the twenty-seven English and Welsh sees had fallen vacant by death: only ten bishops survived, and most of them were over seventy years old.

Because of the virtual eclipse of the episcopate in England during the Commonwealth and Protectorate, when Charles II returned in the early summer of 1660 he had little alternative but choose his ecclesiastical advisers largely from the Laudians who had shared his exile. It has been argued that, while Charles was making declarations in favour of toleration and permitting negotiations to proceed with the leading Presbyterians for the creation of a broad Protestant Church, from the beginning these clerics worked consciously for the restoration of a Laudian Church. Certainly whether by intention or accident, the turn of events furthered the High Churchmen's cause. The King did offer bishoprics to Baxter, Calamy and Reynolds, and deaneries to other leading Commonwealth clerics, which most eventually declined, but behind this front the Episcopalian zealots seized the opportunity of bringing back the institutions of the old Church. With Sheldon and Morley, now respectively bishops of London and Worcester, in power at court most of the influential bishoprics went to the former Laudian exiles. Charles rewarded Cosin with Durham, Laney with Peterborough, Henchman with Salisbury and Sanderson with Lincoln: by January 1661 all the English sees had been filled save two.

The King made most of these episcopal appointments while the Convention Parliament was still sitting, a Parliament which in the autumn of 1660 tried vigorously to protect Puritan parish incumbents. To calm their fears Charles issued his Declaration of Indulgence, though the Laudians seem never to have considered this as more than a temporary political expedient. Just before the end of the year Puritans in the Commons attempted to get the royal declaration passed into law, but failed by a few votes, and the King dissolved this Parliament before it could intervene further in religious matters. The elections for the new Parliament held in the spring of 1661 showed a remarkable reversal of opinion among the governing classes. London, as anticipated, returned four Presbyterians as its representatives, but was quite out of line with most of the rest of the country which almost without exception chose Royalists and supporters of the old Church. Perhaps partly as a gesture towards conciliating London opinion Charles authorized the setting up of the Savoy Conference where he hoped Commonwealth clerics and Laudian divines might yet discover some common ground. In fact at the Savoy, Baxter and the other leaders of the Puritan clergy soon realized their weakness, finding themselves little more than suppliants before the supremely confident Anglican churchmen: before the Cavalier Parliament even met the Church of England had in all essentials already been restored in its old form.

The mood of this Parliament which assembled in May 1661 proved to be vindictively Anglican. It began by ordering the burning of the Covenant and required its members to receive communion kneeling, so once again making religious observance a test of political loyalty. It approved a bill allowing the bishops to return to the House of Lords, and, though the Savoy Conference remained in session, introduced another bill to bring back the Elizabethan Prayer Book. The government, afraid of civil disturbance, now tried to restrain the Royalists, and the King adjourned Parliament before a bill for uniformity could be carried by the Commons. For the first time since the Restoration the King summoned Convocation to meet simultaneously with Parliament to discuss conformity, and, significantly, Parliament looked upon this body, not the Savoy Conference, as representative of English churchmen. When Parliament and Convocation came together again in the late autumn, the Commons appeared in an even more intransigently Anglican temper and members called for drastic action against Commonwealth clergy who would not conform without reservation. They approved the Prayer Book presented to them by Convocation, virtually the Prayer Book of 1559 with minor adjustments to cope with the disruptions of the previous twenty years, and went on to pass the Act of Uniformity which required episcopal ordination of all who held office in the Church and prescribed the use of the Prayer Book in public worship, exclusive of all other forms, from St Bartholomew's day 1662. Between the passing of the Act of Uniformity in May 1662 and the following August some members of the Government, particularly Clarendon, feared the political consequences of widespread ejections of Puritan ministers and advocated some kind of temporary indulgence to avoid confrontations, but neither Sheldon at the head of the Laudian clergy, nor the greater part of the Commons would countenance compromise. So at St Bartholomew tide 936 ministers were deprived for Nonconformity: taken together with those ministers who had already been forced out of their livings since May 1660 this gives a total of perhaps 1800 clergy who lost their benefices.

The Acts concerning religion which Parliament sanctioned during the remainder of this decade continued to illustrate the now firm belief of many gentlemen that religious dissent could be equated with political subversion, and members with mounting shrillness tried to enforce conformity through Parliament. The Conventicle Act of 1664 forbade the holding of meetings for religious worship outside the established Church apart from family gatherings. The Five Mile Act prohibited ministers ejected under the Act of Uniformity from coming within five miles of the parish they had previously served. The new Conventicle Act of 1670 demonstrates the degree of intolerance felt by many members of the Commons.

Despite the known wishes of the King, under this Act a Justice of the Peace sitting alone had the power to hear a case concerning those who had met illegally for religious worship, and to impose a fine of £10 upon a layman; he could fine a nonconformist minister £20, as well as punish the owner of the house where the meeting had been held, and send to prison or seize the property of those who could not pay.

Yet Parliament soon showed that this apparent triumph of the High Churchmen was little more than a mirage: the Church to which members of the Commons professed such devotion diverged fundamentally from the Laudian ideal. Undoubtedly some gentlemen had been won over to a genuine admiration of the Anglican Church because of the sufferings of its clergy between 1640 and 1660, and in the early Parliaments they displayed an enthusiasm for the Church's defence such as would have been inconceivable among the vast majority of the gentry a generation earlier. This capture of the hearts and minds of the younger gentlemen by the Episcopalians may have happened in the 1650s when landowners often gave a refuge in their households to sequestered Episcopalian clergy. Walker, the contemporary chronicler of the troubles of the Episcopalians, believed that young Henry Yelverton subsequently grew up to be a loyal member of the Church of England because his Parliamentarian father, Sir Christopher Yelverton, chanced to befriend Bishop Morton of Durham and made him tutor to his son. Yet it is difficult not to see the intolerant Anglicanism of the members of the Cavalier Parliament more as a means of revenge for previous political defeats and hardships, and as a means of inflicting punishment upon their former political victors, than as an expression of piety in however misguided a form. Whatever their professions their actions proclaimed that the members of the Cavalier Parliament had no intention of restoring to the Church in 1662 the legislative, economic or, above all, the political powers which it had possessed under Laud. The propertied classes indeed wished to re-establish the alliance between parson and squire, but now meant this alliance to be one in which the squire without question had the upper hand.

The Restoration Church settlement can most appropriately be considered as the achievement of an increasingly assertive Parliament. Parliament would not countenance the bringing back of the prerogative ecclesiastical courts, and particularly not the revival of the Court of High Commission. In 1640 the Commons had been bitterly affronted by the Crown's attempt, with the connivance of the churchmen, to tax the clergy through prolonging Convocation after the dissolution of Parliament. This caused. Parliament after the Restoration explicitly to disallow by statute all the canons passed by this Convocation with the result that ecclesiastics after 1660, in default of any more modern canons, had to govern the Church through the outdated Canons of 1604. Bishops indeed regained their seats in the House of Lords in 1661 but were soon made to realize that successive governments expected them to elevate their parliamentary duties above all others. They may have thought of themselves as servants of the Church, but they had to accept being considered the government's servants first. As the number of parliamentary sessions increased in the second half of the seventeenth century, to become almost annual by 1700, so did the amount of time the government reckoned the bishops should spend away from their dioceses on parliamentary duties in London. The general disposition of returning churchmen in 1660 seems to have been reactionary and they positively wanted all Church affairs to revert to their 1640 state. Yet even if their attitudes had favoured innovations, there would have been little chance of the Commons permitting them to embark upon the administrative, judicial or financial reforms that the antiquated structure of the Church so urgently needed.

Parliament, in fact, had never intended to restore to the Church powers which in the last resort it could not control. From the very moment of the King's return, Peter Heylyn, Laud's disciple and biographer, had the foresight to understand that the churchmen had as much to fear from their lay friends as from their Puritan adversaries. 'Questionless,' he wrote in a letter to Sheldon in April 1660, 'some busy members of the House of Commons will thrust themselves into concernments of religion, when they shall find no Convocation sitting to take care thereof.' To curb lay ambitions he urged the immediate re-establishment of Convocation, but Convocation no longer retained in practice the authority he thought it had. In 1661 its members may well have held back from making major changes in the Prayer Book, particularly from substituting the far more Arminian Prayer Book Laud had tried to impose upon the Scots in place of the Elizabethan Prayer Book, out of fear of antagonizing their allies in the House of Commons. As matters stood, the Commons only agreed to accept Convocation's revision of the Prayer Book without debating the proposed

changes by a vote of 96 to 90, going on to make a clear reservation
of their right to discuss any future changes in religion. As in 1646,
when Parliament had refused to give ministers unlimited power to
implement the Presbyterian system of Church government, so in
1662 laymen let it be seen that the final decision over both doctrine
and Church government rested with Parliament.

When the Archbishop, on the King's command, called Convocation in 1661, Sheldon, the chief actor behind the aged Archbishop
Juxon, hoped that it would breathe new life into the decayed
discipline of the Church. Some clergy proposed re-issuing the non-
contentious items from the Canons of 1640 in order to strengthen
the Church's arm; others wanted a reform of the exercise of
excommunication as a judicial penalty and a closer association
of ecclesiastical with civil punishment; but Convocation again did
not go forward with the revision, perhaps to avoid provoking a
clash with Parliament. This indecision lessened the Church's prestige
still further. It had forfeited prerogative courts through which it
had previously overawed the laity, and its ancient courts, which
did come back, had no laws to administer adapted to deal with
the conditions of the later seventeenth century or penalties to
inflict which any longer raised real apprehension or caused much
hardship to the upper reaches of lay society. Parliament ensured
that all the new laws passed against Nonconformists should be
enforced in the Common Law courts, and the business of the
ecclesiastical courts, apart from the still numerous testamentary
and tithe cases, slowly withered away.

Heylyn in his letter to Sheldon in the spring of 1660 went on to
counsel him to take especial care 'to prevent the laity from bringing
the clergy into taxes and payments with them, constantly practised
since the first beginning of the late Long Parliament, [and] not
otherwise to be prevented than by having a bill of subsidy ready
to be presented to the King in the name of the clergy, and by the
King to be delivered unto such of his learned council as shall be
members of that house, before the Commons enter upon that
consideration'. He obviously realized what course of action the
Church needed to take to keep its privileges, but the time had
passed when it had the strength to assert its right to be treated
financially as a separate estate of the realm. In 1664, it seems by
an oral agreement between Clarendon and Sheldon, who had
succeeded as primate on Juxon's death, the clergy surrendered
their right to tax themselves in Convocation. Sheldon may have

agreed to this concession in order to escape a new governmental survey of clerical incomes, thinking that, if the clergy in future were to be taxed by Parliament, he could at least see that they were taxed on the outdated assessment of the Henrician *Valor Ecclesiasticus* and not on a modern valuation. Nonetheless, although he may in some degree have protected clerical livelihoods, this compromise made yet further inroads upon the Church's independence. In the generation between 1664 and the Revolution, Convocations, though formally summoned, conducted no ecclesiastical business of any importance. Churchmen could no longer place any economic pressure upon the Crown and, indirectly, upon Parliament. Yet the decline of Convocation cannot be entirely attributed to lay assertiveness; the clergy themselves must bear some blame. As late as 1689 William and Mary instructed Convocation to deliberate on reform of the liturgy and on the revision of the old canons in order to accommodate them to a Church to which all Englishmen were no longer compelled to belong, but divisions within the two houses of Convocation led to a stalemate. The Convocations which met under Queen Anne similarly degenerated into bitter wrangles between the houses, now consciously modelling themselves upon the Houses of Parliament. This political deadlock in Anne's reign resulted in the failure of Convocation to act at all during the remainder of the eighteenth century until its revival in the radically different circumstances of the Victorian era. The lapse of Convocation, brought about in no small part by the surrender of the right of taxation in 1664, allowed Parliament yet again to extend its authority at the expense of the spiritual power. Legislatively, judicially, as well as financially, the Restoration Church had been forced to capitulate to the laity in Parliament, a far cry from the Laudian concept of an independent Church ruled by the King in partnership with his bishops.[1]

Yet although after 1662 the laity in Parliament on every front achieved this ascendancy over the clergy, they in their turn discovered that they did not have an unlimited power to enforce conformity upon the laity in the nation as a whole. Parliament could pass an Act of Uniformity in 1662, but it still could not resolve the old objections to the ceremonies contained in the Book of Common Prayer, and these objections after the freedom of the Commonwealth period had rooted themselves even more deeply among the laity in general. Attempts to reassert the dignity and authority of the episcopate after the Restoration attracted the populace little more than Laud's ceremonialism had done; indeed some now even professed to find the bishops' antics amusing. Pepys, after watching the elaborate service for the translation of Accepted Frewen from the see of Lichfield to the archbishopric of York on 4 October 1660, commented on the bishops' reception by the Londoners: 'But, Lord, at their going out, how people did most of them look upon them as strange creatures, and few with any kind of love or respect.' These bishops and the clergy who conformed after August 1662 faced the unenviable task of trying to bring the laity back to conformity, and they soon found that they could not necessarily rely on the support even of those who had voted for uniformity in Parliament.[2]

As before 1640 so after 1662 much Nonconformity remained within the established Church, and the very structure of the Church continued to help perpetuate it. The laity's old dislike of baptism with the sign of the cross, kneeling in church, particularly at the receipt of communion, of a distinctive garb for their clergy, all again came to the fore. Some of the people showed a considerable unwillingness to submit their children for public baptism and evaded the ceremonies by asking for a private service. The rector of Clayworth waxed indignant at this apparently new stratagem, reporting how his parishioners requested private baptism on every possible occasion, since then neither surplice, nor godparents, nor the sign of the cross need be used. The reluctance many of the laity had displayed during the Commonwealth to take part in the sacrament of holy communion continued long after 1662. Ralph Josselin, the very imperfectly conformist incumbent of Earl's Colne in Essex, gave communion to only twelve of his parishioners on Easter day in 1665, and here it definitely seems that many of his flock held back rather than submit to an examination of their morals by the minister. Elsewhere refusal to communicate can more positively be linked to dislike of the newly restored ceremonies. At St Helen's in London the congregation would not take communion kneeling from Kidder, their recently instituted minister, and Bishop Henchman advised him not to withhold the sacrament from them on this account. As late as 1681 a hostile observer reported that John Conant, vicar of All Saints, Northampton, another Commonwealth incumbent who had conformed only after years of self-questioning, had been conducting conventicles in his house. He alleged that Conant had given communion to his people sitting, and that he had then had the audacity to certify that those who had so received had taken communion according to the usage of the Church of England.

The re-appearance of the surplice in particular aroused the laity's suspicions. Dean Glanville found that in Cornwall his curate did not wear it so as to gain favour with the people. In 1675 Bishop Croft of Hereford after deliberation came to the conclusion that he should not be over zealous in insisting on the surplice, and it seems that a number of partially conformist ministers, given a tolerant bishop such as this, may have succeeded for years in contriving to avoid wearing it. Not until 1680 did Josselin admit defeat and confide in his diary that he had been forced to put on the hated garment. In the North at Penistone, where he enjoyed the protection of the families of Bosville, Riche and Wordsworth, Henry Swift, though he did not die till 1689 and continued up to his death in possession of the parish living, never wore the surplice at all. Many churches in many parts of England must have been in the same condition as those in the diocese of Bath and Wells which in 1684 had no surplice for the minister, no chalice and no Book of Common Prayer, and had done nothing about railing off the altar.

At the Restoration the bishops had shown no interest in re-organizing the distribution of parishes to accord with the present distribution of population, perhaps partly because the Common-wealth commissioners had attempted such a scheme, and in consequence in certain parts of England, especially in the North-West, the parochial structure still accidentally promoted the development of Nonconformity within the Church. Nonconformity flourished in the chapelries of some of the vast parishes of the West Riding and Lancashire just as it had done in the first half of the century. John Angier, who had taken a prominent part in the Commonwealth Church in Lancashire, officiated at Denton chapel until his death in 1677. Other chapels of ease in the same area, Darwen, Walmsley near Bolton and Gorton also provided havens for ministers who did not conform. As a token gesture a clerk read Common Prayer once a year at Rainsford chapel in Lancashire. When a Latitudinarian bishop felt he could not allow a minister to flout the Act of Uniformity in quite so flagrant a way, the system of lectureships once again provided a means by which a minister might to some extent serve within the Church and yet avoid the requirements of the Prayer Book. Bishop Wilkins permitted John Tilsley who had been ejected from Dean in Lancashire for refusing to conform, to continue to act as lecturer there while Herrick, a founder member of the Lancashire Presbyterian *classis*, who also did not submit, still remained as warden of Manchester College. Even in the South, examples of comprehension can be cited which seem far indeed from the intentions of members of the Commons in 1662. At Southwold in Suffolk until 1680 Anglicans and Dissenters apparently went on sharing the use of the parish church, the Anglicans having a Prayer Book service one Sunday in four, while the Independents together with their minister worshipped there undisturbed on the other three.

In the twilight area between full conformity and deliberate separation chaplaincies in noble and gentry households once more, as in the previous century and a half, offered a refuge for scrupulous clergy from the Commonwealth Church. Dr Jacomb, the former incumbent of St Martin's Ludgate Hill, and a leading member of the London provincial *classis* until its dissolution in 1660, moved into the Countess of Exeter's household. Lord Massarene took John Howe as his chaplain to Ireland. John Flavel lived with the Rolls family at Hudscott Hall in Devonshire. Several Nonconformists followed the example of John Thornton who combined his duties as chaplain to the Russell family at Woburn Abbey with those of tutor to his patron's son. Especially in the North of England, gentry families invited ejected ministers to preach in their private chapels. Oliver Heywood fairly regularly went over to preach in the Rhodes family chapel at Great Houghton Hall, and Jeremiah Crossley continued to minister permanently at the Dyneley chapel which Robert Dyneley had built at Bramhope in Wharfdale in 1649. Some families even erected new chapels after the Restoration in order to gain this freedom of worship. Lady Brooke set up her own chapel at Ellenthorpe where former Presbyterian incumbents often officiated, and at Morley and Stannington certain inhabitants took the initiative in founding chapels in the form of private trusts. As in the Laudian period, churchmen in the last resort could not control the religious activities of influential laymen, and some bishops indeed had little desire to do so.

The reign of Charles II stands in marked contrast to that of Charles I in that now many bishops showed a greater readiness to countenance some irregularities within the Church in the interest of unity than did the governing classes, at least as they expressed themselves in Parliament. Once the Act of Uniformity had been passed some of the High Church bishops tended to sympathize with a limited form of comprehension, since this made the ideal of a national Church more of a reality and circumvented the general toleration preferred by the King. Proposals for a bill, which would have allowed clergy to dispense with certain ceremonies as long as they adhered to the doctrinal articles within the Thirty-Nine Articles, very much on the lines of the Puritan demands in the earlier Elizabethan Parliaments, came from Charles II in 1662. The House of Commons would have nothing to do with them, its members seemingly more rigidly Anglican than the higher clergy, and there can be little doubt that the religious persecution which lasted with intermittent severity from 1660 to 1688 derived its impetus largely from this sector of the laity. The contradiction between the attitude of the governing classes in Parliament and the behaviour of some individual gentlemen in the localities can only be explained satisfactorily in political terms. Active Royalist gentlemen had tasted the wrath of the Parliamentarians when their plots against the Cromwellian government had come to light: after 1660 they vented their animosity on their erstwhile anta-gonists and looked upon some Puritan ministers as the chief instigators of the troubles which had led to the Great Rebellion. Others, perhaps less revengeful, feared that the Nonconformists were only waiting for the opportunity to establish a republic again, and Venner's revolt of January 1661 gave them enough evidence to confirm their predictions. At one and the same time, therefore, members of Parliament as a body could demand and get persecuting legislation, and yet some as individuals on their own estates felt free to dispense themselves from the intentions of this legislation. A gentleman considered himself entitled to judge the political reliability of his own chaplain while professing genuine abhorence of the subversive tendencies of illegal popular conventicles.

So, largely on account of the governing classes' apprehension of the political and social consequences of Protestant dissent, imme-diately after the King's return, there began the period of the great persecution of Puritans. The upper reaches of society generally looked upon Quakers as the most dangerous of the sects because of their belief in inner illumination and their abolition of any distinction between a layman and a minister, their refusal to pay tithes, swear an oath or observe accepted social conventions. Quakers together with the Baptists were among the first to experi-ence their intolerance. Cromwell with difficulty had managed to shield the Quakers from the fierce hostility of his Parliaments;

after 1660 they had few powerful protectors. Early in 1661, some months before the Act of Uniformity had gone before Parliament, prisons were already overflowing with Quakers: in March 1661 reports reached the government of five hundred Quakers in London prisons alone, and of nearly four thousand in prisons throughout the rest of the country. Even before the passing of the first of the Acts which made up the Clarendon Code, magistrates were sentencing both Quakers and Baptists under the sixteenth-century Acts against sectaries, and justices at Aylesbury actually condemned twelve Baptists to death for their Nonconformity, though Charles II intervened to save them and the revered Cambridgeshire Baptist leader, Francis Holcroft. The two Conventicle Acts of 1664 and 1670 in addition made it possible for local Justices to disrupt by force any religious gatherings held outside the bounds of the national Church.

From the accession of Charles II the records of the Nonconformist churches and the diaries of individual Nonconforming ministers abound with tales of persecution. Edward Terrill, in the annals of the Bristol Broadmead Church which he wrote at this time, listed ten different outbursts of persecution directed against his church between 1660 and 1681. As might be expected the dissenting ministers had to endure the worst of the persecution; they bore the chief responsibility of keeping their scattered congregations together at the height of the onslaught and of providing them with the encouragement to stand firm. John Bunyan, the best known of the Restoration Nonconformist ministers because of his popular writings, was arrested in November 1660 on a charge of being about to preach to a seditious meeting, and his imprisonment lasted for twelve years. In the West of England magistrates in 1663 fined John Norman £100 for unlicensed preaching in Bridgwater and, as he could not pay, sent him to Ilchester gaol for a year and a half with John Alleine, five more ministers and fifty Quakers. Alleine continued in prison till 1667 and died in the following year from the effects of his privations. Although, through the compliance of their gaolers, ministers like Bunyan might enjoy special privileges in prison, being allowed out to visit their families and even to preach, the physical conditions in gaol were, nevertheless, so bad and the danger from epidemics so great that it is remarkable that more did not succumb to their imprisonment. In his obituary of one such minister, Thomas Hardcastle, who served the Broadmead Church until his death in Bristol in 1678, Terrill set out the tribulations any of the Nonconforming clergy at this time might be called upon to bear:

> He was a man, as it were a champion for the Lord, very courageous in his work and sufferings. His zeal provoked many, before he came to Bristol. After he had thrown off conformity, he suffered about eight months' imprisonment in York castle; and then, because he would not give bond to preach no more, as some ministers, his fellow prisoners, did, to get free, he was carried thence, out of his county eighty miles, to Chester castle, and there he was kept fifteen months more, close prisoner; and then, by an order from the king, he was released without bonds, and he came to London, and there he was baptised. After that [he] was taken up for preaching, and by the Conventicle Act was six months prisoner in London. And then being called by this church to be their pastor, for the defence of the gospel, [he] was twice imprisoned in Bristol, two six months; still preaching as soon as ever he came forth, and so continued till his death, having been our pastor about seven years and a quarter. He was seven times imprisoned, for Christ and a good conscience, after he left off conformity.[3]

The courage of lay members of dissenting congregations often fell little short of that of their ministers. Soldiers twice disrupted the congregation of James Janeway of Rotherhide and assaulted inoffensive members assembled for worship. Despite the protection of several local gentlemen, Oliver Heywood had his meetings broken up on several occasions and his supporters injured. Particularly because of their supposed connection with Fifth Monarchy men, Baptists of all persuasions came under suspicion after Venner's revolt. Towards the end of 1661, 289 out of 355 prisoners in Newgate were Baptists, and city magistrates did nothing to prevent the mob from raiding the Baptist church in Brick Lane six times in 1662. Congregations would go to great lengths to avoid this kind of harassment, coming together in small groups very early in the morning, building their chapels, as in Stepney in 1674, in the guise of private dwellings, or constructing concealed rooms, even (when the hostility of the local magistrates grew particularly hot) meeting in woods. In spite of these precautions, laymen went on paying heavy fines and enduring periods of imprisonment until the end of James II's reign.

The experiences of the Nonconformist communities in Bristol, which Terrill related in such detail, mirror those of many other dissenting groups elsewhere in England. In Bristol, one of the largest cities in England outside London in 1660, different forms of dissent had become firmly established. Besides the supporters of moderate Puritanism, now not very accurately known as Presbyterians, Independent, Calvinist Baptist, Arminian Baptist and Quaker meetings had been set up there. Quakers and Baptists had to face particularly harsh persecution in 1664, and it may be that local magistrates sent as many as 900 dissenters to prison in that year alone. The passing of the 1670 Conventicle Act spurred the justices on to further persecution, and in 1675 the minister of one of the Independent churches, John Thompson, died in prison. Still this persecution did not succeed in obliterating dissent. During the intermission in 1672, when Charles issued his short-lived second Declaration of Indulgence and Nonconformist congregations could obtain royal licences for worship, in Bristol three Baptist, two Independent and one Presbyterian congregations came out into the open besides several Quaker meetings. Nor did dissent derive its support only from the poorer sections of society as many Anglicans supposed. When Thomas Ewins, an earlier pastor of Broadmead Church, died in 1670, the church could offer Thomas Hardcastle an annual income of £80 raised entirely from voluntary subscriptions. Nine years later Terrill gave substantial property to the church which brought in an additional income of £50 a year designed to relieve the church's poor and supplement the minister's living, so that the succession of learned preachers might be preserved. By 1680 one observer thought dissenters made up two-thirds of the inhabitants of the city, most probably an exaggeration, but in one year Bristol Quakers on their own paid fines amounting to more than £16,000.

In London an influential sector of the mercantile community threw in their lot with dissent, as they did in Bristol, together with some members of the aristocracy and gentry. In 1672 London merchants founded a Tuesday lecture at Pinners' Hall and set up a fund sufficient to pay a lecturer £1 for every sermon: Menton, Owen, Bates, Baxter and Collins, in fact some of the most eminent of the Nonconforming ministers, all preached on this endowment. The next year the membership of John Owen's London church surpassed 170 and counted the Countess of Anglesey, Sir Thomas Overy, Sir John Hartopp, Lady Tompson, Lady Vere Wilkinson besides Fleetwood, Desborough and Berry among its attenders. When Owen died in 1683 the carriages of no less than sixty-seven noblemen and gentlemen assembled at his funeral. In no town, however, does Nonconformity seem to have been more strong between 1660 and 1688 than in Yarmouth where the sympathies of the aldermen virtually halted the implementation of the Clarendon Code. In 1663 two hundred inhabitants of Yarmouth were presented for not receiving communion; four years later when William Bridge, their former pastor, returned to the town the people gave him an immediate welcome, and he at once began gathering large congregations. From early in this decade the town's government had been falling into dissenting hands and the magistrates made little attempt to enforce the provisions of the Corporation Act. Circumstantial evidence tends to confirm contemporary assertions that less than half the aldermen and councillors belonged to the established Church; a further estimate of 1676 gave the Anglican communicants in the town as numbering five hundred; in contrast, the Nonconformist meeting house could hold two thousand, and was often full. In a borough like Yarmouth, where the local climate of opinion so obviously favoured dissent, imposition of conformity far exceeded the powers which the central Government could deploy.

Had it not been for the Exclusion Crisis and the fears it reawakened of popular rebellion, *de facto* toleration for Protestant dissenters might have been achieved before the end of the reign of Charles II. During the 1670s among the governing classes the traditional fear of Popery seemed to be overtaking the fear of Dissent, and in the counties Justices appeared to be losing their enthusiasm for persecution. The uncovering of the Popish Plot further deflected attention from Dissenters towards Catholics. Yet the very intensity and apparent strength of the campaign which the Whigs conducted between 1678 and 1681 to exclude the Catholic Duke of York from the throne provoked a political reaction of corresponding vehemence. The Whigs had not fought their battle within the privileged circle of the governing classes but had dared to involve Dissenters of lower social antecedents throughout the country, especially Dissenters concentrated in towns. Religious allegiance had again become dangerously linked with allegiance to a political party, and moreover, with one which seemed to permit a widening of that sector of society from which the governing elite was drawn. Irrational hatred of Catholics had attained such proportions that gentlemen could believe that a social revolution lay within the bounds of possibility. When Charles II overcame the crisis in 1681, partly by deciding to dissolve Parliament and so denying the Whigs their chief platform, Tories led the reaction and again forced Dissenters into the role of potential rebels against the Crown. The discovery of the Rye House Plot served to confirm the idea of Nonconformists as conspirators against the government, and as a result the years between 1681 and the death of Charles II witnessed another spate of fierce persecution. Militia men again broke into meeting houses; ministers and their congregations had again to face arrests and fines. Francis Bampfield, a minister who had spent nearly ten years from 1663 until 1672 in Dorchester gaol, stood by helplessly in 1683 while soldiers destroyed his London chapel. Sent to Newgate, he died there the following year, and other ministers suffered a similar fate. The Broadmead Church took to meeting in Kingswood to escape notice in Bristol, but still its new minister, John Fownes, could not avoid capture, and he also died in prison in 1685. Another Bristol minister called Knight collapsed and died from exhaustion and his companion drowned when fording a river in an attempt to evade pursuing soldiers. Other areas of England where Nonconformity had grown in strength in the previous decade produced similar reports of vindictive harassment. Even Baxter, in spite of his influential protectors and his well-known reputation as an advocate for conciliation between the Church and more moderate Dissent, was several times brought before the magistrates late in 1684 and bound over in substantial sums.

With Monmouth's rebellion breaking out so soon after the accession of James II, the position of Dissenters worsened yet further. Once again Tories could claim that Protestant Nonconformity should be equated with disloyalty towards the principle of hereditary succession and the duly constituted government of the country, and a further period of persecution of Dissenters ensued. At the trial of Richard Baxter in 1685 Judge Jeffreys let slip the rationalization that lay behind these attacks upon seemingly inoffensive Dissenters. 'He is as modest now as can be,' he exclaimed, pointing to the aged minister, 'but time was when no man was so ready at 'Bind your King in chains, and your nobles in fetters of iron"; and "To your tents, O Israel." Gentlemen, for God's sake, don't let us be gulled twice in an age.' Yet Jeffreys by exaggeration such as this as well as by his brutality, excessive even by the standards of the day, at length alienated many of those who began as his supporters. James II, through his behaviour towards the established Church, unintentionally brought a majority of the governing classes to see the political necessity for ending the physical persecution of Protestant Dissenters. At least in the earlier part of his reign Charles II had quite seriously tried to relieve Dissenters, but Parliament had replied by introducing still harsher laws against Nonconformists, forcing the King to withdraw his Declarations of Indulgence and thereby, after 1681, to acquiesce in Tory intolerance. James, however, by appearing to undermine the dominance of the national Church, achieved by accident what his brother had failed to accomplish by design. Tories found to their consternation that their King by Divine Right would no longer acknowledge his dependence on those accustomed to exercise national or local government, and, even worse, that the Supreme Governor was no longer a professing member of the English Church. In the face of James's actions to promote his co-religionists in Church and State, the Tories set aside their theories of passive obedience.[4]

The attitudes of the more conservative churchmen moved in parallel with this change among the conservative politicians. The bishops whom Charles I, under Laud's tuition, had regarded as the pillars of the monarchy had little choice in the event but give their support to an opposition which eventually succeeded in toppling the throne. On the publication of James's first Declaration of Indulgence in April 1687, and even more after the appearance of his second Declaration the following year, Anglican and Nonconformist church leaders together with many members of Parliament at last recognized a common threat from a Catholic king. The clergy refused to read the second Declaration of Indulgence in their churches, and the seven bishops who had petitioned the King against the Indulgence found themselves in prison. Spontaneous demonstrations took place in the streets of London on behalf of the bishops who temporarily enjoyed a quite unprecedented popularity, and few missed the political significance of the visits of Nonconformist leaders to the bishops in the Tower. Since at the eleventh hour the more conservative Nonconformists had not fallen for James's blandishments and had not accepted his offers of toleration at the expense of the national religious establishment, Tories at Westminster as well as Whigs now conceded the necessity of rewarding Protestant Dissenters with some degree of religious liberty should they accomplish their plan of removing James from the throne. In anticipation of the successful outcome of the political revolution, Archbishop Sancroft devised a rather generous scheme under which most Dissenters could have been included within a re-organized national Church. Yet again events proved that a churchman had under-estimated the strength of the prejudices of the governing classes.

When William and Mary had replaced James II, the Toleration Act passed by Parliament in 1689 fell far short of the liberty Sancroft had envisaged. Parliament rejected a Comprehension Bill which would have provided for conditional re-ordination of Non-conformist ministers and a much simplified form of subscription, in addition to the optional observance of certain Anglican ceremonies and the wearing of the surplice. Had this bill been accepted Protestant Dissenters would have been able to re-enter the political life of the country both at Westminster and in their local areas. The alternative to the Comprehension Bill, the Toleration Act, gave much more limited concessions, and this was the measure Parliament preferred. By the provisions of the Toleration Act of 1689, orthodox, that is Trinitarian, Protestant Dissenters might meet together separately for worship in buildings licensed by the bishops and be freed from the penalties of all laws for the imposition of uniformity passed in the reign of Charles II and his predecessors. The Act made no mention of the laws which continued to exclude Dissenters from all forms of political activity.

The Toleration Act reveals the unwillingness of many in authority to surrender their long-held belief in the necessary connection between loyalty to the State and loyalty to the established Church. Under the requirements of the Test and Corporation Acts, which Parliament did not modify, Dissenters still might not hold office without receiving communion in the Church of England, and Tories formally continued to maintain this position for a further century. Though in 1689 they had granted the case for toleration for Protestants, many seemed unable to reconcile themselves fully to the situation, and some even seem to have looked upon the concessions as merely temporary. Certainly the number of Dissenters taking advantage of the Toleration Act was very frightening to many Anglicans. In the first year of the Act's operation the ecclesiastical authorities registered more than nine hundred places of worship for Dissenters, and between 1691 and 1700 this number rose to well over a thousand. Many Tories, like many of the governing class under Elizabeth, thought the problem of Dissent would not last for more than a generation, and reacted with alarm when they saw Dissenters taking pains to perpetuate a dissenting tradition. This accounts for their particular hostility towards dissenting academies and their attempts in the reign of Anne to put pressure on the bishops to close any school which did not observe the Anglican liturgy. The Schism Bill of 1714 would once more have forced all schoolmasters to obtain an episcopal licence, and only the opportune death of the Queen prevented its enactment. The very fragility of the limited toleration the Dissenters had secured is further shown by other Tory demands. High Church Anglicans could not accept the custom by which Dissenters managed to evade the Test and Corporation Acts and enter politics by occasionally conforming and receiving the sacrament in the Church of England, a practice of long standing with some dissenting ministers like Baxter who regarded it as a gesture of fellowship among Protestants. The Tories introduced their first bill against Occasional Conformity in 1702, though it did not become law until 1711 when the Whigs allowed it to pass, thinking, wrongly, that they could later relieve Dissenters from its penalties. On the change of dynasty with the death of Anne, the Tories lost their predominance in national politics; the Whigs in 1718 procured the repeal of the Occasional Conformity Act, and this desire to thrust Dissenters yet further from public life became the mark of a dying cause. A state of balance had finally been attained between the established Church and Protestant Dissent which persisted for the remainder of the century.

In the person of Sir Roger de Coverley Addison in the reign of Queen Anne depicted his ideal country squire, old fashioned even for the age in which he wrote. Sir Roger chose not only his parson but also the sermons he permitted him to read in the parish church Sunday by Sunday. As landlord to the whole parish he inflicted his religious views upon the villagers, standing up in service time 'when every body else is upon their knees, to count the congregation, or see if any of his tenants are missing'. All matters secular or religious in his little world were governed according to Sir Roger's inclinations. He, 'being a good churchman, has beautified the inside of his church with several texts of his own choosing: he has likewise given a handsome pulpit-cloth, and railed in the communion table at his own expense. He has often told me that at his coming to his estate he found his parishioners very irregular;

and that in order to make them kneel and join in the responses, he gave every one of them a hassock and a Common Prayer book.'[5] Throughout the eighteenth and indeed the nineteenth century actual squires continued to impose their opinions upon their parsons and tenants in very similar ways, and achieved in no uncertain terms that ascendancy within the national Church for which the governing classes had been striving for so long. Yet they could not keep the fruits of victory to themselves. Many other sectors of the laity, having learnt from their experience during the Interregnum, expected a comparable freedom in religion. Dissent had taken lasting root both in populous towns and in the countryside, especially in areas of scattered settlement away from seigneurial control, and from the 1690s in the depths of the country as well as in towns Nonconformist chapels became a new feature in the landscape. By 1714, if not by 1689, the triumph of the laity in the English Church had involved a recognition in the counties as well as at Westminster of the legality of diversity in religious allegiance. The laity had made good their superiority in the national Church; some laymen, more precariously but as it proved permanently, had also established their right to live outside its bounds : an age of religious pluralism had begun.

ABBREVIATIONS

A P C	J. R. Dasent, ed., *Acts of the Privy Council*
Broadmead Records	E. B. Underhill, ed., *Records of a Church of Christ meeting at Broadmead, Bristol, 1640–1687*, Hanserd Knollys Society, 1847
B I H R	*Bulletin of the Institute of Historical Research*
Cal S P Dom	*Calendar of State Papers Domestic*
Ec H R	*Economic History Review*
E H R	*English Historical Review*
Foxe	G. Townshend and S. R. Cattley, eds., *Acts and Monuments of John Foxe*, 8 vols. 1837–1841
H J	*Historical Journal*
J E H	*Journal of Ecclesiastical History*
P & P	*Past and Present*
Strype, *Ecc. Mem.*	J. Strype, *Ecclesiastical Memorials*, I–III, 1721
S C H	*Studies in Church History*, ed., vol. I C. W. Dugmore and C. Duggan, vols II–VI G. J. Cuming, vols. VII–VIII G. J. Cuming and D. Baker, vols. IX– D. Baker
T R H S	*Transactions of the Royal Historical Society*
Y A S	*Yorkshire Archaeological Society*

All books are published in London unless otherwise stated.

NOTES

CHAPTER 1 (pages 9 to 30)

1 A. R. Myers, ed., *English Historical Documents 1327–1485*, 1969, 848–50, 865.
2 R. L. Storey, *Diocesan Administration in Fifteenth Century England*, Borthwick Paper 16, York, second edition, 1972
3 G. W. H. Lampe, ed., *The Cambridge History of the Bible*, II, Cambridge, 1969, 388.
4 K. B. McFarlane, *Lancastrian Kings and Lollard Knights*, Oxford, 1972, 201–6.
5 M. Aston, 'Lollardy and Sedition 1381–1431', *P & P*, XVII, 1960, 12, 13.
6 McFarlane, *Lancastrian Kings and Lollard Knights*, 211.
7 Foxe, III, 141.
8 ibid., 235.
9 J. F. Davis, 'Lollards, Reformers and St Thomas of Canterbury', *University of Birmingham Historical Journal*, IX, 1963, 5.
10 Foxe, III, 585.
11 Aston, 'Lollardy and Sedition', 11.
12 V. H. H. Green, *Bishop Reginald Pecock*, Cambridge, 1945, 141; *English Historical Documents 1327–1485*, 872.

CHAPTER 2 (pages 31 to 52)

1 C. Jenkins, 'Cardinal Morton's Register', in R. W. Seton-Watson, ed., *Tudor Studies presented . . . to A. F. Pollard*, 1924, 48.
2 J. Strype, *Ecclesiastical Memorials*, I, 1721, 82–3, 85.
3 ibid. appendix, 35–7.
4 Foxe, IV, 231, 237–8; A. F. Pollard, ed., *The Reign of Henry VII from Contemporary Sources*, III, 1914, 236; K. B. McFarlane, *John Wycliffe and the Beginnings of English Nonconformity*, 1952, 184–5.
5 P. Heath, *The English Parish Clergy on the Eve of the Reformation*, 1969, 173.
6 ibid., 70–92.

CHAPTER 3 (pages 53 to 80)

1 M. Bowker, 'Lincolnshire 1536: Heresy, Schism or Religious Discontent?', *S C H*, IX, 202–3; A. G. Dickens, 'Secular and Religious Motivation in the Pilgrimage of Grace', *S C H*, IV, 61.

2 A. G. Dickens, *Lollards and Protestants in the Diocese of York*, 1959, 93, 99.

3 A rhyme by Robert Crowley quoted in J. J. Scarisbrick, *Henry VIII*, 1968, 525–6.

4 Foxe, V, 443–9, 465.

5 Foxe, IV, 584; Strype, *Ecc. Mem.*, I, 286–7.

6 Foxe, V, 445–7; G. R. Elton, *Policy and Police*, Cambridge, 1972, 139.

7 K. G. Powell, 'The Beginnings of Protestantism in Gloucestershire', *Transactions of Bristol and Gloucestershire Archaeological Society*, XC, 1971, 147.

8 Foxe, V, 454, 443–7; VI, 26–7.

9 ibid., V, 535.

CHAPTER 4 (pages 81 to 100)

1 H. Robinson, ed., *Original Letters relative to the English Reformation*, Parker Society, Cambridge, 1846, 72.

2 Strype, *Ecc. Mem.*, 11, 74.

3 Robinson, ed., *Original Letters . . .*, 66.

4 F. D. Price, 'Gloucester Diocese under Bishop Hooper 1551–3', *Transactions of the Bristol and Gloucester Archaeological Society*, LX, 1939, 142; Foxe, VI, 643–4.

5 C. Burrage, *The Early English Dissenters*, II, Cambridge 1912, 1–2; *A P C 1550–2*, 198, 206.

6 Strype, *Ecc. Mem.*, III, appendix, 113–6.

CHAPTER 5 (pages 101 to 123)

1 Foxe, VI, 413.

2 A. G. Dickens, *The Marian Reaction in the Diocese of York; Part I, the Clergy*, Borthwick pamphlet 11, York, 10-11.

3   A. F. Leach, *Early Yorkshire Schools*, Y A S, Record Series XXVII, 1899, xxxv.

4   A. G. Dickens, 'R. Parkyn's Narrative of the Reformation', *E H R*, LXII, 1947, 82.

5   Strype, *Ecc. Mem.*, III, 73.

6   Strype, *Cranmer*, 1694, appendix, 195–6.

7   Foxe, VII, 713–4.

8   ibid., VII, 119; VIII, 409, 383, 464, 322–3.

9   ibid., VIII, 125.

10   ibid., VIII, 388, 600, 553; A. F. Pollard, ed., *Tudor Tracts 1532–1588*, 1903, 179.

11   C. Garrett, *The Marian Exiles*, Cambridge, 1938, 41.

12   Foxe, I, 519–20.

CHAPTER 6 (pages 124 to 152)

1   E. Arber, ed., *A Brief Discourse of the Troubles at Frankfort*, 1908, 38–9, 54, 77, 113, 155, 152, 225–6.

2   *Statutes of the Realm*, IV, part I, 354.

3   H. Robinson, ed., *Zurich Letters*, I, Cambridge, 1842, 86–7.

4   ibid., 44–5.

5   W. Nicholson, ed., *Grindal's Remains*, Cambridge, 1843, 203–4, 208, 211, 214.

6   Inner Temple, Petyt Ms 538, vol. 47, fo. 511: a slightly different version appears in A. Peel, ed., *The Seconde Parte of a Register*, I, Cambridge, 1915, 56–7.

7   'An Admonition to the Parliament' in W. H. Frere and C. E. Douglas, eds., *Puritan Manifestoes*, 1907, 16, 19.

8   'A True and Short Declaration' in A. Peel and L. H. Carlson, eds., *The Writings of Robert Harrison and Robert Browne*, 1953, 422.

9   R. G. Usher, ed., *The Presbyterian Movement in the reign of Queen Elizabeth*, Camden Society, 1905, 37.

10   L. H. Carlson, ed., *The Writings of John Greenwood and Henry Barrow, 1591–3*, 1970, 301.

CHAPTER 7 (pages 153 to 174)

1 R. A. Marchant, *The Puritans and Church Courts in the diocese of York 1560–1642*, 1960, 147, 214.
2 B. Brook, *The Lives of the Puritans*, II, 1813, 380.
3 Marchant, *The Puritans and the Church Courts*, 31–2.
4 J. C. Cox, ed., *Records of the Borough of Northampton*, II, Northampton, 1898, 386–8.
5 C. Cross, ed., *The Letters of Sir Francis Hastings, 1574–1609*, Somerset Record Society, 1969, 81.
6 J. Ayre, ed., *The Sermons of Edwin Sandys*, Parker Society, Cambridge, 1841, 448.
7 J. Strype, *Whitgift*, 1718, 461 (in Latin).
8 S. B. Babbage, *Puritanism and Richard Bancroft*, 1962, 83, 224.
9 Cross, ed., *The Letters of Sir Francis Hastings*, 104.
10 Marchant, *The Puritans and the Church Courts*, 142, 157, 180.
11 J. P. Kenyon, *The Stuart Constitution 1603–1688*, Cambridge, 1966, 41.

CHAPTER 8 (pages 175 to 198)

1 G. Gilfillan, ed., *The Poetical Works of George Herbert*, 1853, 208.
2 *Cal S P Dom 1635*, xxx–xlv.
3 T. T. Lewis, ed., *Letters of Lady Brilliana Harley*, Camden Society, LVIII, 1854, xxxii.
4 I. M. Calder, *The Activities of the Puritan Faction in the Church of England, 1625–33*, 1957, xxii, xxiv.
5 Kenyon, *The Stuart Constitution*, 158.
6 J. Raine, *The Fabric Rolls of York Minster*, Surtees Society, XXXV, 1859, 319 n; *Cal S P Dom 1635*, xxxvii.
7 D. Parsons, ed., *Diary of Sir Henry Slingsby*, 1836, 8–9.
8 *Letters of Lady Brilliana Harley*, xxxiv.
9 R. C. Richardson, *Puritanism in North West England*, Manchester, 1972, 138.
10 T. W. Davids, *Annals of Evangelical Nonconformity in the County of Essex*, 1863, 171–3, 168–9, 165, 151, 149.

11   Richardson, *Puritanism in North West England*, 82, 79, 85.
12   E. B. Underhill, ed., *Records of a Church of Christ meeting in Broadmead, Bristol, 1640–1687*, Hanserd Knollys Society, 1847, 4, 5–6, 18.
13   Kenyon, *Stuart Constitution*, 167, 169.
14   *Letters of Lady Brilliana Harley*, 111, 115.

CHAPTER 9 (pages 199 to 221)

1   C. Hill, *God's Englishman*, 1970, 126.
2   W. K. Jordan, *Development of Religious Toleration in England*, III, 1938, 21; Kenyon, *Stuart Constitution*, 231–2.
3   A. G. Matthews, *Walker Revised*, Oxford, 1947, xv.
4   W. A. Shaw, ed., *Minutes of Manchester Classis*, Chetham Society, New Series 22, 1891, 114; J. Horsfall Turner, ed., *Oliver Heywood's Autobiography*, Brighouse, I, 1882, 79.
5   B. Hanbury, *Historical Memorials*, II, 1841, 55.
6   *Broadmead Records*, 28, 30.
7   G. F. Nuttall, *Visible Saints*, Oxford, 1957, 52–3; A. T. Jones, *Notes on the Early Days of Stepney Meeting 1644–1689*, 1887, 4.
8   *Apologetical Narration*, 1643, 8, 24; Nuttall, *Visible Saints*, 64.
9   Hill, *God's Englishman*, 68; *Commons Journals*, III, 626.
10   G. F. Nuttall, *The Holy Spirit in Puritan Faith and Experience*, Oxford, 1946, 116; C. H. Firth and R. S. Rait, eds., *Acts and Ordinances of the Interregnum*, II, 1911, 822.
11   J. M. Lloyd Thomas, ed., *The Autobiography of Richard Baxter*, 1925, 71.
12   *Autobiography of Richard Baxter*, 136, 138.
13   E. Freshfield, ed., *Vestry Minute Book . . . of St Bartholomew Exchange, 1567–1676*, 1890, xxviii; Jones, *Notes on . . . Stepney Meeting 1644–1689*, 17–18; Nuttall, *The Holy Spirit in Puritan Faith and Experience*, 115.

CHAPTER 10 (pages 222 to 242)

1   N. Sykes, *From Sheldon to Secker*, Cambridge, 1959, 36.

2 R. Latham and W. Matthews, ed., *Diary of Samuel Pepys*, I, 1970, 259.
3 *Broadmead Records*, 388.
4 J. M. Lloyd Thomas, ed., *The Autobiography of Richard Baxter*, 1925, 263.
5 D. F. Bond, ed., *The Spectator*, I, Oxford, 1965, 460–1.

BIBLIOGRAPHY

CHAPTER I (pages 9 to 30)

W. A. Pantin in *The English Church in the Fourteenth Century*, Cambridge, 1955, provides a general introduction to the Church in England in the high Middle Ages, while there is a wealth of material on monks and friars and much else relating to ecclesiastical history in D. Knowles, *The Religious Orders in England*, I and II, Cambridge, 1955 and 1961. R. B. Dobson, *Durham Priory, 1400–1450*, Cambridge, 1973, in meticulous detail places one religious house in its local community. There is a good county study, D. M. Owen, *Church and Society in Medieval Lincolnshire*, Lincoln, 1971, and a valuable national survey, R. L. Storey, *Diocesan Administration in Fifteenth Century England*, Borthwick Paper 16, York, second edition, 1972. The ability of the laity to participate actively in the Church was governed in some degree by the accessibility of education; the most recent discussion of the extent of lay education is N. Orme, *English Schools in the Middle Ages*, 1973.

The best general account of Wyclif and Lollardy is still K. B. McFarlane, *John Wycliffe and the Beginnings of English Nonconformity*, 1952, although he considerably modified his opinion about the limited social appeal of Lollardy, and hence of its significance, in his later, posthumously published *Lancastrian Kings and Lollard Knights*, Oxford, 1972, which contains an important re-appraisal of educated lay piety at the turn of the fourteenth century. The Twelve Conclusions and other key Lollard manifestoes, as well as many more documents of direct relevance to church life in this period, are printed in A. R. Myers, ed., *English Historical Documents 1327–1485*, 1969. J. A. F. Thomson, *The Later Lollards, 1414–1520*, 1965, has written a useful but rather negative account of the extent of Lollardy. Other interpretations of Lollardy which stress its spiritual aspects are still in article form : M. Aston, 'Lollardy and Sedition, 1381–1431', *P & P*, XVII, 1960, 1–37; J. F. Davis, 'Lollards, Reformers and St Thomas of Canterbury', *University of Birmingham Historical Journal*, IX, 1963, 1–15; M. G. Snape, 'Some evidence of Lollard activity in the diocese of Durham in the early Fifteenth Century', *Archaeologia Aeliana*, fourth series, XXXIX, 1961, 355–61; E. Welsh, 'Some Suffolk Lollards', *Proceed-*

ings of the Suffolk Institute of Archaeology, XXIX, 1964, 154–65; A. Hudson, 'Some aspects of Lollard book production', *SCH*, IX, 1972, 147–57, and A. Hudson, 'The Examination of Lollards', *BIHR*, XLIV, 1973, 145–59. The Elizabethan martyrologist had access to records which have subsequently perished, and despite its obvious bias, S. R. Cattley, ed., *The Acts and Monuments of John Foxe*, III and IV, 1837, is an irreplaceable sourcebook for fifteenth-century lay nonconformity.

G. W. H. Lampe, ed., *The Cambridge History of the Bible*, II, Cambridge, 1969, includes a concise description of English translations of the Bible in the Middle Ages; there is a much fuller account in M. Deanesley, *The Lollard Bible*, 1920.

The standard biography of Pecock is V. H. H. Green, *Bishop Reginald Pecock*, Cambridge, 1945, but see also E. F. Jacob, 'Reynold Pecock, Bishop of Chichester', *Proceedings of the British Academy*, XXXVIII, 1951, 121–153. There are further articles on the reactions of other churchmen to Lollards: R. M. Haines, ' "Wilde Wittes and Wilfulnes"; John Swetstock's attack on those "poyswunmongeres", the Lollards', *SCH*, VIII, 1953, 143–153, and A. K. McHardy, 'Bishop Buckingham and the Lollards of Lincoln Diocese', *SCH*, IX, 1972, 131–145.

The Book of Margery Kemp, ed., W. Butler-Bowden, 1954, is the precocious religious autobiography of an eccentric but in all essentials orthodox laywoman of the early fifteenth century.

CHAPTER 2 (pages 31 to 52)

For Lollardy Thomson, *The Later Lollards* remains the standard work but for accounts of Lollard trials reference needs also to be made to Foxe, volume IV, and J. Strype, *Ecclesiastical Memorials*, I, 1721; there are further transcripts of trials in H. Maxwell-Lyte, ed., *Registers of Oliver King*, Somerset Record Society, LIV, 1939; C. Jenkins, 'Cardinal Morton's Register', in R. W. Seton-Watson, ed., *Tudor Studies presented . . . to A. F. Pollard*, 1924; *British Magazine*, XXIII, XXIV, XXV; A. F. Pollard, ed., *The Reign of Henry VII from Contemporary Sources*, III, 1914; all these are listed and discussed in Professor A. G. Dickens's most helpful article, 'Heresy and the Origins of the English Reformation', in J. S. Bromley and E. H. Kossmann, eds., *Britain and the Netherlands*, II, Groningen, 1971, 120–25. In addition there are important articles elsewhere: J. F. Davis, 'Lollard Survival and the Textile Industry in South East England', *S C H*, III, 1966, 191–201; J. Fines, 'The post-mortem condemnation for heresy of Richard Hunne', *E H R*, LXXVII, 1963, 528–31; J. Fines, 'Heresy trials in the Diocese of Coventry and Lichfield, 1511–12', *J E H*, XIV, 1963, 160–174; I. Luxton, 'The Lichfield Court Book: a postscript', *B I H R*, XLIV, 1971, 120–25.

Besides Professor Knowles's invaluable works on the monks and friars, *The Religious Orders in England*, II and III, Cambridge, 1961, there have been some very good new studies of the parish clergy since he wrote: P. Heath, *The English Parish Clergy on the Eve of the Reformation*, 1969, and a rather more specialized mono-graph, M. Bowker, *The Secular Clergy in the Diocese of Lincoln 1495–1520*, Cambridge, 1968. The key work on chantries is K. L. Wood-Legh, *Perpetual Chantries in Britain*, Cambridge, 1965, and for further details on London and York see J. A. F. Thomson, 'Piety and Charity in late Medieval London', *J E H*, XVI, 1965, 178–195, and R. B. Dobson, 'The Foundation of Perpetual Chantries by the Citizens of Medieval York', *S C H*, IV, 1967, 22–38. A particularly violent episode in the rivalry between the secular and regular clergy is described by F. R. H. Du Boulay, 'The quarrel between the Carmelite Friars and the Secular Clergy of London, 1464–68', *J E H*, VI, 1955, 156–74.

Mrs J. Simon has written a succinct account of new develop-ments in higher education in *Education and Society in Tudor England*, Cambridge, 1966.

CHAPTER 3 (pages 53 to 80)

Professor A. G. Dickens's *The English Reformation*, 1964, in which he largely concentrates upon the Henrician and Edwardian Reformation, is in itself a most illuminating and sympathetic study and provides an excellent guide for further reading. His *Lollards and Protestants in the Diocese of York*, Oxford, 1959, includes among much else a detailed description of the career of Sir Francis Bigod. In addition Professor Dickens has written on Cromwell's contribution to the introduction of Protestantism in England in *Thomas Cromwell and the English Reformation*, 1959. Although in his work on Cromwell Professor G. R. Elton has not specifically turned his attention to religious reform, his *Policy and Police: the Enforcement of the Reformation in the Age of Thomas Cromwell*, Cambridge, 1972, and *Reform and Renewal: Thomas Cromwell and the Commonweal*, Cambridge, 1973, are very valuable for their consideration of Cromwell's attempt to implement the Acts of the Reformation Parliament, control social unrest and translate into practical policy some of the ideas of the Henrician commonwealthmen. Full extracts from the Acts of the Reformation Parliament are in G. R. Elton, *The Tudor Constitution*, Cambridge, 1960. Behind the servant towers the master, and the authoritative biography of Henry VIII is now J. J. Scarisbrick, *Henry VIII*, 1968, very important for Henry's attitude to religion in general and the royal supremacy in particular.

W. A. Clebsch, *England's Earliest Protestants, 1520–1535*, New Haven and London, 1964, has written a very useful and detailed account of the theology of the first English Protestant clerics; for lay attitudes Foxe, and Strype, *Ecclesiastical Memorials*, I, 1721, continue to provide rich source material.

In *The Religious Orders in England*, III, Cambridge, 1961, Professor Knowles describes the process of the dissolution of the monasteries, while J. Youings, *The Dissolution of the Monasteries*, 1971, is particularly good on the economic problems of the transfer of land and includes an up-to-date bibliography.

The standard narrative account of the Pilgrimage of Grace, M. H. and R. Dodds, *The Pilgrimage of Grace, 1536–7*, Cambridge, 1915, 2 vols., can now be supplemented by a series of articles on the causes of the revolts: A. G. Dickens, 'Secular and Religious Motivation in the Pilgrimage of Grace', *SCH*, IV, 1967, 39–64; C. S. L. Davies, 'The Pilgrimage of Grace Reconsidered', *P & P*, XLI, 1968, 54–76; M. E. James, 'Obedience and Dissent in Henrician England: the Lincolnshire Rebellion, 1536', *P & P*, XLVIII, 1970, 3–78; M. Bowker, 'Lincolnshire 1536: Heresy, Schism or Religious Discontent?', *SCH*, IX, 1972, 195–212.

Other articles particularly relevant for any consideration of the social and economic impact of religious change upon English society are J. J. Scarisbrick, 'Clerical Taxation in England, 1485–1547', *JEH*, XI, 1960, 41–54; H. J. Habakkuk, 'The Market for Monastic Property, 1539–1603', *EcHR*, second series, X, 1958, 362–80; M. Bowker, 'The Commons Supplication against the Ordinaries in the light of some Archidiaconal *Acta*', *TRHS*, fifth series, XXI, 1971, 61–77; K. G. Powell, 'The Beginning of Protestantism in

Gloucestershire', *Transactions of the Bristol and Gloucestershire Archaeological Society*, XC, 1971, 141–157.

CHAPTER 4 (pages 81 to 100)

Compared with the abundance of new work relating to the religious history of the reign of Henry VIII relatively little has been written recently on that of the reign of his son, with the important exception of A. G. Dickens in *The English Reformation*: the accounts of religious events in Foxe and Strype are therefore all the more valuable. Although his definitions of the theological position of the Edwardian Protestant reformers have been rather widely questioned, C. H. Smyth, *Cranmer and the Reformation under Edward VI*, Cambridge, 1926, remains useful, particularly for the activities of the continental reformers in England. It can now be supplemented by P. Brooks, *Thomas Cranmer's Doctrine of the Eucharist*, 1965. The letters and other writings of the reformers themselves are accessible through the publications of the Parker Society; especially relevant in the context of this chapter is H. Robinson, ed., *Original Letters relative to the English Reformation*, Cambridge, 1846. C. Burrage has similarly made the attitudes of unorthodox Protestants known in *The Early English Dissenters*, 2 vols., Cambridge, 1912.

There is as yet no study in print of the administration of another Edwardian bishop equal to an article by F. D. Price, 'Gloucester Diocese under Bishop Hooper, 1551–4', *Transactions of the Bristol and Gloucestershire Archaeological Society*, LX, 1939, 51–151, though in her Cambridge 1972 PhD thesis, 'The Bishops of Ely and their Diocese during the Reformation Period, c. 1515–1600', Mrs F. M. Heal has interesting additional information on both episcopal administration and episcopal lands, some of which should shortly appear. Professor Dickens has edited the reactions of a conservative Yorkshire priest to the Edwardian changes, 'Robert Parkyn's Narrative of the Reformation', *EHR*, LXII, 1947, 58–83, and Dr D. M. Palliser has published a study of the reputedly conservative city of York, *The Reformation in York, 1534–1553*, Borthwick Paper 40, York, 1971, and more recently still in *Reformation and Resistance in Tudor Lancashire*, Cambridge, 1975, Dr C. Haigh has described the coming of Protestantism to an undoubtedly conservative county.

On the risings of the reign see S. T. Bindoff, *Ket's Rebellion, 1549*, The Historical Association, 1949, and A. Vere Woodman, 'The Buckinghamshire and Oxford Rising of 1548', *Oxoniensa*, XXII, 1957, 78–84.

A seminal book on the economic plight of one bishopric is P. M. Hembry, *The Bishops of Bath and Wells 1540–1640*, 1967, while I have examined the state of affairs at York in 'The Economic Problems of the See of York: Decline and Recovery in the Sixteenth Century', *Agricultural History Review*, XVIII, 1970, Supplement, 64–83.

CHAPTER 5 (pages 101 to 123)

The partnership between Mary Tudor and Pole to restore Catholicism in England has lately received considerable attention from historians. What was the standard biography of Pole, W. Schenk, *Reginald Pole, Cardinal of England*, 1950, can now be supplemented by D. Fenlon, *Heresy and Obedience in Tridentine Italy: Cardinal Pole and the Counter Reformation*, Cambridge, 1972, and a Cambridge PhD thesis, 1972, by R. H. Pogson, 'Cardinal Pole: Papal Legate to England in Mary Tudor's reign'. Dr Pogson has published part of his research in two articles, 'Revival and Reform in Mary Tudor's Church: a question of money', *JEH*, XXV, 1974, 249–65, and 'Reginald Pole and the priorities of government in Mary Tudor's Church', *HJ*, XVIII, 1975, 3–20. There is a further article by J. H. Crehan, 'St Ignatius and Cardinal Pole', *Archivum Historicum Societatis Iesu*, XXV, 1956, 72–98. Professor Knowles has much on Marian Catholicism generally, as well as specifically on the refoundation of monasteries, in his *Religious Orders in England*, III, Cambridge, 1959. In addition to his book which describes some of the political opposition Mary encountered, *Two Tudor Conspiracies*, Cambridge, 1965, Dr D. M. Loades has written a valuable article on 'The Enforcement of Reaction 1553–1558', *JEH*, XVI, 1965, 54–66. One aspect of the administration of an important Marian bishop is analysed in A. M. Jagger, 'Bonner's Episcopal Visitation of London, 1554', *BIHR*, XLV, 306–311.

On the Marian martyrs Foxe retains pride of place: the substantial accuracy of his accounts which other historians have since confirmed was first demonstrated by J. F. Mozley, *John Foxe and his Book*, 1940. Strype in *Ecclesiastical Memorials* and *Memorials of . . . Thomas Cranmer*, 1694, includes contemporary material Foxe did not print. In *The Oxford Martyrs*, 1970, Dr Loades has recounted the trials of Cranmer, Ridley and Latimer. Although her thesis concerning the planned nature of the Protestant exodus from England has not won general acceptance, C. H. Garrett, *The Marian Exiles*, Cambridge, 1938, contains very useful biographical material. There are some recent local studies; A. G. Dickens, *The Marian Reaction in the Diocese of York: Part I, the Clergy*, and *Part II, the Laity*, Borthwick Papers 11 and 12, York, 1957; H. E. P. Grieve, 'The Deprived Married Clergy in Essex 1553–61', *T R H S*, Fourth Series, XXII, 1940, 141–169; J. E. Oxley, *The Reformation in Essex to the death of Mary*, Manchester, 1965; K. G. Powell, *The Marian Martyrs and the Reformation in Bristol*, Bristol, 1972.

CHAPTER 6 (pages 124 to 152)

A great deal has been written on the Elizabethan Church in the last twenty years. M. M. Knappen, *Tudor Puritanism*, 1939, is still of value, particularly on the theoretical and political aspects of Puritanism, but it must now be read in conjunction with Professor P. Collinson's very important and detailed book, *The Elizabethan Puritan Movement*, 1967. There is also a good new study on the Separatists: B. R. White, *The English Separatist Tradition*, Oxford, 1971. Professor J. E. Neale's work, especially his *Elizabeth I and her Parliaments*, 2 volumes, 1953, 1957, contains much of relevance to the religious history of the reign. The chief account of Catholicism remains A. O. Meyer, *England and the Catholic Church under Elizabeth*, 1915: the reprint of 1967 has a helpful introduction by Dr J. A. Bossy. Dr Bossy has also written a highly influential article: 'The character of Elizabethan Catholicism', *P & P*, XXI, 39–59. In *Papists and Puritans under Queen Elizabeth I*, 1967, P. McGrath points out interesting parallels between Catholicism and Puritanism. I have tried to illustrate with documents the theory behind the royal supremacy and its working in practice in *The Royal Supremacy in the Elizabethan Church*, 1969.

Many of the most necessary original sources for Elizabethan religious history are accessible in Victorian or twentieth-century editions. The Parker Society published, among much else on the reign, H. Robinson, ed., *Zurich Letters*, I, Cambridge, 1842; J. Bruce, ed., *Correspondence of Matthew Parker*, Cambridge, 1853; W. Nicholson, ed., *The Remains of Edmund Grindal*, Cambridge, 1854. There is much original material on Puritanism in E. Arber, ed., *A Brief Discourse of the Troubles at Frankfort*, 1908; W. H. Frere and C. E. Douglas, eds., *Puritan Manifestoes*, 1907; A. Peel, ed., *The Seconde Parte of a Register*, 2 volumes, Cambridge, 1915; R. G. Usher, *The Presbyterian Movement in the Reign of Queen Elizabeth as illustrated by the Minute Book of the Dedham Classis 1582–1589*, Camden Society, 1905. In addition to C. Burrage, *The Early English Dissenters*, 2 volumes, Cambridge, 1912, a new series of editions of Separatist writings is in progress: among the most useful are A. Peel and L. H. Carlson, eds., *The Writings of Robert Harrison and Robert Browne*, 1953; L. H. Carlson, ed., *The Writings of Henry Barrow 1578–90*, 1962; *The Writings of Henry Barrow 1590–1*, 1966; *The Writings of John Greenwood and Henry Barrow 1591–3*, 1970. For an example of English contemporary propaganda against Catholics, and the riposte it provoked, see R. M. Kingdon, ed., *The Execution of Justice in England by William Cecil and A True, Sincere and Modest Defense of English Catholics by William Allen*, Ithaca, New York, 1965.

The continuing vigour of ecclesiastical courts throughout the sixteenth and early seventeenth century has been demonstrated in two books by R. A. Marchant, *The Puritans and the Church Courts in the Diocese of York 1560–1642*, 1960, and *The Church under the Law: Justice, Administration and Discipline in the Diocese of York 1560–1640*, Cambridge, 1969. R. G. Usher, *The Rise and Fall of the High Commission*, Oxford, 1913, is in many respects outdated and should be read in the reprint edition of 1968 which has an introduction by P. Tyler.

Historians have also recently been paying considerable attention to the Church in the localities, and one of the first of these studies to appear in print is R. B. Manning, *Religion and Society in Elizabethan Sussex*, 1969: with the publication of Dr Haigh's *Reformation and Resistance in Tudor Lancashire* it is now possible to compare religious life in two very different counties. An instructive article on crown patronage is by R. O'Day, 'The Ecclesiastical Patronage of the Lord Keeper, 1558–1642', *T R H S*, fifth series, XXIII, 1973, 89–109; she has also described the diocesan administration of one Elizabethen bishop, 'Thomas Bentham; a case study in the problems of the early Elizabethan Episcopate', *J E H*, XXIII, 1972, 137–159. F. Heal had written on the economic situation of

Elizabethan bishops, 'The Bishops and the Act of Exchange of 1559',
H J, XVII, 1974, 227–246.

CHAPTER 7 (pages 153 to 174)

Much of Dr Hill's work relates directly to the religious history of
the reigns of James I and Charles I, and particularly valuable here
are C. Hill, *Economic Problems of the Church*, Oxford, 1963, and
Society and Puritanism in Pre-Revolutionary England, 1964. There
is as yet no modern work on Jacobean religious history to match
those of the Elizabethan period, but the article by N. Tyacke,
'Puritanism, Arminianism and Counter-Revolution' in C. Russell,
ed., *The Origins of the English Civil War*, 1973, provides an exciting
foretaste of his forthcoming book. W. M. Lamont, *Godly Rule:
Politics and Religion 1603–60*, 1969, contains many stimulating
ideas. W. Haller, *The Rise of Puritanism*, Columbia, 1938, concentrates largely on the sermon literature of the first half of the
seventeenth century. W. K. Jordan, *The Development of Religious
Toleration in England*, Cambridge, Mass., II, 1936, includes much
besides religious thought for the period 1603–40. B. R. White, *The
English Separatist Tradition*, remains useful for the early seventeenth century, as does C. Burrage, *The Early English Dissenters*.

Of the more specialist studies, particularly helpful are R. A.
Marchant, *The Puritans and the Church Courts in the Diocese of
York 1560–1642*, 1960, most detailed on the seventeenth century;
P. J. Seaver, *The Puritan Lectureships*, Stanford, 1970, which relates
chiefly to London; J. B. Babbage, *Puritanism and Richard Bancroft*,
1962. Professor Collinson's *The Elizabethan Puritan Movement*,
1967, extends as far as the Hampton Court Conference on which
Professor M. H. Curtis has written a revisionary article, 'Hampton
Court Conference and its Aftermath', *History*, XLVI, 1–16. On the
expansion of the universities in the seventeenth century some very
stimulating work is being carried out by Professor L. Stone who
has published some of his preliminary conclusions in *Past and
Present*; see especially L. Stone, 'Educational Revolution in England',
P & P, XXVIII, 1964, 41–80; and 'Literacy and Education in England
1640-1900', *P & P*, XLII, 1969, 69–139.

Diaries and collections of letters written by laymen begin to be
available by the late sixteenth century and among those particularly enlightening on the attitudes of lay patrons are D. M. Meads,

ed., *The Diary of Lady Margaret Hoby 1599–1605*, 1930, and C. Cross, ed., *The Letters of Sir Francis Hastings 1574–1609*, Somerset Record Society, 1969.

CHAPTER 8 (pages 175 to 198)

A new study on Arminianism in England is very much needed. A. H. W. Harrison, *The Beginnings of Arminianism to the Synod of Dort*, 1926, concentrates upon the rise of the opposition to Calvinism in the Netherlands, while his *Arminianism*, 1936, treats the growth of Arminianism in England only in a very general way. Until the appearance of his book, *The Rise of English Arminianism*, Dr Tyacke's article, 'Puritanism, Arminianism and Counter Revolution', in C. Russell, ed., *The Origins of the English Civil War*, 1973, is therefore all the more valuable. W. M. Lamont, *Godly Rule*, 1969; W. K. Jordan, *Development of Religious Toleration in England*, II, Cambridge, Mass., 1936; and J. P. Kenyon, *The Stuart Constitution*, Cambridge, 1966, all contain information of Arminianism. The standard biography of Laud is H. R. Trevor Roper, *Archbishop Laud*, revised edition, 1962.

Much more has appeared recently on the Protestant opposition to Arminianism. In addition to C. Hill, *Economic Problems of the Church*, and *Society and Puritanism in Pre-Revolutionary England*, and Marchant, *Puritans and the Church Courts in the Diocese of York*, all cited previously, important studies are R. C. Richardson, *Puritanism in North West England*, Manchester, 1972; R. Howell, *Newcastle on Tyne and the Puritan Revolution*, Oxford, 1966; I. M. Calder, *Activities of the Puritan Faction of the Church of England 1625–33*, 1957; and, though very much older, useful for its command of original material, T. W. Davids, *Annals of Evangelical Nonconformity in the County of Essex*, 1863. For a recent biography of Preston see I. Morgan, *Prince Charles's Puritan Chaplain*, 1957.

P. Slack links civic Puritanism, social control and opposition to Laudian policy in 'Religious protest and urban authority: the case of Henry Sherfield, iconoclast, 1633', *SCH*, IX, 1972, 295–302. E. R. C. Brinkworth gives an account of ceremonial changes in Buckinghamshire in 'The Laudian Church in Buckinghamshire', *University of Birmingham Historical Journal*, V, 1955–6, 31–59. In *Family, Lineage and Civil Society: a study of Society, Politics and Mentality in the Durham Region 1500–1640*, Oxford, 1974, M. E. James sets out the conflict between Arminians and Puritans in county Durham in the early seventeenth century.

There is considerable comment on the contemporary religious situation in both T. T. Lewis, ed., *The Letters of Lady Brilliana Harley*, Camden Society, LVIII, 1854, and D. Parsons, ed., *The Diary of Sir Henry Slingsby*, while Edward Terrill graphically describes the genesis of an Independent church in E. B. Underhill, ed., *Records of a Church of Christ meeting at Broadmead, Bristol, 1640–1687*, Hanserd Knollys Society, 1847.

CHAPTER 9 (pages 199 to 221)

The most comprehensive history of the Church in England between 1640 and 1660 is very old, but it still contains information of value: J. Stoughton, *History of Religion in England*, I and II, 1867; W. K. Jordan, *The Development of Religious Toleration in England*, III and IV, Cambridge, Mass., 1938 and 1940, covers the same period and has considerable detail on all the different religious confessions. Otherwise, most historians have approached the religious history of the time from a denominational standpoint. The definitive, but somewhat turgid, account of English Presbyterianism is W. A. Shaw, *A History of the English Church during the Civil Wars and under the Commonwealth*, 2 vols., 1900. R. S. Bosher in *The Making of the Restoration Settlement: the Influence of the Laudians 1649–1662*, 1951, has written a lively account of the Episcopalians who refused to conform during this period. The two illuminating studies by G. F. Nuttall, *The Holy Spirit in Puritan Faith and Experience*, Oxford, 1946, and *Visible Saints: the Congregational Way 1640–1660*, Oxford, 1957, surmount denominational boundaries; and now easily the most scholarly and sympathetic discussion of the radical sects is C. Hill, *The World Turned Upside Down*, 1972. In addition to a wealth of helpful articles in the various journals of the denominational societies two articles deserve special mention: J. F. Maclear, 'The making of the lay tradition', *The Journal of Religion*, XXXIII, 1953, 113–136, and M. James, 'The political importance of the tithe controversy in the English Revolution 1640–1660', *History*, XXVI, 1942, 1–18. One of the most recent biographies of Cromwell is C. Hill, *God's Englishman*, 1970, though for Cromwell's religious policies also useful is R. S. Paul, *The Lord Protector: Religion and Politics in the life of Oliver Cromwell*, 1955. The two biographical studies compiled by A. G. Matthews provide a fund of information on both the clergy who were ejected from their livings in this period and also those who served in the Commonwealth Church: *Calamy Revised; being a revision of Edmund Calamy's Account of the Ministers and others ejected and silenced 1660–2*, Oxford, 1934, and *Walker Revised; being a revision of John Walker's Sufferings of the Clergy during the Grand Rebellion 1642–1660*, Oxford, 1968. Mrs M. Spufford in *Contrasting Communities*, Cambridge, 1974, has traced the religious history of selected Cambridgeshire villages in the sixteenth and seventeenth centuries: her work is particularly detailed and informative from 1640 onwards.

The period is rich in original records. Among those most accessible in print are: on Presbyterianism, C. E. Surman, ed., *The Register Book of the Fourth London Classis*, Harleian Society, nos. 82 and 83, 1953, and W. A. Shaw, ed., *Minutes of the Manchester Presbyterian Classis*, Chetham Society, 20, 22, 24, 1890–1; on Independency, E. B. Underhill, ed., *Records of the Church of Christ meeting at Broadmead Bristol 1640–1687*, Hanserd Knollys Society, 1847, and E. B. Underhill, ed., *Records of the Churches of Christ gathered at Fenstanton, Warboys and Hexham 1644–1720*, Hanserd Knollys Society, 1854. T. Edwards, *Gangraena*, 1646, a Presbyterian's view of sectarianism, well repays study. Lastly there are many contemporary diaries and autobiographies, and among the most representative of varying religious positions are: J. Horsfall Turner, ed., *Oliver Heywood's Autobiography*, I, Brighouse, 1882; L. Hutchinson, *Memoirs of Col. Hutchinson*, Everyman edition, 1965; J. M. Lloyd Thomas, ed., *The Autobiography of Richard Baxter*, 1925; E. Hockcliffe, ed., *Diary of the Rev. Ralph Josselin 1616–1683*, Camden Society, Third Series, XV, 1908; E. S. De Beer, ed., *Diary of John Evelyn*, 6 vols., Oxford, 1955.

CHAPTER 10 (pages 222 to 242)

The fullest account of the return of Anglicanism is R. S. Bosher, *The Making of the Restoration Settlement*, 1951, but it should now be read in conjunction with A. Whiteman, 'The Restoration of the Church of England', in G. F. Nuttall and O. Chadwick, eds., *From Uniformity to Unity 1662–1962*, 1962. The late Professor N. Sykes remains the great authority on the established Church in the later seventeenth and in the eighteenth century and, among his many books, the one which relates most to the Church in the reigns of the later Stuarts is *From Sheldon to Secker*, Cambridge, 1957. More recently G. V. Bennett, 'Conflict in the Church', in G. Holmes, ed., *Britain after the Glorious Revolution 1689–1714*, 1969, has written sympathetically of the problems of the Anglican clergy both before and after the Revolution of 1688.

On the clergy ejected in 1662 A. G. Matthews, *Calamy Revised*, Oxford, 1934, has become the essential reference book. A general discussion of nonconformity is given in G. R. Cragg, *Puritanism in the period of the Great Persecution 1660–1688*, Cambridge, 1957, but this can still be usefully supplemented by the older, and more episodic, but more detailed book by C. E. Whiting, *Studies in English Puritanism from the Restoration 1660–1688*, 1931. M. Spufford, *Contrasting Communities*, is valuable for Nonconformity in Cambridgeshire after the Restoration. A new and influential article linking rural Dissent and the forms of rural settlement by A. Everitt, 'Nonconformity in Country Parishes', appeared in the *Agricultural History Review*, XVIII, 1970, Supplement, 178–199.

Some of the church books begun during the Commonwealth were continued during the persecution, and among these *Broadmead Records* is one of the most detailed. Similarly, many diaries or autobiographies of clergy and laity cover both the Interregnum and the reign of Charles II; some of the most instructive are R. Latham and W. Matthews, eds., *Diary of Samuel Pepys*, I– , 1970– ; J. Horsfall Turner, ed., *Oliver Heywood's Autobiography*, Brighouse, I, 1882; E. Axon, ed., *Oliver Heywood's Life of John Angier of Denton*, Chetham Society, New Series 97, 1937; R. Parkinson, ed., *The Life of Adam Martindale*, Chetham Society, IV, 1845; E. Hockcliffe, ed., *Diary of the Rev. Ralph Josselin 1616–1683*, Camden Society, Third Series XV, 1908; J. M. Lloyd Thomas, ed., *The Autobiography of Richard Baxter*, 1925.

INDEX